# THE TRIUMPH OF SATYAGRAHA

## About the Author

**Thomas Panakal,** Ph.D., from School of Gandhian Thought and Development Studies, Mahatma Gandhi University, Kottayam, Kerala, India. He later studied at Columbia University. An experienced and prolific writer, Dr. Panakal has to his credit several books and novels in addition to more than 250 articles.

His interest in Indian history and heritagestarted to take roots in high school. The author strongly believes in the India's highly peaceful heritage and its major contributions to the progress and harmonious existence of mankind.

# THE TRIUMPH OF SATYAGRAHA

An analysis of Mahatma Gandhi's Influence
on the Civil Rights Movements in
The United States of America

**Thomas Panakal**

**CONCEPT PUBLISHING COMPANY PVT. LTD.**
**NEW DELHI-110 059**

**ISBN: 978-93-5594-544-0**

First Published 2023

*Published and Printed by*

Concept
Since 1974

**Concept Publishing Company Pvt. Ltd.**
A/15-16, Commercial Block, Mohan Garden,
New Delhi-110059 (India)
*T* : +91-11-41101460
*E* : publishing@conceptpub.com, *W*: www.conceptpub.com

**Cataloging in Publication**--Courtesy: D.K. Agencies (P) Ltd. <docinfo@dkagencies.com>

**Panakal, Thomas, author.**
The triumph of satyagraha : an analysis of Mahatma Gandhi's influence on the civil rights movements in the United States of America / Thomas Panakal.
pages cm
Includes bibliographical references and index.
ISBN 9789355945440

1. Gandhi, Mahatma, 1869-1948--Influence. 2. Civil rights movements--United States. 3. African-Americans--Civil rights--History--20th century. 4. Passive resistance--United States. 5. United States--Race relations. I. Title.

LCC E185.61.P36 2023 | DDC 323.1196073 23

The Man of the Millennium

# FOREWORD

It gives me immense pleasure to write a foreword to the book entitled "The Triumph of Satyagraha: An Analysis of Mahatma Gandhi's influence on the Civil rights Movement in the United States of America" written by a well-known reputed scholar and my friend Dr. T. Panakal. Mahatma Gandhi is very close to my heart and I have dedicated my life in the cause of Gandhi.

Mahatma Gandhi popularly known as Bapu or Father of the Nation is tallest among the leaders of the world of the 20th century ever produced. He is remembered all over the world for his love for peace, non-violence, truth, honesty, pristine purity, compassion and his success in using these instruments to bring together the entire population and helping the country to attain independence from the colonial power and show the new way to the world. Gandhi was a creative man and responding to the challenges of his time and setting example for present and future generations. Albert Einstein, the great scientist rightly said that **"Generations to come will scare believe that such a one as this ever in flesh and blood walked upon this earth".**

Step by step, Gandhi reached at the pinnacle of existence, where no one has reached before. In fact, Gandhi, who motivated millions of people during his life time, continues to inspiring people around the globe. Gandhi changed the course of history and created history. He was a man of principles, great convictions and always practiced what he preached. There was no dichotomy between theory and practice and between public and private life. He left an everlasting impact on the world at large because he always spoke and understood the language of the masses, socially deprived and downtrodden. Even after sixty-eight years of his death Gandhi continues to attract the attention of scholars, social activists, media, policy makers and dreamers not only in India but throughout globe.

Present world is passing through a critical phase of human history and is in search of an alternative. Liberalisation, privatisation and globalisation are not only reshaping the economy of the people and nation but fundamentally reshaping culture, ideology, attitude and life style of the people across the world. Everywhere one can see the fundamental change. Small is being replaced by mega. Invisible became visible. There is a mad race for materialistic development resulting in alienation of people from society and nature and resorting to violence of different type. Everywhere structural violence has increased. Service and need is replaced by greed. Ethics and honesty is no longer pivotal in public life. There is crisis after crisis, corruption after corruption and ultimately people are sufferer. Marxism provided an alternative to Capitalism. Due to inherent contradiction Marxian experiments failed. Liberalism and neo-liberalism are also not able to solve the human miseries. People's hope lies in Gandhism which provides an alternative.

The Gandhian principles are capable of mitigating the greatest challenge of the modern age. The most urgent need of today is the abolition of human suffering. Gandhi's philosophy becomes pertinent in the present world due to the complexity of human behaviour. His philosophy, laying stress on the goodness of human nature, unity of mankind, service of man, application of moral principles considered valid for individuals to group life and inter-state relations, the non-violent process of change, social and economic equality, economic and political decentralization, tries to resolve the various kinds of tensions that disturb domestic and international harmony. It is capable of strengthening the forces of love, creativeness and joy of life and beauty. It takes an integrated view of man and emphasizes his spiritual nature. Gandhi provides an answer and an alternative, which is above all, a ray of hope, a vision for future and a blue print for individual, state and society. The interpretations of Gandhian thought and perspective needs to be reiterated again and again till the masses learn to adopt and practice it in their thought and deed.

Gandhi provides solution to the contemporary dilemmas and conflicts arising out due to failure of developmental paradigms and failure of leadership. Even the welfare state is not responding as it was expected. The tragedy of modern India is that the important aspects of the Gandhian philosophy are not given serious attention. The ruling elite never realized that Gandhi was much ahead of time. The quest of humanity for social justice and sustainability will remain a dream until and unless humanity realizes what Gandhi meant when he said, that economics is untrue which ignores and disregards moral values. Gandhi in his various speeches and in his articles written throughout the freedom struggle spoke highly of democratic decentralization and rural development. In the 22nd July, 1946 issue of *Harijan,* Gandhi stated that **'Independence must begin at the bottom'.** He said, **"the swaraj of my dreams is the poor man's swaraj. The necessaries of life should be enjoyed by you in common with those enjoyed by the princes and the moneyed men. But that does not mean that you should have palaces like theirs. They are not necessary for happiness. You or I would be lost in them. But you ought to get all the ordinary amenities of life that a rich man enjoys. I have not the slighest dought that swaraj is not Poorn Swaraj until these amenities are guaranted to you under it."**

Gandhi is simple everything else is complex. He is an author, thinker, philosopher, though not in modern sense but beyond that. His writings, running into hundred volumes, known as *Collected Works of Mahatma Gandhi,* contain a wide range of views on different issues concerning humanity, spirituality and cosmology.

Like Fakir he led a simple life and committed to moral and political values. His life is symbol of pristine purity and based on highest order of transparency. He was experimenting with Truth. In fact his relentless experiment after experiment with truth and changing contexts may not have lent his writings a propositional form. However it contains deep philosophical proposition containing all aspects including man, nature and spirituality. Works on Mahatma Gandhi are both voluminous and diverse. More than 450 biographies are written by well known authors including Nobel laureates and in almost all the languages of the world.

There is a need to provide a platform and forum where different interpretations of Gandhi can be brought together in debate, thereby elevating the understanding of Gandhi. One must come out from the cocoon of caste, class, gender, regions, ideology and religion. There is no need of garlanding of Gandhi rather need of the hour is to follow the basic tenets of Gandhi that is love, compassion, honesty, self-esteem and integrity. One must go beyond the comparative, expository, and even dialogical axes, to bring to centre stage the idea of debate. Differences are the pre-requisite to a debate, and a living debate involves intellectual activity. Truth is not seen as given but has to be arrived at through arguments and counter-arguments.

Through his creativity Gandhi became a great man in diverse sense and in many ways. It is difficult to understand a great person. Bhavbhuti, a great scholar of Sanskrit, rightly said 'who indeed can claim to know and understand the mind of the great?' This is true in case of Gandhi. Gandhi was a man of public. His approach was humane. He inspired masses and masses inspired him. Gandhi is byproduct of global culture and he later on influences entire globe by his thought and action.

*Hind Swaraj* is the Gandhian bible, it is the sacred book the Father of the Nation gave to country, truly the *Gita* of the nationalist era. Through Hind Swaraj Gandhi wanted to establish **self-esteem of individual** and **moral regeneration of India.** In other words Gandhi through Hind Swaraj wanted to transform (a) **India as a nation and polity** and (b) **Indians.** *Hind Swaraj* **is a source book for evaluation of India and Indians.** It is a manual of action for people. *Hind Swaraj* is a critique of excessiveness of materialistic Western society. It is a pointer to down side of modern civilization, i.e. colonialism, neo-colonialism, violence, alienation etc. It is also a pointer to Political democracy because political democracy without social democracy is not a democracy at all. Criticism on Railways, Lawyer and Doctors must be seen as down side of colonialism and neo-colonialism. *Hind Swaraj* provides an alternative how an oppressed class can fight. It provides a way to fight against oppression, injustice, extremism, violence etc. It also provides alternative to individual, society and state. One can honestly say that Indians love to talk about Hind Swaraj but not understood it properly nor transformed its idea or philosophy on ground. It is a source book for evaluation of India and Indians in the post-independence India.

Of course, in order to come out of the present malaise and dilemma, the only remedy lies in adopting Gandhian path to resolve conflicts. Arnold Toynbee has rightly observed: **"At this supremely dangerous moment in human history, the only way of salvation for mankind is the Indian way—Emperor Ashok's and Mahatma Gandhi's principles of non-violence and Sri Ramakrishna's testimony to the harmony of religions. Here we have an attitude and spirit that can make it possible for the human race to grow together into a single family and in the Atomic Age this is the only alternative to destroying ourselves."**

Gandhi had two dreams in his life. The first dream was liberation of India from the British rule, while the second was liberation of Indians from oppression and injustice, from inequity and inequality, from discord and disharmony. To quote his own words: **"I shall work for an India in which the poorest shall feel that it is their country in whose making they have an effective voice, an India in which there should be no rich class and no poor class of people, and an India in which all communities shall live in perfect harmony. This is the India of my dream."**

His first dream was fulfilled but the second was not. According to the Mahatma, the true time for celebration would be when the second dream is fulfilled. Gandhi was a leader of his people, unsupported by any authority; a politician whose success rested, not upon craft or guile, but simply upon the moral grandeur of his soul; a fighter who pushed back the mightiest empire on earth without the use of force; a spirit of profound wisdom and captivating humility, armed with only an iron will and inflexible resolve; and a frail man who confronted the brutality of military strength with the dignity of a simple human being. To the Mahatma, Truth was God and non-violence was religion. At his memorable trial for sedition in 1922, he said: **"Non-violence is the first article of my faith. It is also, the last article of my creed. In non-violence bravery consists of dying, not in killing".** His compassion and humanity were as boundless as the universe. **"Gather together,"** he said, **"under one banner all men from all religions and races of India and infuse into them the spirit of solidarity and oneness to the utter exclusion of all communal and parochial sentiments."** And again: **"My Hinduism is not secularism. It includes all that I know to the best of Islam, Christianity, Buddhism, and Zoroastrianism. Truth is my religion and Ahimsa (the principle of nonviolence) is the only way of its realization."** Gandhi held the view that the life of a good citizen was the life of *Karma* action in the service of the country. **"My writings should be cremated with my body"**, he said. **"What I have done will endure, not what I have said or written."**

The hatred and fanaticism which consumed the body of the Mahatma did not touch his great soul. Indian systems and ideologies may be relevant at one time and irrelevant at others. But teaching of this great and benign lamp of wisdom and humanity are for endless time. He gave us the priceless gift of self-respect and the sense of dignity as a nation. **The last interview which the Mahatma gave was in the early afternoon of 30 January, 1948 to Margaret Bourke an American from the *Life Magazine*.** She asked him whether he would persist in his theory of non-violence in the event of a nuclear attack on a city. The Mahatma's reply was that if the defenceless citizens died in a spirit of nonviolence, their sacrifice would not go in vain. They might well pray for the soul of the pilot who thoughtlessly sprayed death on the city. This was his last message of compassion to mankind. He completely identified himself with the Indian masses. He observed: **"We must first come in living touch with them by working with them and in their midst, we must share their sorrows, understand their difficulties and anticipate their wants. With the pariahs we must be pariahs and see how we feel to clean the closets**

**of the upper classes and have the remains of theirs to be thrown at us. We must see how we like being in the boxes, miscalled houses, of the labourers of Bombay. We must identify with the villagers who toil under the hot sun beating on their bent back and see how we would like to drink water from the pool in which the villagers bathe, wash their clothes and pots, and in which their cattle drink and roll. Then and not till then shall we truly represent the masses and they will, as surely as I am writing this, respond to every call."**

The Indian masses responded to the Mahatma's call in a spirit of total surrender. He said to them that **"real Swaraj will come not by the acquisition of authority by a few but by the acquisition of the capacity by all to resist authority when it is abused."** He repeatedly used to mention that through realization of freedom for India, we would try to carry on and fulfil the mission of the universal brotherhood. He was really involved in achieving the broadest good of humanity at large.

Gandhi lived in a world of wars, colonialism, survival of the fittest, and eye for eye, Gandhi's truth and nonviolence appeared to many, as weapons of the weak. They gathered around him as co-workers and followers only when it appeared to work as a potent force against violence appearing in different garbs: injustice, exploitation, colonialism, and wars, to mention a few. Gandhi's weapons proved more powerful but least destructive *vis-à-vis* the conventional weapons of war. His satyagraha evoked world wide attention and crossed the borders of India to reach many other countries, the USA, Russia, China, European Union, and South Africa included. It proved beyond doubt that his means of fighting injustice ennobled both sides and left them in win-win situation. Globalization of Gandhian praxis did not go far enough to usher in a civilization of peace and harmony. It remained a movement which petered off when war mongering returned with a big bang in the form of modernization and globalization. Modernization means Westernization and globalization means deprivation of the rights of the people to fully participate in production and consumption of the goods and services they need and use. It converts people from being prosumers to consumers.

The relevance of Gandhi remains undiminished today. In fact, his ideas and approach to political, economic and social issues are more relevant now than even in his life-time. The policy makers, politicians, intellectuals and scientists must remember in thought and action the Talisman of Mahatma Gandhi:

**"I will give you a Talisman. Whenever you are in doubt, or when the self becomes too much with you, apply the following test.**

**Recall the face of the poorest and the weakest man whom you may have seen, and ask yourself, if the step you contemplate is going to be of any use to him? Will he gain anything by it? Will it restore him to a control over his own life and destiny? In other words, will it lead to swaraj for the hungry and spiritually starving millions? Then you will find your doubts and yourself melting away."**

We shall like to conclude that Gandhi's spoken words, writings, and work done by him will resonate for centuries to come. At the same time we must remember the **seven social sins which Gandhi wrote in *Young India* of 22.X.1925.**

**Politics without principles**
**Wealth without work**
**Pleasure without consciences**
**Knowledge without character**
**Commerce without morality**
**Science without humanity**
**Worship without sacrifice.**

What breath is to life, Gandhi is to humanity and civilization. As long as there is strife, hostilities, ethnic cleansing, religious unrest, internal conflicts and threats of military occupation, people will turn to Gandhi. His usefulness will not end unless conflict ceases, radical discrimination ends, women are empowered and poor live with dignity.

This is modest attempt but a well researched timely book. Panakal always thinks new and researches in the new emerging areas. It is a unique and fundamental work on the subject. I congratulate the author for his tremendous hard work.

**Anil Dutta Mishra**

# ACKNOWLEDGEMENTS

It would have been next to impossible for me to complete the research for the present dissertation without the active cooperation of and advice from several important individuals and institutions. The Thesis is the final product of everything the candidate has, in the past, learned from interactions with others.

My special thanks are due to Rev. Dr. A.K. Chirappanath, the thesis guide, Mahatma Gandhi University, for his valuable assistance and helpful criticism without which the present study could never have been completed. Prof A.K. Chirappanath was of great inspiration for me for more than three years.

I am grateful to the professors of The School of Gandhian Thought and Development Studies for their timely advice and recommendations in carrying out the research.

My thanks are also due to Mr. T.P. Antony, Rtd. teacher of Teacher Training Institute, Cochin, who painstakingly went over the dissertation in its entirety. His corrections, suggestions and additions, despite his heavy schedule, were invaluable to me.

I also wish to express my heart-felt gratitude to Mr. P.V. Mathew and his team of computer experts of the Vikas Computer Centre, Kumaranalloor, Kottayam, for composing the entire text and for meeting the technical requirements of the University. Their efforts were invaluable.

The candidate also wishes to express his profound gratitude to the librarians at Mahatma Gandhi University, Concordia and McGill Universities in Montreal, Canada, Library of Black Studies, Atlanta, U.S.A. and the University of West Indies, St. Augustine, Trinidad, West Indies. The travels were instrumental in the multidimensional study of the problem of Gandhiji's influence on the historic Civil Rights Movement in the United States of America, the second largest nonviolent campaign in the world after Gandhiji's successful Satyagraha movement, which he launched in India for justice, peace and liberty.

A major section of King Centre in Atlanta is devoted to the memory as well as Gandhiji's nonviolent philosophy with his huge portrait, charkha, home-spun cotton, large pictures of Jawaharlal Nehru and those of other Indian leaders who had played key roles in India's-Gandhiji's-nonviolent struggle for freedom. The museum shelves also contain elegantly hand-written tribute to Gandhiji's ideals and his words of wisdom embracing generation regardless of national barriers, boundaries and hurdles.

During his field research in the Southern parts of the U.S.A., the candidate had had the cooperation of several individuals at King Centre, different research facilities and museum in gathering the data vital to the dissertation. The interviews with several Afro-Americans and others in Montgomery, Atlanta and Birmingham have lent a new dimension to the present study.

Inasmuch as the Indian settlers constituted a minority within an oppressed majority, it is relevant here to consider their situation to measure the disabilities in relation to the problems of the indigenous African majority. The situation presented problems in terms of the struggle by the Indian community for justice, which Gandhiji had placed at the centre of his non-violent campaign: Satyagraha. Gandhji's uninterrupted stay in South Africa signified a revolution, revealing the rekindling of India's soul. It was a remarkable portrayal of the manner in which an unarmed community could overcome various hurdles in an alien land to gain access by peaceful means. That Gandhiji filled South Africa with the strong echoes of the best in Indian heritage and civilization that he proved himself, by his example, a credit to the country, that he was able to harmonize divergent forces, that he made himself responsible for transforming the Indian community, that he instilled into India's heart a lasting spirit of reconciliation and that he dispelled an air of intense gloom by beams of light is a fact recognized by everyone.

The author also expresses his gratitude to his wife, J. Ann Panakal, and the family for the encouragement he did receive on myriad occasions. Encouragement adds vitality to the mind, especially when it comes from the family.

**June 30, 2021** **Thomas Panakal**

# Contents

## BIBLIOGRAPHY

# LIST OF ILLUSTRATIONS



## DIAGRAMS

# Abbreviations

| | | |
|---|---|---|
| ACMHR | : | Alabama Christian Movement for Human Rights |
| CO | : | Colonial Office |
| IOL | : | India Office Library |
| KKK | : | Ku Klux Klan |
| MIA | : | Montgomery Improvement Association |
| NAACP | : | National Association for the Advancement of Colored (Negro) People |
| NAI | : | National Archives of India, New Delhi |
| SCLC | : | Southern Christian Leadership Conference |
| SNCC | : | Students for Nonviolent Coordinating Committee |
| TA | : | Transvaal Advertiser |
| WCC | : | White Citizens' Council |

# INTRODUCTION

Mahatma Gandhi, affectionately and respectfully called Gandhiji, is the history's most renowned proponent and father of Satyagrah to implement socio-political changes with malice towards none. His campaign, which had galvanised millions of Indian people for freedom and justice from an alien mismanagement, had been the largest in the globe, by any account. The peaceful campaign culminated in victory over the British sworn in policies of conquest, misrule, steal, divide and leave. England had parallel *modus operandi* in other parts of the globe and in different forms in England with murders, decapitations and unseating regimes.

Gandhiji had adhered to a policy which had been firmly rooted in India's spiritual values and a web of strong traditions. If we forget the richness of our heritage, we will become poor in our thinking—and living below the poverty line.

Gandhiji, the quintessential Indian, had strong faith in *Bhagavad Gita* and Indian philosophy as did others in his homeland and also in other lands. Rev. Dr. Martin L. King had been the illustrious Indian leader's most renowned disciple outside India. Salt Satyagraha had left a strong impact on his mind. On February 3, 1959 the American pilgrim landed in New Delhi and declared, "TO OTHER COUNTRIES I MAY GO AS A TOURIST, BUT TO INDIA I COME AS A PILGRIM. IT IS BECAUSE OF MAHATMA GANDHI, A GREAT MAN OF OUR TIMES." In his tool-box the special American traveller had familiarised himself with the philosophy of Jeremy Bentham and other social thinkers. Nevertheless, the Gandhian road map offered him the best opportunity to rid America of racism, the lynching of black people, police strangling them to death on footpaths, at door fronts with blood stains. Rev. M.L. King used the peaceful Gandhian recipe to stop endemic racism in America, the lynching of black people and to end razing to the ground their places of worship and educational institutions. Besides Dr. King, India has had numerous admirers in the world. Voltaire, the noted French philosopher (November 21, 1694—May 30, 1778) of the French revolutionary era, stated: "I am convinced that all good things have come down to us from the river Ganges (implying India as a whole)." Carl Von Clausewitz (June 1, 1780—November 16, 1831), the German military thinker, admired Indian laws on war forbidding ill-treatment of widows or harming those who ventured out from the army camps to fetch water. Clausewitz stated that such laws must have originated from the members of a highly developed society. **Max Mueller,** the German scholar (1823-1900) admired India for its wisdom and classical works. Mark Twain, the American prolific writer (1835-1910) said: "India is the birth place of human speech. Our most valuable instructive materials in the history of man are gathered up only in India".

Colonisation is a double edged weapon. Colonisers would do anything to realise their imperialistic goals in their land and in foreign countries. For instance, the British cut off the hands of the talented Bengali weavers to eliminate competition against the British imports of textiles into India. In those days the Indians had no access to pension. Yet, our forefathers were taxed to pay for the pension of the retired British agents. Students in colleges were beaten up for anti-British activities. Their blood was splashed on the wall of the university class room. The activists were forced to carry books on their heads under the hot sun forcing them to walk to the police station. Gandhiji said: "The British rule in India is evil." He knew the underpinnings of colonialism. Edmund Burke, the Irish parliamentarian in the British House of Commons (1766-1794), an economist, astute diplomat, a powerful orator and philosopher, succinctly said "When the power of love overrules the love for power, the world will know peace." Brit succinctly said, "Britain the law breaker in India should not be the law maker in India. (nextpara) India's welfare was uppermost on Gandhiji's mind and gave his life to this cause." Nehru, another great leader, wrote in his last will and testament: "I have received the special thing called love from the people of India and I do not know how I can repay it." How many world leaders can make such profound statement? Perhaps none.

Gandiji's codes of conduct for Satyagrahis among others were: (1) Not to provoke opponents in negotiations; (2) Abstinence from alcohol, and (3) Help your opponent when his life is in danger even at the expense of your own life. He also unambiguously said, "The day the power of love overrules the love of power the world will know peace." If you want to preserve civillization, you have to act in a civilized manner. Gandiji did **The Salt Satyagraha, a product of the Gandhian genius, sealed the fate of the British rule in India *vis-à-vis* its colonial grip.**

Gandhiji peacefully demolished colonialism in India and the British closed down its colonial offices stretching all the way from the idyllic valleys of Kashmir to the sandy beaches of Kanyakumari. Salt was sharper than the sword...and suddenly exactly so.

Hu Shin, the former Chinse ambassador to the United States said, "India conquered and dominated China for over 2,000 years without ever having to send a single soldier across her borders." This is also true of the Indian influence much more than that of China in other Asian lands."

Towards the second half of the last century, all the exit polls in India indicated that British rule was on its death bed gasping for life. Britain had lost its grip and enforcement. In a wider sense Gandhiji influenced Rev. Dr. M.L. King in the process. Britain woefully lacked enforcement.

Law is powerful. Law without enforcement law is soup in your hand.

**June 30, 2021** **Thomas Panakal**

## CHAPTER-I

# PROLOGUE

The present work discussing Mahatma Gandhi's profound influence on the historic Civil Rights Movement launched by Rev. Dr. Martin Luther King Jr., in the United States of America is born out of the investigator's years of reflection on and commitment to Gandhian ideals in India and the Afro-American struggle in the United States of America. The American leader's campaign was based on the **ideals of Non-violence and reconciliation based on universal LOVE as espoused by Gandhiji in contemporary times.**

A frightening aspect of our times is the escalation of arms race. Even though virulent national spirit is on the wane in contrast to the last century, arms race is ironically continuing creating the need for non-violent solutions of the problems as advocated by Gandhiji.

The living standards of those who peddle arms with no qualms in open and black markets go up a clear sign of political corruption. The economic condition of the people of the nations that buy the weapons decline as capital is diverted to purchase arms rather than utilize it to buy food for the needy, machinery for reconstruction, money to improve infrastructure for building hospitals. The world's developed nations are also trying to combat some of these vital issues while the developing nations can ill-afford the heavy expenditure of arms race.

It is fallacious to assume that the storage of the massive weapons of annihilation would necessarily lead to a stable world order. On the other hand, the more arms individual nations pile up, the more instability their existence would create. Normal man-to-man relationships become corrosive resulting in suspicion and rivalry in the world. The arms peddlers or the International supermen of Death are only interested in fomenting the crisis with their minds and bodies focused on profits not only in the United States. In the door-to-door sales of the weapons of mass destruction, these men defy laws.

Mankind has entered a new millennium. Our collective concern should be a total denunciation of violence as shown by Gandhiji in the last century to heal the old wounds. In the last century, Gandhiji was the greatest exponent of non-violent resistance as the best avenue to resolve socio-political problems that still plague us. His legacy should be the world's legacy to strip the universe of needless conflicts and arm race.

The present dissertation concerns itself with three basic aspects:

(i) The early history of Afro-Americans and their arduous struggle for justice.
(ii) Gandhiji's non-violent crusade in South Africa, the birth-place of Satyagraha.
(iii) To what extent Rev. Dr. King applied the Gandhian vision in the United States to rectify racial injustice, marking the culmination of historical convulsions in that country.

The decorous study of a topic should be relevant to the needs of the time either to benefit from the manner by which a new thought has been expounded or how an innovative ideal is applied to resolve current problems. The relevance of the present study is as follows:

(i) Gandhiji demonstrated the effectiveness of non-violent means to achieve socio-political objectives in South Africa for the first time in the panorama of man's history. After South Africa, he came to India to topple the largest colonial nation in the world by employing the most peaceful and potent tool: Satyagraha.
(ii) The human energy can be channelled either to remodel or destroy life and if we are unwilling to direct the available resources for peace and consonance, the consequences of our collective reaction would be prodigious. The posterity would be burdened with the ponderous outcome of our misjudgements.
(iii) Gandhiji, more than any other individual in our times showed by his own example, the power of Non-violence over the brute force of violence to help eradicate injustice by launching the history's largest non-violent crusade, an important milestone in history. Hence the relevance of the study. Gandhiji tried

to show the world/mankind **the universality of Satyagraha based on love and non-violence.**

(iv) The Gandhian principles can be effectively applied to usher in an era of peace and co-operation on a global level.

We can take solace from the fact that India was the first country in the world, and perhaps the last, to rout the world's largest colonial empire in the most non-violent manner known to mankind manifesting itself in the form of Gandhian Satyagraha, the product of Gandhiji's political genius with a doughty mind and a spiritual connotation without parallel. It would have been fatuous to liberate a nation with its strong spiritual heritage from the bonds of colonial rule by advocating violence even though any method of self-defence is globally justified. The quintessence of the Gandhian spirit is the total rebuff of force. Gandhiji believed in compassion, and not coersion.

Furthermore, India's answer, in our times, found its stamp of approval in the history's second largest non-violent campaign under the stewardship of Rev. Dr. Martin Luther King for democratic rights for Afro-Americans. The Afro-American leader not only desired justice for his people but also strove for changes in the attitude of the rest of the society by advocating peaceful means. **Thus the Indian perspective appears to be applicable in the entire global context for peace and justice.**

The nature of war has gone through cycles of change. During the time of *Mahabharata* (seven times as large as Iliad and Odyssey combined) wars had been waged at a specific time, on specific days agreed upon by the adversaries as enunciated by the moral principles of war. Today, war challenges time as the concept of time is alien to modem brigades and a band of illegal feudal warlords. Also today war is global. It is more destructive and morally repugnant than at any period in history. Therefore, the saga of violence and history's compulsions to overcome the substantive issue of violent methods, as shown by Gandhiji, are crucial to unmask the deleterious nature of violence and war, with its ghastly results.

Gandhiji never equated non-violence with inaction, but considered it a strong and a polished tool to counter evil humanely believing in action as exemplified during his public life and to show the importance of the dignity of labour. His belief in action was as old as the teachings contained in *Gita*. On seeing the relatives on both sides of the battlefield, Arjuna decided not to fight while Lord Krishna revealed the importance of performing one's duty, "for action is superior to inaction." (*Gita*, Chapter 3, verse 8).

The Gandhian philosophy of Non-violence can be applied to all spheres of life be they local or global, personal or social by appealing to reason and the **fundamental goodness of humans** who have the same aspirations in life irrespective of their lands of birth. Gandhiji had intense faith **in the fundamental goodness of the human being** and that faith had formed the nucleus of his entire career. In the absence of Gandhian vision of Non-violence and its impact on Rev. Dr. King, his most renowned disciple outside India, attempts by America's civil rights leader would not have received the stamp of strong approval that they did. The Afro-American society, without his non-violent leadership would have turned its eyes to the violent doctrines openly preached by other Afro-American leaders. In the absence of the Gandhian methods espoused by Rev. Dr. King, the Civil Rights Movement in the United States would have been hit with severe racial turbulence. **The hypothesis is that Gandhian Satyagraha can be applied now and in the future to resolve socio-political conflicts right from personal to international realms.**

The study makes a humble effort to prove the hypothesis. Therefore, the present study is undertaken by stressing the need for non-violent social action for a more peaceful society in view.

What are the justifications of the study on Gandhiji's influence on Rev. Dr. King's campaigns for justice? The present study can be justified on the following principal grounds:

(i) Gandhiji, deriving his inspiration from the Sermon on the Mount, the spiritual values of Gautama Buddha and many humanistic thinkers attempted to prove the power of love and compassion over the swarthy forces of malignity, still conceding that his "ideals are as old as the mountains and hills." Those ideals should be practised on a broader scale than had been the case with their sharply etched symbols of harmony and reconciliation.

(ii) Gandhiji and Rev. Dr. King, who under the sway of the former have shown the universe, hungry for a peaceful formula of stability, that Non-violence is a highly potent force to effect changes in society. Their ideals should receive wider acceptance to save the planet from the jaws of destruction.

Non-violence is much more powerful than violence and therefore, it is applicable in personal, social, national and international spheres. In fact, non-violent methods are practised in a wide variety of ways in different societies. These methods and the progress resulting from them are not given adequate attention. Individuals, everywhere in the universe, want to work in a peaceful environment and the building blocks of civilization are laid in an orderly and non-violent atmosphere. Violence tramples on civilization. War destroys it completely. Accordingly, this study attempts to present Gandhian Satyagraha as a viable method for the transformation of the society/world without hurting the neighbours.

Violence and corruption are ubiquitous in society compelling individuals to raise questions on the validity of the legal system, which seems unable to combat such social evils. People should be truthful and should espouse true means, as did Gandhiji, without resorting to violent and corrupt means. An eye for an eye would make the whole world blind. A tooth for tooth would make everyone toothless.

Training in Non-violence and the development of a culture of peace are significant to sustain human values and to ensure the continuity of our civilization, now and in the future. One can feel a compelling need to confirm this stark reality and to seek peaceful solutions.

Scientifically, man has made great progress that by turning a red button, a few switches or by activating laser beams, an individual is capable of killing his adversaries who may be living thousands of miles away, not to mention irreversible damage to property. The person who pulls the trigger would not injure even his fingertips. The film, *Day After,* graphically exposes our minds to the unequivocal frivolity of the policies that would precipitate a crisis of immense proportions.

Non-violent methods of action, against corruption, exploitation and all vestiges of injustice appear to be the best alternatives to violent agitation that frequently erupts in the world. Therefore, the present study is undertaken as a research programme for a serious and scientific analysis.

Gandhiji's spiritual foundation may be traced back to his family which is quite strong in India. His father was the ruler of a principality and wanted his son to follow his footsteps. His mother wanted him to grow up as a *Sanyasi.* What was the natural outcome of the parental influences?

He eventually became a saint among politicians and a politician among saints, a preeminent status no political figure has attained transforming him into a unique individual. The idea of fasting, a proven expression of self-sacrifice and the one, which Gandhiji had used on myriad occasions breaking international records, had been an enduring legacy from his own mother. He risked his own life on several occasions for his love of India.

The Gandhian ideology was transformed into action throughout his life while its main components were (a) Faith in God, (b) Faith, and (c) Non-violence. "I may live without air and water, but not without God," Gandhiji said in 1931 as his faith in God had evolutionized his public career.

A scientific study should have clear objectives for a proper analysis. The objectives can be divided into general and specific and both are interconnected.

The study attempts to make a systematic assessment of Gandhiji's influence on Rev. Dr. King's non-violent campaigns, to show to what degree the Afro-American leader applied the Gandhian philosophy in the United States and to point out the universal applicability of Satyagraha.

**Specific Objectives**

1. To study the different aspects of the Civil War and the Emancipation Proclamation of Afro-Americans in order to bring to limelight their miserable situation as slaves stripped of even a thin coating of individuality.
2. To illustrate the results of the newly gained freedom by means of a non-violent struggle.
3. To study Gandhiji's *modus operandi* in South Africa.
4. To assess the technique of Satyagraha applicable to situations from personal to international situations.
5. To assess the racial climate in the United States in the past and today.
6. To compare the problems as they had existed in South Africa with those faced by Afro-Americans.
7. To evaluate Rev. Dr. King's peaceful methods based on Gandhian ideology.
8. Finally, the researcher, based on the non-violent activities of Gandhiji and Rev. Dr. King, would make an effort to establish the power of *Satyagraha* as an effective instrument to resolve conflicts and the universality of its application. Human beings have to live with other human beings resulting in

> constant interactions; such interactions are to be facilitated in a peaceful atmosphere as shown by Gandhiji.

The American civil rights advocate emphasized—and did not turn away from Gandhiji's non-violent route by attempting to convert the minds of those who had been inimical to the constitutional rights prerogatives of Afro-Americans.

It is important to note that in a violent world, Gandhiji tried to show the significance of tossing out the door violent means to settle social and political problems.

Violence has been a serious societal problem from ancient times down to the modem era, more so in some regions of the world than in others. In 513 B.C., Heraclitus argued that war was the father of all progress. According to Cicero and Plutarch, war was an instrument of the swift dissemination of culture. Cicero declared that since "Rome has acquired the possession of the world by war, it has to employ force to keep the universe from collapsing." Nietzche even said: "I do not advise you to work, but to fight. A good war halloweth a cause."

Gandhiji denounced the use of violence and devised the extremely strong tool of Satyagraha to topple the British rule for freedom. Freedom is to the mind of man as light is to his eyes. The Indian Satyagraha was history's largest non-violent campaign for justice. Outside the Indian subcontinent Rev. Dr. King, more than any other individual, had embraced the Gandhian philosophy turning it into the cardinal aspect of his homegrown Satyagraha. Rev. Dr. King, accepting Gandhian ideology with verve embarked on the American crusade for freedom. In the aftermath of Gandhian non-violent movement to defeat the British rule in India, the American civil rights leader's peaceful struggle was perhaps the most popular movement in the world for the twin goals of freedom and equality.

Moreover, Gandhiji's peaceful campaign also served as an appropriate model for the Afro-American struggle obfuscating the skeptical views of the opponents. The non-violent Satyagraha technique appears to be an effective instrument to resolve social conflicts even in developed countries like the United States. This shows the significance of the exploration. This also shows the need for the exploration.

An analytical evaluation is possible only within a theoretical framework. Consequently, it is necessary for one to be precise about the theoretical framework upon which analysis is based.

The methodology for the present analysis is as follows:

The researcher relies on books by and on Gandhiji and Rev. Dr. King. In addition, the researcher travelled to the southern parts of the United States conducting interviews, visiting museums, honouring Gandhiji and Rev. Dr. King in Atlanta (Georgia) collecting data essential for the analysis. Conclusions are drawn from Gandhiji's non-violent struggle in South Africa, his campaign in India and Rev. Dr. King's study of the Gandhian doctrines. Systemic analysis is made with the focus on Gandhian Non-violence and its impact on Rev. Dr. King's just campaign to cleanse the American society of its racist impurities.

The present study is divided into three segments.

Segment 'A' would discuss the Emancipation Proclamation, the multifarious problems Afro-Americans had to face during American's infancy. Segment 'B' dwells on Gandhiji's activities in South Africa. The Government of South Africa was chiefly interested in cheap Indian labour, and not in the welfare of the Indian settlers determined against countenancing the Indians as citizens of that country. Segment 'C' would delve into Rev. Dr. King's non-violent campaign in the United States and the fruits it has brought to Afro-Americans. Thus the present study is a contextual analysis of the activities of two great world leaders who believed in *ahimsa.* Segment 'A' is significant for a clear understanding of harsh experience of black America in the past in relation to its struggle and the progress in our times. The contrast is startling.

Rev. Dr. King's summed up his indebtedness to the Gandhian methods by stating in New Delhi that to other nations **"I may go as a tourist and to India I come as a pilgrim. It is because of Gandhi, a great man of our times." Satyagraha is the soul of India.**

In the past, a plethora of books has been written on Gandhiji's life and activities providing a comprehensive analysis of his non-violent and extremely egalitarian philosophy and its implications for our age, an age of bombs and scud missiles.

No study of Gandhiji's life and its message for our age would be complete without reading his Autobiography which explains various aspects of his life and the true meaning of Satyagraha. In the same manner, Gandhiji's own works such as *My Philosophy of Life, Satyagraha in South Africa* and *Young India* are windows to his philosophical thinking, his indebtness to God and non-violent activities.

Louis Fischer's *The Life of Mahatma Gandhi: His Life and Message* provides detailed accounts for students on Gandhian ideals. G.P. Misra and B.C. Das have written an important book titled: *Gandhi in Today's India*, describing his ideals and their application in modern society.

Of all the works at our disposal discussing the problems of Afro-Americans and their attempts for democratic rights in their own land of birth, perhaps few books are as important as *Stride Toward Freedom* written by none other than the chief architect of America's civil rights movement, Rev. Dr. King who, in this monumental work, explains Gandhiji's influence on his own campaign. James Melvin Washington has compiled the essays and speeches by Rev. Dr. King in a voluminous work under the appropriate title, *Testament of Hope: The Essential writings of Martin Luther King, Jr.*, covering a decade, 1957 to 1967.

*The Negroes in the United States* by Franklin Frazier vividly explains the historical background of Afro-Americans and their struggle for equality. In 1860, slavery had full legal sanction under the Constitution of the United States.

This is an extensive study and it would be next be impossible to analyze the entire history of violence or all the aspects pertaining to the problem of non-violent principles and their application. Consequently, an objective evaluation of all the issues relating to violence and non-violence is beyond the realm of the present investigation. The researcher acknowledges his limited access to and knowledge of the entire history of violence and non-violence. What he says in the present study is what he has learned from others—and nothing more.

The study is limited to a fraction the principles of Gandhiji and how Rev. Dr. King applied them in the United States as a pragmatic option. Still, special attention is paid in the first segment to the problems faced by Afro-Americans in the early days of American history for justice and the hurdles they had to overcome followed by an analysis of Gandhian principles and their application in South Africa. In the third segment Rev. Dr. King's non-violent attempts in Montgomery, Selma and Birmingham are evaluated to attain freedom for his people, to travel as human beings on the bus in Montgomery without being victimized by racist attitude, to attain voting rights in Selma or for job opportunities in Birmingham.

After briefly explaining the relevance of the topic, the crucial issues to be analyzed and the Indian perspective, an attempt will be made in the opening chapter to discuss the important issue of the Civil War, and its vast implications for Afro-Americans. The problem of (Negro) Afro-American suffrage could only come to the surface with the dawn of emancipation as the slave was far from being treated as a citizen, without even a veneer of individuality suffering dour disabilities. America has yet to appreciate the fine and gentle qualities of Afro-Americans to build the bridges of racial harmony without which no society can function to its full capacity. The Afro-Americans were the first group in America, or in the world outside India, to embrace Gandhian ideology on a mass level.

The power that stems from the barrel of a gun will be broken to pieces by more guns and bayonets. In this successful attempt for peace and justice, Gandhiji believed in the principle of *Pax et reconciliation pro amnibus*—peace and reconciliation for all.

SEGMENT-A

# CHAPTER-II

# THE CIVIL WAR AND THE EMANCIPATION OF AFRO-AMERICANS

## ARTICLE -I

### (A) The Slave Status

Scarcely a year before the outbreak of the Civil War in the United States of America, it was manifest from a set of resolutions adopted in the Senate that the slave status of the Afro-American people had been established for a long period. One of the resolutions sponsored by Southern leaders was adopted as early as May 24 -25, 1860, spelling out:[1]

> Slavery is lawful in all the territories under the Constitution; neither Congress nor a local legislature can abolish it there; the federal government is duty bound to slave owners as well as to the holders of other forms of property in the territories; it is a violation of the Constitution for a state or a combination of citizens to intermeddle with the domestic institutions of any other state 'on any pretext whatsoever, political, moral, or religious, with a view to their disturbance or subversion,' open or covert attacks on slavery are quite contrary to the solemn pledges given by the states on entering the Union to protect and defend one another for the common objective.

Ascertaining the imperative need to continue the practice of slavery, a practice which was as dark as soot, the resolution went on to say, echoing the orthodox reading of the situation[2]:

> That the inhabitants on any territory on their admission to the Union may then decide whether or not they would sanction slavery thereafter; that strict enforcement of the fugitive slave law is required by good faith and the principles of the Constitution.

The Republican Party's triumph at the polls in November 1860, helped transform the nation's political climate to a considerable degree marking a clear signal for the secession of the so-called planter aristocracy[3] and following the eventual withdrawal by the Southern legislators, the Republicans, who were a minority in the Senate, were in absolute control of the Federal Government. Although the vast majority of the Republicans were opposed to the planter class, there was no unanimity of views on the distant horizon on the fate of the status of Afro-Americans.

## (B) The Conservative Wing

Even though Abraham Lincoln was the dexterous spokesman of the conservative block of the Republican party, the conservative wing, on the whole, showed little or no interest in enhancing the status of Afro-Americans as different factions in the party were chiefly interested in implementing the legislation necessary to fit the nation's nascent industrial development.[4] Franklin Frazier pointed out the dilemma inherent in the system:[5]

> On the other hand, the Radical Republicans were divided into two distinct factions; the Old Radicals who were not simply interested in making the industrial-capitalist class quite dominant, but who were also concerned with the rights of the Negro; the New Radicals were, on the other hand, interested in the triumph of the rising industrial class.

Both factions among the Radical Republicans had reached the unanimous conclusion that the Civil War could only be won by emancipating Afro-Americans mainly to undermine the political and economic power wielded by the planter aristocracy. The radical elements in the Republican Party, represented chiefly by such distinguished individuals as Thaddeus Stevens and Charles Summer, had started a lengthy campaign for the abolition of slavery and in the general election held in 1852, the Free Soil Party was not in a position to garner even five per cent of the total number of votes. Beard made the following observation concerning this crucial development[6]:

> After Garrison had been at work for more than a century, by a decision of more than three to one, even the mildest plank in the anti-slavery platform had been overwhelmingly repudiated by the country at large.

Such was the attitude prevailed in favour of the perpetuation of slavery in the United States during the latter half of the eighteenth century. One has to reckon with that historical background if one has to grasp the true implications of the dilemma being faced by the descendants of the slaves in today's America and Rev. Dr. King's non-violent attempts to remedy the situation. The following historical facts would further illustrate this point. Let us analyze them now.

The first and the most critical test of the overall status of the Afro-American during the Civil War was directly concerned with his employment as a soldier and when the war erupted, the Secretary of War even refused to accept the service of the Afro-Americans, but with no qualms in accepting the services of others with open arms. In 1861, General W.T. Sherman began operations on the coast of South Carolina, a Southern state, where anti-Afro-American sentiments were quite pervasive. The General had been instructed to use the "contraband" as he "may deem most beneficial to the service, this, however, not being a general arming them for service."[7] Although he had been given the authority to rely on his own discretion, Sherman was, nonetheless, dauntless in his refusal to unlock the doors to Afro-Americans to join the armed forces, providing an example of blatant racial discrimination common in the country. A sizable number of Northern officers had even permitted several slave owners to retrieve escaped slaves who had been forced to seek refuge within the Northern lines.[8] The action by the officers resplendently reflected the anti-Afro-American sentiments rife in the country, opposed to granting the Afro-American social recognition, let alone giving him even a vestige of equality. He had to live without a ray of justice. It is striking that despite the growth in democratic ideals during the three decades prior to the outbreak of the American Civil War, the Afro-American residing outside the state of New England was deprived of the umbrella of legal protection in contrast with the rest of the society. W.E. Burghardt Du Bois made the following observation concerning this point[9]:

> To the Northern masses the Negro had been a curiosity, a sub-human minstrel, willing and naturally a slave, and treated as well as he deserved to be. He did not have sense to stage any revolt and assist Northern armies, even if Northern armies were trying to emancipate him, which they were not. The Northerner shrank at the very thought of encouraging servile insurrection against the whites.

The United States was not the only nation where African slaves had to face severe hardships since, in the last century; hundreds of slaves were brought to the West Indian island nation of Jamaica to toil in the sugar cane fields where they were inhumanly treated. W. Payne provided the following graphic illustration of the great sufferings they had to endure[10]:

> Shame to the planters; it was among them that Negroes received the worst treatment. And during the eighteenth century it was generally considered in Jamaica alone **light punishment to hang the blacks in chains, leaving them to starve to death.** (Emphasis added).

Payne goes on to describe in more poignant terms the different forms of mistreatment of slaves in Jamaica:[11]

> The mistreatment of numerous African slaves was indeed widespread. There were many forms of execution; **the more approved method of execution was by torture over a slow fire.**

## (C) The Emancipation Proclamation

When the pivotal problem of the emancipation of Afro-Americans came up for any serious discussion, a handful of members of Congress supported the enlistment of Afro-American soldiers as their view was predicated on the assumption that such a step would help them prove their right to equal status. Nonetheless, the majority of the members of Congress supported the measure from a negative standpoint that it might help to erode the political power of the South. It was only after the Emancipation Proclamation and when urgent need was felt to replenish the Union troops in the State of Louisiana that the enlistment of Afro-American soldiers received credibility as an explicit policy of the North.

It is pertinent to observe in the present context that Abraham Lincoln had by now given vent to his view on the question of the emancipation of Afro-Americans to whose cause he had devoted his life. "My paramount object," Lincoln wrote in August 1862,[12] "in this struggle is to save the Union, and not either to save or destroy slavery."[13] Furthermore, he stated that whatever steps he had adopted "about slavery and the coloured race,"[14] he did so under the overwhelming assumption that it would help preserve the Union with the firm wish that all men everywhere would be free."[15] Lincoln, later in the month, admitted to a Chicago audience that slavery was **"at the root of the rebellion, or at least its *sine qua non*."** The emancipation of the Afro-American, he admitted, would also improve the Union's cause in Europe;[16] but he had little or no confidence in the ability of Afro-Americans to become soldiers, further expressing the view that if they were armed, their guns would slip into the hands of the Southern rebels.

That did not mean that Lincoln was not fully committed to the emancipation and on January 1, 1863, nine days after his famous speech in Chicago, **Abraham Lincoln issued his preliminary Emancipation Proclamation, his irrevocable declaration liberating Afro-Americans from the clutches of servitude and bondage for the first time in the history of the United States. The proclamation marked the dawn of a new era in the lives of Afro-Americans since their forefathers had arrived from the African shores.**[17] He said that no nation could move forward if it was half free and half slave.

Lincoln's proclamation unequivocally stated that those who had been held as slaves within the states in rebellion against the United States were free.[18] Now, the emancipated Afro-American was admonished to refrain from violence and to accept employment at reasonable wages. This admonition against violence made by Lincoln may be considered a precursor to Rev. Dr. King's own entreaties to the black community based on Gandhian non-violence.

## ARTICLE -2

### (A) A State of Bewilderment

Lincoln's decisive action signalled a turning point in the history of race relations in the United States, a harbinger to further improvement in the life of Afro-Americans, in succeeding years.

And now to the race-conscious free Afro-Americans, especially those residing in the North, the Emancipation Proclamation, in effect meant the debut of a new status in America's political and social fabric leading to cycles of transformation. The announcement of freedom, on the other hand, had resulted in a state of bafflement among the vast majority of illiterate slaves on the Southern plantations, forcing one ex-slave to state that the proclamation of freedom and equality sounded "Wce Greek" to him. His aged mother whispered to her flustered offspring[19]:

> Son, we have been slaves all our lives, and now Mr. Abe Lincoln done set us free, and say we can go anywhere we please in the country, without getting the pass fiom Marse cage like we used to have to do.

An Afro-American clergyman narrated the following story on the general effects of the historic announcement of freedom for the slaves on the cotton plantation where his grandfather had held a responsible position[20]:

> The slaves were in the fields chopping the cotton and chanting the rhythm of the day as a testimony to the drowsy overseer that they were doing his

> bidding "Massah" Ridley was on the porch of the "big house" fast asleep. The Yankees had ridden up to the mansion, and the horses put their hoofs on the low and the mailed porch as if at home. By this time, "Missus" Ridley had come from the house. Ridley summoned his wife and spoke slowly with a tear in his voice: "Call all the niggers together ..." (Nigger is a highly derogatory term that could infuriate an Afro-American today).

The minister went on to explain[21]:

> The slaves did not understand anything, although they had heard rumours that they may be free some time. Few could read, and none had access to newspapers, and as they left the field they wondered who was to be whipped or who was to be sold off or what orders were to be given. Half-starved and half afraid, they wended their way through the fields in one silent mass of praying creatures.

Despite the discernible lack of knowledge and the whole ramifications of freedom, the slaves knew that they had stepped into a different world. The clergyman described that "Dr. Ridley was weeping bitterly ... His words were stilled with sobs. The slaves were awe-stricken; they had never seen a white-man cry. Only slaves had tears, they thought."[22]

We also have the following moving narration[23]:

> But the slaves did rejoice and loudly too. Some cried; some jumped up and cracked their heels. Charlotte took her children up in her arms and shouted all over the field: "Chillun, didn't I tell you many times that God would answer prayer?"

The general pattern of behaviour of the Afro-American toward his master at a time of great quandary created by the Civil War was, to some degree, the result of the nature of the relationships, which had developed between the slave and his master. The slaves who had been treated well and who had forged close relationships in the same household with their masters generally remained loyal. On the other hand, field slaves and those living in towns were likely to take full advantage of the favourable climate in order to free themselves from the iron grip of control that was external and formal. We shall now the specific aspects of the problem.[24]

First, bands of slaves forthwith left the plantations from the firm control of their masters and the news spread that they move about freely as a crucial test of individual freedom. Freedom opens the doors to choices in life. Booker T. Washington had this to say[25]:

> After the coming of freedom, there were two main points upon which practically all the people in our place agreed, and I find that this was also true all over the South: that they must change their names, and that they must leave the plantation for at least some days or weeks in order that they might feel sure that they were free.

Secondly, in the aftermath of the collapse of the network of the plantation system under the growing impact of incessant warfare and the defeat of the Southern armies, the spirit of submission tended to fade away with the consequence that the traditional and the emotional links between the slave and the master began to break up.[26]

Radical changes in society are bound to break traditional ways of social interactions as it is particularly true when the traditional patterns of societal orientation have had a strong hold on the individuals some of whom would raise serious questions on the need for such changes. Others would endorse changes since they find in them seeds of growth. Certain changes are aimed at improving the existing conditions even though the objectives may not be fully realized. Individuals always search for means to improve the prevailing conditions as a means to lighten the burden on life or to provide greater momentum to social and political development.

Thirdly, when we analyze the traditional channels of control on the Life of the Afro-American, it becomes quite obvious that the breakdown of the accepted norms of control under the slave regime showed signs of demoralizing him. As Sherman's columns of army swept through the narrow and intertwined streets of the State of Georgia, thousands of Afro-Americans from the plantations were also marching shoulder to shoulder in huge columns. But it was unfortunate that the demoralization, which had resulted from the trauma of war, had driven mothers to leave their children severely exhausted and dying by the way side; in a few extreme cases parents even put their children to death as they had become too heavy a burden to bear.[27] General H.W. Slocum, who had been commanding the left wing of the Army of the State of Georgia, has provided the following glaring account[28]:

> Negro men, women and children joined the columns at every mile of our march, many of them bringing horses and mules, which they had cheerfully turned over to the quartermaster's departments. I think at least thousands of these people had also joined the two columns at different points.

A large number of Afro-Americans were so old and frail that they were in no position to endure the ordeal under the blazing sun. "Others were too young to endure the fatigue of the long march," according to H.W. Slocum, "that they were left in the rear of the column. More than one-half of this number, reached the coast with us after a strenuous march."[29]

In the march countless number of Afro-Americans, according to C.D. Goodson, flocked to army camps and cities in search of employment to eke out a paltry existence or to store up experience in life.[30] When the troops captured Savannah in the State of Georgia, hundreds of Afro-Americans from the adjacent plantations swarmed into the city. The exodus of the hordes of refugees into various army camps and the surrounding regions created problems of discipline and sordid social condition. An educated clergyman, who had worked among the freed Afro-Americans in the neighbouring State of South Carolina, described the demoralization in the following manner[31]:

> This whole section with its hundreds and thousands of men, women and children just broken forth from slavery, was so far as these were concerned, lying under an almost absolute physical as well as moral interdict. There was none to baptize their children, to perform marriage or even to bury the dead. A ministry had to be created at once, to ease the situation that had existed at the time.

### (B) Urgent Appeal to Philanthropists

In the face of such a harsh dilemma, General Sherman sent out an urgent appeal to a number of philanthropists of the North to come to the rescue of the poverty-stricken refugees. In quick response to the general's appeal, Freedman's Aid Societies soon sprang up in New York, Boston and in Philadelphia. In March 1863, Edward L. Pierce, an official delegate of the aid society, sailed from New York along with other men and women who were said to constitute what was considered "the first missionary expedition to propagate industry, religion and education among the contraband at Hilton Head in the State of South Carolina."[32] The group comprised forty-five men and fifteen women whose job it was to encourage agriculture and eventually some of the same missionaries became teachers. The majority of them served as superintendents, distributing food and clothing among the needy and the disabled.

The number of teachers and superintendents soon increased to approximately one hundred in a few months as there were about four thousand freedmen toiling on some 15,000 acres of corn and potato fields by summer.[33] The missionaries and teachers formed the nucleus of a group that was to devote itself to preparing the Afro-American to shoulder the added obligation of citizenship.

The situation created by the Afro-American refugees in camps and urban areas brought about changes in the attitude of the Government, as their plight required the officials to assume additional obligations over the lives of the former slaves. The Afro-Americans, who had managed to escape from the control of their owners, were still treated as "contraband" as though they were mere commodities being transported from one town to another.[34] After the slaves living in the adjacent areas had learned of their plight they, including women and children, flocked to the army camps. The men were put to work. The Southern planters had also fled, leaving cotton crops and hundreds of slaves in virtual limbo. Edward L. Pierce explains the aims of the Secretary of the Treasury[35]:

> A special agent to visit this district for the sole purpose of reporting upon the conditions of the Negroes who had been abandoned by the white population, and of suggesting some plan for the organization of their labour and the promotion of their general well-being.

After studying the agent's report, the Treasury commissioned Edward Pierce to take charge of the freedmen as he had already demonstrated considerable skill in handling analogous situation in the State of Virginia. An evaluation of the problems faced by contraband is significant to our study.

No sooner had the Union army advanced into the country's other regions than they confronted the problem of the so-called contraband who had come to the army camps. The presence of slaveholders in the western region even confounded the situation forcing the commander of the Department of Military to issue an order to the effect that fugitive slaves were not to be allowed to enter the camps and that the unemployed men were to be turned away. But the move resulted in a storm of protest in Congress and it manifested itself in the refusal to obey the order by several subordinate officers in the eastern region of the United States. Although General Butler had made several attempts to ban the fugitive slaves from the Union camps in the State of Louisiana, he was compelled to modify the orders, employing them first as labourers and, as time went on, as servants and soldiers. Du Bois commented[36]:

> Through the wages and bounty money thus received [during the war], a large fund of something between five and ten millions of dollars was distributed among the freed men.

The author conceded[37] that the amount represented a "mere pittance per capita, but enough in some cases to enable the recipients to buy a little land and start as small farmers."[38] Yet, the wages paid out to the servants and labourers in the army camps and the bounties the soldiers did receive were not ample for the recipients to establish themselves as free workers. It became apparent that the freed slaves still had to face depravation despite the changes in the wake of the new era of freedom. There was no noticeable change for many years in the lives of Afro-Americans, who still face serious challenges in social and economic spheres in the most affluent country in the world.

In order to assist the freed Afro-Americans, a bill had been introduced in Congress in 1863 providing for the establishment of a department to assist them and it was only after receiving a flood of petitions from Freedmen's Societies that Congress finally gave any serious thought to it. The Afro-Americans lived all the while in poverty, depravation and ignorance. Charles Summer at last endorsed the implementation of a bill for the formation of a department to handle the problem of the black man in a thorough manner.

The black man had not been considered an individual with flesh and blood, let alone a citizen with basic privileges and rights which other people enjoyed with no reservations.

As nothing else could be expected from a society which had largely closed its eyes to the plight of Afro-Americans, Summer's bill was defeated. Another bill enacted in 1865 saw the birth of a Bureau of Refugees, Freedom, and Abandoned Lands in the War Department, to be known as Freedman's Bureau which was to last during the Civil War and for another year thereafter. And what were the aims of the Bureau?[39]

> The Secretary of War may direct such issues of provisions, clothing and fuel as he may deem needful for the immediate and temporary shelter and also the destitute and suffering refugees and their wives and children.

## (C) Additional Obligations

Furthermore, the President named the commissioner to fulfil the following additional obligations[40]:

> To provide the loyal refugees and freedmen, such tracts of land within the insurrectionary states as shall have been abandoned, or to which the United States shall have acquired title by confiscation or sale, or otherwise, and to every male citizen, whether refugee or freedman, as aforesaid, there

> shall be assigned not more than forty acres of such land and the individual to whom it was so assigned shall be protected in the use, and general enjoyment of the property for the term of three years at an annual rent that should not exceed six per cent upon the value of such land, as it was appraised by the state authorities in the year eighteen hundred and sixty, for the chief purpose of taxation and if no such appraisal can be found, then no rental shall be based upon the estimated value of the land in the said year, to be ascertained in such manner as the commissioner may by regulation prescribe.

It was also stipulated that at the end of the prescribed term or at any time during that term, the occupants of any parcel of land may purchase the same and receive the title necessary to complete the transaction by paying "for the value of the land, as ascertained and futed for the purpose of determining the annual rent aforesaid."[41] Du Bois points out the serious problems faced by the Freedmen's Bureau in carrying out its obligations[42]:

> .....to make as rapidly as possible a general survey of conditions and needs in every state and locality; and to relieve immediate hunger and distress; to appoint state commissioners and upwards of 900 Bureau officials; to put the labourers to work at regular wage; to transport needed labourers, teachers and officials.

The Bureau was saddled with the responsibility of opening up schools, to pay bounty to Afro-American soldiers and their families burdened with financial stress in addition to building hospitals and clinics.[43] Even at its very inception, the Bureau had its quota of trouble in carrying out the assigned responsibilities for the well-being of the Afro-American community. Referring to the gloomy picture, General Howard makes the following observation[44]:

> Many were afraid to remain on the soil, which they had tilled as slaves, lest by some trick they might find themselves in bondage again. Others supposed that the Government would either take the entire supervision of their labour, or divide up among them the land of the conquered owner and **furnish them with all that might be necessary to begin life as an independent farmer.**

The impetuous collapse of the rebellion, inevitably making the historic proclamation of emancipation a universal truism, hit the society with the force of a tidal wave breaking up the traditional links of life. The impact of the change was so strong that even the well disposed and many humane landowners were at a loss as to how to lay the foundation for a new society and how to realign the new social structure. It is against this background that we have to analyze the relevant facets of contemporary Afro-American society and its struggle for justice. Denying justice to a collectivity would result in social upheavals and in our times Rev. Dr. King, under the strong influence of Gandhiji, has turned the persistent yearning of Afro-Americans into a mass campaign based on sound Gandhian philosophy to extinguish the smouldering flames of racial conflicts.

An analysis of the first wave of Afro-Americans and the difficult racial problems they had faced *vis-à-vis* other groups of people who came to America falls within the scope of the present study. The Analysis is vital for a clear understanding of the socio-political issues they had faced in the past. We have to evaluate three main points here:

(i) In contrast to the Pilgrim Fathers and other countless men and women who had willingly landed on the American shores, including the famous Ellis Island in New York, in search of an oasis of freedom, the African people were bundled up in ships and sent into the land of the free as chattels.

(ii) As a supreme paradox, they failed to find even a spark of freedom in the land of liberty, but they found bondage and repression instead.

(iii) The main objective here is to discuss the early phase of the arrival of Afro-Americans and its implications by attempting to establish the correlationship with the social status they gradually began to gain in the American society. This change in social attitudes was largely brought about by the new laws.

### (D) The Saga of Jamestown

A Dutch ship, brought the first batch of slaves from Africa into America as early as 1620, arriving at Jamestown in Virginia. Many of them were transported across the open sea against their will. During the hazardous voyage, many had died of self-inflicted wounds as their reaction had been spasmodic, certainly sulky, and even today the general effects of that historical background are visible to a great degree to any observer, including the researcher widely travelling in the South interviewing people and gathering relevant data to complete the study. Understandably, this propensity is more conspicuous in the South than in the Northern parts of the United States. This correlation between the developments in the past and the problems faced by the present generation should receive adequate attention to indicate that the Afro-Americans of the current generation have made considerable progress, progress that has surpassed the hopes of their ancestors.

England, by the virtue of the Treaty of 1713, had been a world leader in the trafficking of slaves; a scourge, which assumed colossal proportions stretching even to the world's most remote corners. The boundless selfish economic interests had nourished the roots of slavery. We shall now evaluate the specific policies of the local Governments in the United States towards slavery and in doing so the following important aspects should be carefully analyzed.

First, ever since slavery began to take roots in the rich American soil, the local Governments, notwithstanding the concepts of liberty and equality, remained inimical to the malediction of the human bondage imposed on Afro-Americans. The first census taken in 1790 showed that 670,000 slaves lived in the State of Georgia and Virginia as sharecroppers, indebted for life to the landlords. The legal system served in several states served as a vehicle of repression. **Obviously, the Afro-Americans' toils had proved vital to the opulence of American settlement, a fad not fully appreciated in Canada and the United States, where slavery became a reality of life more than anywhere else in the globe.**

Second, the United States was also a land of slaves. Its economy had always been interlinked to the toil of slaves as roots to the trees. Its earlier development speaks of a heart-renting story of the great grandfathers of the present day Afro-Americans. This economic dimension is pivotal to the proper understanding of and knowledge about the contemporary state of Afro-Americans. Their social status was greatly enhanced as a result of the non-violent resistance put up by Rev. Dr. King in our times, under the sway of the Gandhian ideals, in gaining new grounds in the legal and educational spheres. Their progress is something newfangled in American society.

Third, the great ancestors of Afro-Americans residing in urban centres and also in the isolated countryside had suffered great indignities during the slave and post-emancipation era. As far as the English colonial settlements were concerned, the horrid paradox had been to make the early Afro-American first a slave, then a servant while the racial metamorphosis stopped with his evolution into a second-class citizen.

Since the arrival of the first batches of African slaves, exploitation stretched out its lethal tentacles. The prolific virgin soil with all its potentialities and the scarcity of labour together with the greed inherent in human nature created a situation in which the hapless slave from Africa fell an easy prey to every kind of oppression and exploitation. The Maryland Colonial Assembly without any qualm imposed in 1664 "by the force of law the status of perpetual slavery upon the slave and their offspring."

These historic aspects are crucial to our study and in the researcher's travels in the South and his numerous interviews with people—black, white and of mixed origin—have led him to believe that the residue filtered from the past still exists in the minds of the segregationists and the Afro-Americans in the South. This is particularly so in large cities such as Birmingham, Alabama, Atlanta and Georgia. The moving portraits on the museum walls in these cities speak volumes of the horrible conditions faced by Afro-Americans in the past.

Still the segregationists of the present day cannot shut themselves off from the realization that Afro-Americans under the non-violent leadership of Rev. Dr. King have once again exemplified the efficacy of non-violence in the past.

The social trends prevalent in the past had much to do with the continuation of slavery in the United States. American planters and landlords would certainly have preferred their own serfs and servants from Europe to African slaves in the expectation that they would hold on to the traditional patterns of servitude familiar to them in rural Europe. Nevertheless, trading in slaves was common among the landlords as the following two important documents would speak for themselves reflecting the social order in existence then:

### *Document -1*

> About the last August, came in a Dutch man-of-war that sold us twenty Negroes, and Japazaous, the king of Patawomeck, came to Jamestown to desire two ships to come to trade in his river, for a more plentiful year of corn had not been in a long time, yet very contagious, and by the treachery of one Poule, in a manner turned heathen, we were quite jealous the savage would surprise us.
>
> Experienced in the new African slave trade, the Dutch merchants were indeed prepared to aid many of the settlers by providing the black labour .... Still, it was certain that the Negroes were meant to be the lowest serving class.

***Document -2***

> Section 91 of the Body of Liberties of Massachusetts was itself so hedged with implicit qualifications that Massachusetts did not find great difficulty over the years in accommodating its own interests to the slave trade prevalent at the time.

Today's Afro-Americans, in a broad sense, are struggling against the adverse effects of two basic aspects, viz. (i) the racial residue from the past and (ii) the forces that, to some degree, still keep them from the mainstreams of life in the United States.

Throughout the history of the United States, Afro-Americans (and Red Indians or the North American Indians) have suffered beyond words could express. Afro-Americans have been lynched. They have been beaten up. Their houses and churches have been blown up. They have long been denied permission to churches, schools, social clubs, hotels and motels. Governments even used trained dogs to quell their persistent campaigns for equality, which formed the foundation of a democratic society. It is extremely doubtful whether any community has suffered as much as the Afro-Americans (and Red Indians) have.

Alluding to the conditions of Afro-American community in the remote past, Howard observed[45]:

> In every state many thousands were found without employment, without homes, without means of subsistence, crowding into towns and about military posts, where they expected to find protection. It greatly shook and also shattered the previously existing social systems.

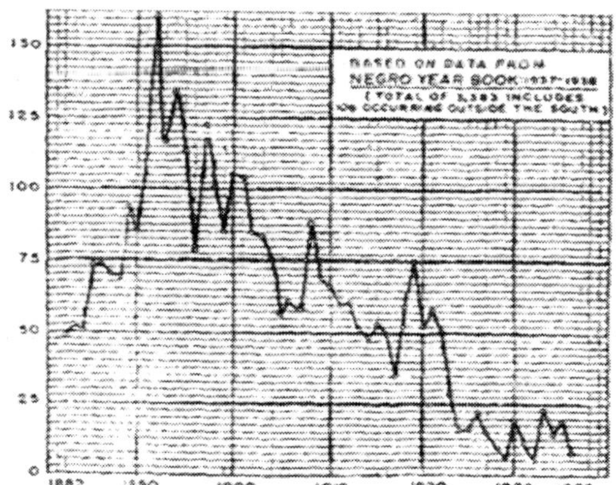


Afro-Americans lynched in the United States
(1882-1936)

Afro-Americans then, and now more than ever, wanted to be in charge of their destiny and resented being dictated to by others.

As a result of the persistent struggle over the last several decades, the Afro-American people have made great progress. Rev. Dr. King's non-violent methods gave their struggle a humane face in addition to international recognition.[46]

It is time that we moved the investigation to the question of suffrage and its impact on the Afro-American community. The next chapter will delve into the important issues of suffrage and the hurdles the black people faced in their search for justice. We will further discuss judicial and legislative attitudes towards Afro-American voter registration for franchise and the mounting opposition to such policies.

## SUMMARY

1. In the years following the outbreak of the civil war United States Senate endorsed a number of resolutions indicating that the slave status of the Afro-American had become an accomplished fact.
2. Two factions among the Radical Republicans unanimously agreed that victory in the Civil War could come only with the emancipation of the slaves eroding the power of the planter aristocracy in the South. Their motive was more negative than positive. But all is well that ends well.
3. During the initial phases of the Civil War, the American Secretary of State refused to accept the services of Afro-Americans.
4. President Lincoln issued his preliminary Emancipation Proclamation on January 1, 1863. The final proclamation declared that all persons who had been serving as slaves within the states which were in rebellion against the United States were free. The emancipated Afro-Americans were admonished to refrain from violence and to accept employment at reasonable wages.
5. The historic Emancipation Proclamation meant improved status in American life to the race-conscious Afro-Americans.
6. The general pattern of Afro-Americans' behaviour towards their masters during the crisis in the wake of the Civil War was largely determined by the nature of the relationship which had developed between the master and his slave.

7. Many slaves fled the plantations as soon as they heard that they were free men. But others were not aware of the full ramifications of the newly won freedom.
8. As an aftermath of the Emancipation Proclamation, hundreds and thousands of black people had flocked to the army camps in cities in search of employment. Still, others did so to gain a new experience in life as slavery had been their fate in life.
9. The success and/or failure of Afro-Americans in establishing themselves as free men and women capable of self-direction largely depended on their intelligence and competence. This is also true of all individuals regardless of race or the colour of the skin.

**Notes and References**

1. *Charles* A. Beard and Mary R. Beard, The Rise of American Civilization, (New York: 1927), Vol. 11, p. 29.
2. *Ibid.*, pp. 29-30
3. The victory of the Republicans at the polls in November 1860 marked the secession of the planter aristocracy. Even though the Republican Party was opposed to the owners of the plantations, there was no unanimity of views in the party on the question of the future status of the Negro. More details in A.H. Shannon, *The Racial Integrity of the American Nep.* (Nashville, Tennessee: Parthenon Press, 1951).
4. See Louis M. Hacker, *The Triumph of American Capitalism,* (New York: 1940). p. 340.
5. Franklin Frazier, *The Negro in the United States,* (New York: McMillan Co., 1957), p. 104.
6. Beard and Beard, op. cit., Vol. 11, p. 24. Please also see, Richard Sterner, *The Negro's Share,* (New York: Harper and Brothers, 1943). Especially Chapters 5 and 7.
7. Bell Invin Wiley, *Southern Negroes,* p. 296, (New Haven: Yale University Press, 1938).
8. W.E. Burghardt Du Bois, *Black Reconstruction in America,* (New York: 1935), p. 60.
9. Du Bois, *Ibid.,* p. 56.
10. W. Payne, *Africa and Colonialism,* (Boston: 1921), pp. 210-11.
11. *Ibid.,* p. 169. Also in Stretson Kennedy, *Southern Exposure* (New York: Doubleday and Company, 1946). The author explains the

hardships Afro-Americans had to endure in the seventeenth and eighteenth centuries in the United States.

12. W. Payne, op. cit., p. 196.
13. In August, 1862, Lincoln made his position clear in a letter to Horace Greeley.
14. Merwin Roe (ed.), *Speeches and Letters of Abraham Lincoln, 1832-1865,* (New York: 1907), p. 194.
15. The Negroes were called coloured people or members of the coloured race: Today they are generally known as black people or Afro-Americans.
16. Merwin Roe, op. cit., p. 195.
17. As a result of the Union blockade of the textile industry, both England and France adopted a favourable attitude towards the South. John Bright in England, for one, said that Civil War was a struggle for emancipation and democracy. See Beard and Beard, op. cit., Vol. 11, pp. 81-84 and Karl Marx and Frederic Engels, *The Civil War in the United States,* (New York: 1937) pp. 3-12 and 40-42.
18. The Thirteenth Amendment to the Constitution of the United States abolishing slavery came into force on December 18, 1865. In January 1865 a resolution for the amendment to abolish slavery was first introduced in the Senate.
19. Thomas A. Higginson, *Army Life in a Black Regiment,* (Boston: 1870), p. 250.
20. Mark Fisher, *The Master's Slave*—Elijah John Fisher (Philadelphia, 1922), pp. 6-8.
21. J. Vance Lewis, *Out of the Ditch: A True Story of an Ex-slave,* (Houston, Texas, 1910), p. 9.
22. Miles Mark Fisher, op. cit., p. 19. When the Union army advanced, it could generally rely upon the Afro-Americans, particularly the field slaves, to engage in espionage activity and provide important information.
23. J. Vance Lewis, op. cit., p. 97. At the same time, the general attitude of subordination was still so strong among some slaves that they were fearful to assert their newly acquired rights and privileges. When some slaves were informed of their freedom, they were in great suspense and awe.
24. *Ibid.*, p. 19.

25. Booker T. Washington wrote even after the slaves were free, they were not sure of their new status. *Up from Slavery,* (New York: 1902), p. 23.
26. L.J. Coppin, *Unwritten History,* (Philadelphia: 1920), pp. 91-92.
27. Elizabeth Pearson, *War Letters from Port Royal, Written at the time of the Civil War,* (Boston: 1906), pp. 293-94.
28. As quoted in Ekbeth Botume, *First Days Among the Contraband,* (Boston: 1893), p. 79.
29. *Ibid.,* p. 80. It is quite striking to note that some freed slaves were too old to be independent and continued to live in small houses. Their 'employers' paid them what they deemed their services were worth. The freed slave was never able to throw off the terrible burden of fear he always had of his master over the years. Other details in Vann C. Woodward, *Origins of the New South, 1877-1913.* (Baton Rouge: Louisiana State University Press, 1951).
30. Carter G. Woodson, *A Century of Negro Migration,* (Washington, D.C., 1980). According to one estimate, some 40,000 Negroes came from Southern plantations to the District of Columbia in 1864. p. 105.
31. T.G. Steward, *Fifty Years in the Gospel Ministry,* Philadelphia: 1922), p. 33.
32. Botune, op. cit., pp. 19-21.
33. Pearson, op. cit., "Introduction", p. VII.
34. After General Butler used the term "contraband" in reference to the escaped slaves, the term was applied to Negroes whom the Confederates had used for military purposes. Eventually, the term was applied to all slaves of disloyal owners. In Wiley, op. cit., pp. 176 77.
35. Edward L. Pierce, *The Negroes at Port Royal,* (Boston, 1862).
36. *Ibid.*
37. W.E.B. Du Bois, "The Negro Landholders of Georgia," *Bulletin of the Department of Labour,* No.35 (Washington, 1901), p. 647.
38. *Ibid.,* pp. 450-53.
39. Edward L. Pierce, op. cit., p. 137.
40. *Ibid.,* p. 67.
41. *Ibid.,* pp. 120-23.
42. W.E.B. Du Bois, op. cit., p. 197
43. Du Bois, *Ibid.,* p. 225.
44. Quoted in *Black Reconstruction in America,* W.E.B. Du Bois, (New York: Harcourt, Brace and Company, Inc.,) p. 224.

45. *Civil Rights and the American Negro: A Documentary History,* Alfred P. Blazer and Robert L. Sengerin (New York: Trident Press, 1961), pp. 12-14.
46. In W.E.B. Du Bois, op. cit. p. 201. Also see Merton E. Coutler, "The South During Reconstruction: 1865-1877 (Baton Rouge: Louisiana State University Press, 1947). The author explains the dilemma faced by the freed slaves during the period of reconstruction and its overall effects on their social attitudes. In the past, the helplessness of Afro-Americans, on the one hand, and the paternalistic attitude of the white-skinned society, on the other, indicated the terms on which the accommodation of the races had been established. In subsequent periods despite the racial turmoil and the denial of civil rights, five decades after Emancipation, 90 per cent of Afro-Americans were still residing in the South and there had been discussion among Afro-American leaders of a large exodus from the South. The issue of Afro-American leaving the South could not be settled either in discussions or in theoretical arguments while the masses of Afro-Americans chose to remain in the South which was the region where they were in a position to secure a livelihood. Added to that was the fact that the majority of Afro-Americans in the North had a precarious existence the reason being that they had not been able to gain a foothold in industry (Alfred H. Stone, *Studies in the American Race Problem, and later* (New York, 1998, pp. 151-205). A large part of Afro-American population continued to find its chief means of livelihood in agriculture, as did their ancestors.

# CHAPTER-III

# AFRO-AMERICAN SUFFRAGE: CHALLENGES AND QUESTS

## ARTICLE-1

### (A) Social Constraints

Since the slaves had been completely deprived of the status as citizens, it was inconceivable that the Afro-Americans would be granted suffrage during the pre-emancipation era. Even the free Afro-American, as previously noted, had faced serious social limitations as only in a handful of Northern states was he permitted to exercise franchise. That prevailed in a country, which had proclaimed Declaration of Independence guaranteeing justice, liberty and equality for all citizens irrespective of colour! Even today, two centuries after the epoch-making proclamation, the Afro-Americans do not have equality or fraternity in several parts of the country. Thus, Rev. Dr. King's attempts, based on the enlightened Gandhian ideals, were directed against the eradication of such social evils the aim of which was to keep them in the swarthy comers of ignorance and servitude. The remnants of such a policy practised in the past can still be found in the South and the North alike. According to Maurice Davie, "at the time of the Civil War only states, all in the North, made no discrimination in suffrage..."[1] The author continues, "New York permitted Negroes to vote, but there was a special property qualification on them."[2] How severe were the requirements? To what degree did the regulations keep the Afro-Americans in obsequious social condition? Three important aspects deserve our attention here.

(1) Extra-legal means were employed to reduce or altogether eliminate the Afro-American vote as such means became the obvious

symbols of the general social attitude towards the Afro-American. After 1890, the highly questionable practices were replaced by a series of far-fetched legal prerequisites, which in reality took away the Afro-American's right to vote further pushing America's black community into disgrace and humiliation. Amendments to the state constitutions restricting the franchise were introduced with dexterous subtlety under the pretext of meeting the requirements of the Constitution of the United States.

(2) The educational requirements were administered in a discriminatory manner and Gunnar Myrdal makes the following comments germane to the problem[4]:

> ...relatively seldom is a white man 'insulted' by being given the test when he mispronounced a single word. Even the professors at Tuskagee and other Negro universities have been disfranchised by failing to pass these tests.

(3) The laws were applied much more stringently to Afro-Americans than to others as the net result of the flagrantly discriminatory policy was to secure an electorate devoid of Afro-American voters. Hence no office holders or representatives to speak on their behalf in Congress. "From the Southern stand-point," Maurice Davie says, "these measures constituted the New Reconstruction or the restoration of white supremacy."[5] The pigmentation of the skin had much to do with the perpetuation of discriminatory practices and other forms of political and economic subjugation in the United States as history stands witness to this fact carved out in granite.

## (B) What were the Restrictive Measures?

Several deliberate measures were introduced to proscribe Afro-American suffrage in the nineteenth century. While some policies were patently discriminatory others were indeed subtle with clear racial overtones, sufficiently clear for impartial minds to see.

In a clear attempt to reduce the number of Afro-American voters and, at the same time, not to disqualify others, many states had adopted a device. The device barred an individual from meeting the educational and property requirements to continue as a voter for life based on three basic criteria, viz. (i) if he had been a voter in 1866; (ii) a veteran who had fought in the Civil War; and (iii) the lineal descendant of such a voter or soldier provided that he had registered prior to a specific date.

These stipulations were in violation of constitutional assurances as Afro-Americans were not eligible to vote before 1866.[6] Maurice Davie observes.[7]

> In an effort to circumvent the decision, the state of Oklahoma passed a statute in 1916, re-enacted in 1932, requiring everyone eligible to register to do so within twelve days or to be barred from registering thereafter.
>
> However, the statute had also provided that all those who had voted in 1914 were registered automatically. As Negroes had been disfranchised by the grandfather clause in 1914, they stood automatically franchised by the new Act.

The infamous "grandfather clause", a retrograde clause at best, had precluded the Afro-American voters from exercising franchise on the basis of the absence of suffrage before 1866. According to the preeminently prejudicial "grandfather clause," an individual should have voted in the year 1866, when the black people were even barred from looking at a polling station.[8]

The strong wave of opposition to the black suffrage also had its regional differences and referring to the egregious disparities, H.D. Price remarks[9]:

> A logical point at which to begin the analysis of opposition to the problem of Negro registration is by comparing areas where Negroes make up a large proportion of the population with areas where there are relatively few Negroes. On a national scale, the differences between the racial attitudes of the predominantly white North and attitudes of the South are obvious to an impartial observer.

## ARTICLE -2

### (A) Divergent Criteria

Besides the legal and pseudo-legal apparatus which had been in force to cripple Afro-American suffrage, other methods were employed, methods such as intimidation, trickery and severe forms of discrimination in the actual enforcement of the law. The Afro-Americans, needless to say, had nowhere to turn for justice and equality as both had been denied them based on the prevailing social outlook and the discriminatory attitude. In the election held in Florida separate booths were set up for the blacks, supervised by white-skinned officials. The Afro-American lines moved at a snail's pace that the majority of would-be black voters, after patiently waiting in line for hours, were unable to exercise their franchise on time. Those who had attempted to register in the election in the southern State of Louisiana, were required to give their age precisely, so precisely as to years, months and even days. Those who had failed to give out the exact information were barred while others were required to provide no such information. And yet another dubious method was to require the Afro-Americans to register only on one day rendering them virtually impossible to travel from distant regions to the office. Many were given the most inexcusable and flimsy reasons for not permitting them to register to vote. The story was told of a white man living in the North quering an Afro-American if he could exercise franchise and his cryptic reply was: "Oh, yeah, sir, I can vote all right—that is, I can vote if I can get registered, but I have been trying to get registered for the past ten years, and I'am always just too late or just too early."[10] There was more. In certain instances, the Afro-Americans were tested as to their basic knowledge of the Constitution while others, were not tested at all. In at least one instance a voter was required to recite the first paragraph of the Constitution verbatim and its proven implications to the populace. The black man's impetuous reply was: "Boss, Ah guess that means us niggers don't vote." Still startling was the truism that if a black American attempted to exercise franchise in one region of the South, where others remained hostile to him, he certainly ran the risk of losing whatever position he had previously held in the community or even being forced out of the neighbourhood. His life will be threatened. His property may be sabotaged. Thomas Bailey gives the following account of the life of Afro-Americans in their quest for rights on the jagged road to equality while drifting into a state of almost stupor.[12]

> There are numerous instances or Negroes who attempted to register or vote, and being driven away, beaten, even killed. Generally, the opposition takes the form of intimidation.

The enemies of the Afro-American suffrage resorted to a number of extra-legal methods to prevent the blacks from voting and the Afro-American society[13] had to face different shades of injustice. Referring to the inherent social contradictions, Maurice Davie explains[14]:

> Many had intended to terrorize the Negro citizens who might seek to cast ballots in the elections held in Dennison, Texas, in the fall of 1932...Riots on election day in which both whites and Negroes have been killed have occurred in different sections of the South.

It is against this background that we have to assess the message of Rev. Dr. King, who was well aware of the historical precedents of the discriminatory attitudes towards the Afro-American in the United States. In the early sixties he stepped up his non-violent struggle for Afro-American franchise in Birmingham and Selma. He rightly chose the just path of Gandhian non-violence having fully imbibed its meaning and relevance in the light of the highly successful experiment conducted by the Indian saint to solve a parallel crisis in India. While other black leaders in the United States advocated violence to wipe off the stains of the past, Rev. Dr. King strictly adhered to the Gandhian non-violent philosophy with the whole-hearted approval of thousands of followers who looked upon him as their servant and guide. The American civil rights leader knew that his ancestors had been subjected to various strands of injustice in their quest for equality and one of the most repressive measures was the infamous poll tax. Its principal objective was to restrict the Afro-American suffrage effectively—and severely—as the levy had far-reaching repercussions.

### (B) The Infamous Poll Tax

The poll tax was one of two chief legal arms aimed at restricting the Afro-American suffrage in the South, a device that had also received the strongest political challenge. In 1948, the legal requirement in Alabama, Arkansas, Mississippi, South Carolina, Tennessee, Texas and Virginia was the payment of the poll tax as a precondition to vote.[15]

The poll tax, was a payment of money rather than a tax in the strict sense of a levy the payment of which was strictly enforced. It required the payment of one dollar to two dollars on an annual basis in order to cast the ballot and in some states such as Alabama, Mississippi and Virginia. The tax had been cumulative with the unerring requirement that arrears should be paid with interest added on to the tax. Its serious result was those who had defaulted were forced to pay as much as thirty to forty dollars to vote. William Nolan comments on the payment of the inglorious and dreaded tax[17]:

> Thus it may be necessary to pay as much as thirty to forty dollars in order to vote. Moreover, in four states the tax must also be paid six to ten months ahead; that means it comes due long in advance of voting day, at a time when few people are thinking of election.

The payment varied from state to state, although its purpose, regardless of the variations, was to obstruct the path of Afro-American suffrage with unnecessary roadblocks. William Nowlin points out[18]:

> Some states had required that the receipt for the payment of the poll tax be produced when one voted; some required receipts for the preceding two and three years; while others, like Alabama, insisted on receipt for every year since attaining voting age.

The amount of poll tax the black voters were required to pay may not appear too large to many; but it had been unquestionably prohibitive to the meagre budget of an Afro-American farmer or to any average labourer whose annual income was less than hundred dollars. "The poll tax," according to Davie, "did not produce much revenue, nor did it act as a qualitative guarantee for electors."[19] He refers to the actual objective of the poll tax, a razor sharp racist tool, in the following penetrating observation[20]:

> It is openly admitted in every state that a large number, in some instances a vast majority, of the poll tax receipts are paid for by politicians who hold them and vote for them wholesale.
>
> The poll tax is only partially a racial question but fundamentally, it is a weapon against progressive politics, another device to maintain the *status quo*...

## (C) An Obtuse Apparatus

Furthermore, the abhorrent poll tax had generally been regarded as an obtuse socio-political apparatus to maintain control by a minority of middle class individuals. They had controlled the local political engines and its industrial and commercial blood vessels, a control that they would safeguard at any cost. The murky side of the imposition of the poll tax was evident in the presidential election held in 1932 when only 22.2 per cent of eligible citizens cast ballots[21] in the poll-tax states as against 70.7 per cent in states without the poll tax. Meanwhile, in the 1936 general election the percentages were 22 in the states with the poll tax as against 72 in those without the tax. Thus, it was easy to conclude that the poll tax had reduced the process to a mere travesty in the South, unlocking the narrow portals to economic feudalism at its worst. The victims had largely been Afro-Americans who were swimming with five bricks in two hands in a vast ocean of inequality.

It was quite natural for an individual, any individual, who had owed his election victory to a small cadre of individuals of a particular state to represent the interest of that minority. In the case of the specific situation in the South, the interests were not those of the Afro-Americans, but of the white skinned people whose interests took precedence to the exclusion of the indigencies of black America at large. Corruption and disregard for law and order had been common in the voting procedures in many parts of the South mainly to safeguard the vested interests of the men in power of the accomplished lectures of the racist doctrines. Black man's social equality was as irrelevant as beauty in a prison guard. Maurice Davie talks about the racist sermons.[22]

> ...much of the voting is carried on with a comption and disrespect for law that is found in few other areas of the country at the time. In some regions the situation was much worse than in others...Southern politics has remained provincial and reactionary.

The political activities in the South, tainted by racism, had remained clannish to keep the Afro-American voters in the shadow of subjugation while Rev. Dr. King had devoted his life for the eradication of the political malaise following the non-violent path as did Gandhiji in India.

Virginius Dabney, a liberal Southern publicist makes the following blunt remarks on the general impact of the notorious poll tax on the Afro-American community[23]:

> Nearly every notorious known political mountebank, who has arisen in the twentieth century, has been chosen by a poll tax electorate in the South with no sense of improving the conditions for the Negro.

Regarding the somber lack of interest in the Southern states in fostering progressive measures for Negroes and others, Myrdal tells us that all modem reform movements which had deeply penetrated the rest of the nation such as women's suffrage and economic equality, the labour legislation, collective bargaining, child welfare, civil service reform, police and court reforms "have until recently, hardly touched the greater part of the South except in so far as the Federal government has imposed them from outside."[24] The Federal Government often failed the South.

Gunnar Myrdal has well stated[25]:

> For a hundred years this region which played such an important and distinguished role in the American Revolution and in the early history of the Republic, has not contributed to the entire country anything approaching its fair share of contribution to fresh political thinking as well as forward-looking political initiative in national issues. It has, on

the whole, served as a reactionary drag against the forces of change and progress.

Paul Lewinson argues that the strong conservative outlook of the South working against progress was "directly tied up with the Negro problem in several ways."[26] Rev. Dr. King, decades later, was combating the residual effects of the Southern conservatism in a non-violent manner to secure voting rights for America's black people and to gain access to colleges and public places such as clubs, coffee shops and hotels. The Afro-Americans, more than any other discernible social group, were the victims of the Southern orthodoxy which had no qualms in resorting to violent means to achieve its dismal objectives. **The American leader's on emphasis non-violence facing waves of opposition was one of the most significant aspects of his nationwide struggle for justice for Afro-Americans-on-violence to erase the social scars of racism and violent agitation, under the aegis of Gandhian ideology.**

One can discern a number of other crude instruments, which were employed to disfranchise the Afro-Americans and to rob them of their elemental human rights. Myrdal, regarding that decisive problem, states[27]:

> The devices inaugurated to disfranchise Negroes, the one-party system, the very low political participation on the part of the white masses, and other peculiarities of Southern politics—all tend to provide a disproportionate power base to a number of classes, groups and individuals who did feel that their main interests tied up with conservatism on social issues. But there is also a more direct connection between Southern conservatism and the distinct Negro problem. For constitutional and many other reasons, social reform measures would have to include Negroes, and this was resented.

It was a matter of much consternation that the born enemies of social reforms would generally work against the evolution of changes in society by rationalizing that reforms would ultimately enhance the status of Afro-Americans who wanted to attain equality, a situation which the South vehemently opposed. The people in the South, also in the North, objected to giving them any semblance of equality, lest the reform should loosen their traditional grip on the political and economic pulse of the nation.

But in the nation one could see a tidal wave of opposition to the blind disregard of justice to Afro-Americans including the imposition of the dreaded poll tax. Presidents Theodore Roosevelt and Harry Truman supported the attempts to abrogate the tax, and so, to give black America a face-lift in social identity. The nefarious revenue and the forces which had given it life and form had to face a wall of federal opposition on three principal grounds. What were those grounds? We shall study these now as they were windows for a clear understanding of the forces working against the sharply etched symbols of discrimination still facing opposition from Southern leaders, who might strangle political reforms with a thick rope.

(i) Bills were introduced in both Houses of Congress to eliminate the poll tax in Federal elections. Although the bill was passed on three different occasions in the House, the Southern Senators defeated it in the Senate by a fillibuster.

(ii) State campaigns were launched to repeat the poll tax in every poll-tax state. The campaigns had the support of the Southern Conference for Human Welfare, the Southern Regional Council, the Committee of Editors and Writers of the South and other local groups.

(iii) Court proceedings were instituted to test the constitutionality of the poll tax as it applied to Federal elections as well as to challenge the Congressional Apportionment Act.

These measures were necessary to remove the remaining unsightly finger marks of bondage in the South, which, without much external pressure, would not have implemented reforms to improve the life of the Afro-American who, according to the Southerners, were destined to remain in the lowest layer of social hierarchy. The claim of many Southerners as members belonging to a higher cultural and social group was a fallacy and the tax had its slow and painful death eventually opening up new doors of opportunity for the Afro-Americans, albeit at a snail's pace.

### (D) The Unjust Primary Election

One of the main planks of Rev. Dr. King's campaign was his strong plea for fairness in the system of elections in the United States. He had been fully aware that the Afro-American society had to overcome serious ethnic problems to register to vote or to exercise the franchise. When a person does not have the right to vote in a democratic nation, he is relegated to the status of a sub-human being. In the United States the Afro-Americans, who had been deprived of the franchise had neither the rights nor the privileges accorded to others, in addition to being denied the necessary means to facilitate changes vital to make headway in society. Social advancement is no easy task to accomplish.

Before we evaluate the effects of the convoluted system of primary elections on American Negroes, it is important to amplify them since they do not exist in many democratic countries and to establish their linkage with the present study.

At the outset, the primary election is a system of selecting a candidate to run for a public office. In a primary election each political party holds an election among its own members to choose the best available candidate to run for office in the general election. Any member of the patty may declare as a candidate for public office but only the winning candidate is formally qualified to represent as a serious candidate. The main advantage of this system is that it enables a political party to screen the individuals and choose the best candidates for office. Several primary elections take place before the general election and they provide reliable indications on the possibilities of individuals and ultimate chances of victory in the election.[28]

It is important to understand the effects of the primary election on Afro-Americans and their struggle to remove its serious limitations Rev. Dr. King directed his non-violent campaign to wipe off the racist tinge in the primary election system excluding his people from voting in America. One of the cardinal objectives of his peaceful formula was to enhance the political status of the black people as an appropriate avenue to attain justice based on the peaceful Gandhian philosophy.[29]

Referring to the manner by which Afro-Americans were excluded from the primary election, Maurice Davie says:[30]

> The most effective way by which Negroes have been excluded from voting in the South is the so-called white primaries whereby no Negroes are permitted even to vote in a party election, depriving them of their rights.

The National Association for the Advancement of Coloured People, known under its acronym NAACP,[31] had strongly opposed the racism built into the system, contesting it in the courts on a number of occasions involving Texas. In Texas, the Afro-Americans had been kept under subjugation for years and where they had been kicked, killed, lynched and denied admittance to public places. The black Americans, seething with discontent stemming from the lack of individual freedom had resisted, frequently with force, such impudence. Rev. Dr. King urged them to opt for Gandhian non-violence to attain justice as many stumbled around in the pursuit of equality.

In that pursuit and under the system of a single party dominance in Southern states, Afro-Americans had no access to primary election. They were permanently disfranchised. A decade or so later Rev. Dr. King expressed strong objections to that system in his interminable speeches and demonstrations in the United States. He argued that it had kept the black people away from attaining their rightful place in the American society although the Supreme Court of the United States, by a unanimous vote, had declared the law in Texas unconstitutional, besides being an open violation of the Fourteenth and Fifteenth Amendments. Henry Moon says: [32]

> The effects of the denial of freedom and opportunities to the Afro-American people are still visible in the United States in terms of their relatively low professional and educational profile without disregarding the fact that many have made considerable progress in various fields in the past.

Much of the progress can be attributed to the non-violent struggle launched by Rev. Dr. King whom Gandhiji had inspired although some of Dr. Kings critics called his ideas utopian. The Afro-American leader had every constitutional right to demand franchise and the non-violent approach had the added advantage of giving his campaign full constitutional validity.

The rejoinder by several white-primary states to such central decisions by the nation's highest court varied considerably. Texas and Louisiana, for instance, desisted from sticking to the discriminatory system with the result that Afro-Americans voted in the 1944 election in growing numbers for the first time since the Civil War had ended. The development added a glorious chapter to the annals of Afro-Americans in their arduous struggle to strip the political system of its iniquitous policies layer by layer. Each layer had blood stains.

## ARTICLE -3

### (A) "The Growing School of Thought"

The Southern liberals, on the other hand, strictly adhered to the traditional view to maintain the hold, that no black person should exercise franchise under any circumstance. Virginius Dabney maintained that there was a "growing school of thought in the South which held the view that any man, irrespective of his ethnic background, qualified to vote should be allowed to vote"[33] and that it was an extreme step for election officials "to disqualify thousands of Negroes arbitrarily while permitting thousands of white illiterates to troop to polls."[34] He goes on to state:[35]

> It is the firm view of this element that an educated and respectable Negro is a greater asset to the community and more deserving of the franchise than an unlettered white swine herd from the pine barns. It cannot be said that such a view is held by anything remotely approaching a majority of several Southern whites, but that view is undoubtedly gaining in favour. As Reconstruction and its many atrocities recede further and further into the background, more and more white Southerners are coming to feel that the loud cry of "white supremacy," raised too frequently in the past, is in the twentieth century mere rawhead and bloodybone with no substance or meaning.

Even in this century the black people in the United States (and Canada) do not have the freedom to purchase houses or to reside in certain areas of the country as they lack the legal authority to effect changes in the system which had been designed to keep them in the narrow economic and social back alleys. Despite the existence of the political system, which had been hostile to the interests of the Afro-American, the race issue, the result of a constricted vision, has caused to have its traditional political appeal. Since the days of Reconstruction, a number of key developments occurred with their net effect on the changing attitudes in the South, a detour from the traditional viewpoints, which Professor William G. Carleton explains in the following words:[36]

> ... the steady decline of the Negro population in relation to the white, the softening influence of education, the growing sense of Negro responsibility, the growing consciousness that the poor white man and the poor black man share a number of economic problems in common, the growth of New Deal ideas in spite of protestations to the contrary, the ever broadening influence of membership in mixed unions, and the participation in two world wars for democracy in a single generation.

Even so, there were individuals in the South steadfastly holding on to their obsolete viewpoints on race relations. They argued that Afro-Americans did not deserve equal status in the society, nor the right to vote, considering them without a scintilla of hesitation as the true descendants of erstwhile slaves with the taint remaining in their psyche. When Rev. Dr. King plunged into his Gandhian non-violent campaign for voting rights in the South, these misguided people, largely full-time converts to the Southern conservatism, virulently resisted him, stymieing his non-violent efforts for equality for Afro-Americans. And in the process their half-baked views constituted a malignant attack on justice.

### (B) Governmental Function

On March 16, less than a decade before Rev. Dr. King began his famous march in Atlanta, in the State of Georgia, the issue of Afro-American registration came up. **The black people were not permitted to register to vote and the denial of justice to his people compelled the American civil rights leader to act with celeb after having embraced the Gandhian ideology.** When the South had historically acted against the interests of Afro-Americans, other regions of the country were under thick racial clouds. Concerning that key aspect J. Tom Watson, Florida's Attorney General, says:[37]

> The political parties in Florida do not perform a governmental function, neither do they, or either of them, constitute a governmental agency. Such parties came into being not as the children of statutes, but only as a result of the direct exercise of the free will, and the choice of those citizens who compose them. Blacks do not have that choice.

The Attorney-General pointed out that the Democratic Party in Florida "has provided that only white persons may become members of such party."[38] Expectedly, the reaction to the Supreme Court's decision on the Democratic primary election varied widely, but it inflamed the emotions of those who had opposed the recognition of Afro-Americans on an equal basis. Those segregationists learned about racism from their mothers' laps. In the state of South Carolina one key legislator was quoted as saying of the prospective Afro-American voter. Well fight him at the polls if we have to bite the dust as did my early ancestors!"[39] In Florida, Tom Conely, Chairman of the Democratic Executive Committee, stated in less virulent terms: "We'll certainly resist if possible any attempt to have Negroes vote in our primaries."[40] Ironically, Senator Claude Pepper, who had been known for his proposed support for the cause of the Afro-American, made some of the strongest arguments in defence of primary election, which virtually precluded the black people from political activities. Paradoxically, Pepper was locked in a primary fight in which his alleged sympathy for Afro-Americans in different states had already become a perennial source of concern.

Other states, opposed to granting the voting right to Afro-Americans, have devised a variety of nasty schemes for their exclusion. Referring to this problem, H.D. Price states:[41]

> Arkansas sought partial evasion by establishing separate primaries for state and for national officers on the highly dubious assumption that the decision might not even apply to the state office and that a system of four primaries would prove workable.
>
> The sovereign state of Georgia which has been at odds with the Supreme Court off and on since 1795, refused to register Negroes as Democrats until after an important Georgia test case had been finally decided by the federal courts.
>
> Alabama adopted a special constitutional amendment subsequently held unconstitutional which had delegated wide discretionary power over registration to several local boards of registrars.

## (C) A Serious Caveat

The most serious caveat to the Supreme Court's decision may have come from South Carolina where the Palmetto state repealed *en masse* its laws governing the primary election system. "This device," Price adds, "send to prevent Negroes from voting in the 1946 South Carolina primaries, but they moved to challenge the system in the federal courts."[42]

In 1944, no Afro-American residing in Florida had the right to vote in the Democratic primary elections even though more than 20,000 people had been legally registered to participate in the general election. A decade later American's staunch Gandhian raised his strong voices against the excess of that system. The murky picture began changing and by May 1956, the total number of Afro-American registrations in the state of Florida had soared to 137,535 of whom 128,437,[43] had been registered as card carrying members of the Democratic Party, able to vote in the Democratic Party. The qualitative change, which had occurred in the mid-fifties, was soon accompanied by a quantitative increase in the matter of registration and in this case the swing in the attitude of the South towards Afro-American voting is significant to our study. It was an encouraging result of the non-violent efforts of Rev. Dr. King who, in the fifties, had embarked on peaceful Gandhian style demonstrations to clear up the system of the smudges of social inequities. His clarion call received a rousing response from millions of his dissipated fellow Afro-Americans, who armed with non-violence, became a force—a force to be reckoned with producing remarkable results. What were the results? Blauser and Zengerin have convincingly answered the question:[44]

> The period, 1957 to 1968, had witnessed the most dramatic series of changes in the general status of the Negro in America since the Civil War and Reconstruction, and finally, the United States Congress had passed four significant pieces of legislation touching on voting, the school desegregation, the national employment practices and public accommodation ...

Analyzing the socio-political changes which had taken place during the same period in terms of Afro-American rights, H.D. Price succinctly says:[45]

> No longer are the Negro voters limited to the local, state and presidential primary candidates, for members of the Democratic Executive Committee and in an increasing number contested general elections.

The general attitude in the South, regarding the issue of the black suffrage was one of determined opposition with the result that Afro-Americans, with a few recent exceptions, had been effectively kept out of the political arena for three main reasons. First of all, the people in the South had been strongly inclined to continue the unlawful political condition, as they had no inkling to give up the white supremacy, a concocted idea. Secondly, they were eager to safeguard the oligarchic control, which characterized social life in the South. Thirdly, granting suffrage to Afro-American citizens was tantamount to granting them potential social equality, a development which the South had always resented. People in the South, had long viewed the exclusion of the Afro-American from gaining political control as a measure of self-defence with scant concern for the veritable aspirations of the black society. In many ways, the Afro-Americans outnumbered others in a number of counties in the South and elsewhere they were sufficiently numerous to tilt the balance of power if the white-skinned people should split on political issues, something that often occurred in the wide world of politics in the United States. Besides, the South having lost its political cohesiveness was no more "solid" than the North. So, the Afro-American cry for equality could well be projected to create a facade of cohesion.

The argument that the Afro-Americans lacked education and experience and so unfit for equal treatment was merely a convenient rationalization. Rationalizations being subjective are prone to errors. (European colonizers advanced this view to maintain control over the people in Africa, also in Europe and Asia). Criticising the viewpoint that the black community had lacked education and skill in political matters, M.R. Davie points out that "what the Negroes are asking is merely that the laws be applied impartially,"[46] and referring to the problem of illiteracy the author makes the following cogent remarks:[47]

> There are great number of Negroes in the South capable of passing the literacy test, but who are nevertheless excluded. The demagogic point of view is that the Negro should not vote no matter what his accomplishments might be.

A concrete example of such erroneous perspective which prevented Afro-American from exercising the constitutional right to vote was echoed in the odious view expressed by Senator Vardaman on the Senate floor, a legislative hall, with reverberations in the country:[48]

> The God Almighty never intended that the Negro should share with the white man in the government of this country, and you cannot improve upon the plan of God Almighty to defeat His purpose, either by legislative enactments.

Based on this spurious notion the Southerners had argued that the Afro-Americans did not take interest in political issues as they remained unconcerned about the "sacred right of suffrage" while several Afro-Americans themselves complained about the passivity of their brethren. The root cause of all this was the deliberate attempt on the part of the whites to keep the black community away from political affairs, lest they should gradually gain upper hand in the influential world of politics. The silly argument was falsified when Afro-American who migrated from the South to the North started showing genuine interest in politics when they found themselves free to do so, opening up new vistas in their lives in many regions.

Available signs in several regions in the South now are indicative of the development that the appeal of the race issue is on the wane, and the aggregate effect of a variety of factors is making itself felt in the attitude of the southerners. Professor W. Carleton says that one of the causes for the changing attitude was "the steady decline of the Negro population in relation to the white.. ."[49]

### (D) The Northward Migration

The racial picture in the North was different from that in the South as the northern region, in comparison, was racially much more tolerant than the South; the Afro-Americans could not only exercise their franchise about the same proportion as the rest of the society but also held public offices in increasing numbers. The Southerner resented the enhancement of their social status especially when many of them came to hold important public oftices in the South, making the community a force to be reckoned with. M.R. Davie says:[50]

> Whereas in the deep South there is not a single member of the legislature, a single judicial officer, or a single member of the city council who is colored [Afro-American], a large and increasing number of state and city offices were held by Northern Negroes. This situation has been indeed marked since 1930.

One can also notice distinct political preference among Afro-American voters who often supported the Democratic Party which, they felt, would work for their cause as opposed to the Republican Party which could not win their trust. The black members in the legislative assembly were elected from the constituencies where the majority of voters were blacks. Nonetheless, in the case of John Adams Jr., a lawyer from Omaha (State of Nebraska in the South) and of African background was elected to the unicameral body of the legislative assembly in 1936. A white-skinned leader opposed him in an electorate with a considerable number of white-skinned voters, a development that was inconceivable in the South of the yester-year providing more than a window into the racial mores of the South. In the North, Afro-Americans were elected or named to a number of important state commissions and agencies to which they had rendered laudable service, a positive aspect of the suffrage of Afro-Americans. M.R. Davie points out:[51]

> Negroes have also been elected or appointed to various state commissions and boards. Elective or appointive positions in the public services are held by Negroes in every major city in the North.

These positions, included "such offices as city councilmen, judges, prosecuting attorneys, members of the board of education, Civil Service Commissions and other official bodies."[52] Despite the upward political mobility being gained by Afro-Americans in the North, persistent white resistance hampered progress. Rev. Dr. King took up the issue and it should be said to his credit that with *ahimsa* and self-sacrifice, true to a Gandhian disciple he fought the menace. He succeeded in breaking up the ice to a considerable degree. He integrated his non-violent campaigns in the South into the proven Gandhian way for social justice for Afro-America.

The fact that Afro-Americans became more numerous and were more conscious of their political rights and privileges to further their cause accounted much for their newly gained political strength in the North and in the emerging political process they began to develop group cohesiveness. In the past, the Afro-American society had blindly supported the Republican Party platform demonstrating, at the same time, a strong degree of hesitation to aspire to public office. The paradox in such an attitude had been that the Republican Party, being sure of the blind Afro-American support, and the Democrats not expecting it, had expressed no concern for the black man's vote. Compelled by the predicament and spurred on by many Afro-American leaders, the black people began channelling their support strictly on racial lines, thereby creating more unity than other ethnic communities on important issues, which had been placed before the electorate. The increasing race prejudice generally found among white-skinned people against Afro-Americans (the prejudice also exists among white-skinned people one of strata against another) had at least one bright side as it turned out to be an important incentive to cultivate a strong sense of solidarity among Afro-Americans making it an important part of their concerted struggle for justice in the United States. The Afro-American was no longer a political paw on the chessboard. His ballot could swing to either side of the political spectrum and be quite decisive in the power game.

The final result of Afro-Americans' burgeoning political strength, the product of his role in participatory democracy, was seen in the development that black man began to secure better treatment, new employment opportunities in civil service positions which remained a significant outlet for white-collar workers, but denied to back people. In a broad analysis of the situation which was yet not flawless, M.R. Davie points out the following:[53]

> He [Afro-American] has pressed for Federal anti-lynching laws, Federal aid for Negro education in the South, and repeal of the poll tax. His position is still far from one of equality, and so long he is discriminated against on account of his race and as long as his civil rights are denied, there will continue to be a Negro vote.
>
> ... There are some Negro leaders who believe that race interests have been superseded by class interests and that the Negro's interests as a wage earner were of greater importance than his race consciousness.

Even in the midst of racial solidarity and the principal concern with his own economic and social welfare, Afro-American, on the whole evinced little enthusiasm in responding to the call of the radical groups to react strongly to the issues affecting him. Yet in the process they had developed more solidarity than other social groups on different issues placed before the electorate. The fact remained that despite the emergence of the Afro-American solidarity, the black people demonstrated little or no tendency to respond to the political and economic overtures of the radical groups which, motivated more by the desire to furbish their pedantic political ideology than by any genuine interest in or sympathy for the Afro-Americans cause made a bid for the black mans support. The Socialist party, not at all a 'powerful entity,' ceased the opportunity promising them strong anti-lynching regulations as well as the implementation "of Constitutional guarantees of economic, political and legal equality for the Negro," the demands which the black people had been making for years. "Equal rights for Negroes" was an important slogan on the Communist platform adopted by party rank and file with unanimous voice. The Communist Party, quite vociferous during the horrid depression era renewing their attempts to muster Afro-American support, obliterated the colour barrier within its own party ranks so thoroughly that it could not entertain even a lingering hope of substantial white support.

Although the Communists tried to woo Afro-American voters, black people held on to other conservative viewpoints on political and economic issues. They still hoped to win their inherent political rights within the framework of the much-acclaimed American Constitution. The extreme unpopularity of Marxian ideology in the United States made it too unpalatable to a growing number of Afro-Americans to swallow the Communist pills for a quick relief from heartburn. Hence the fumy notion, "it is bad enough being black without being red." Throughout America being red had carried the stigma of a general lack of patriotic sentiments and engaging in subversion. One can also hypothesize that the religious background of the Afro-Americans made the Communist ideology a hard pill to swallow besides its avowed denial of individual freedom for which the black people, since the abolition of slavery, had been clamouring. The antipathy for the Communist platform on the part of Afro-American was quite natural under the prevailing condition in America.

The apologists for the virtual denial of voting right to the Afro-Americans in the South argued that the black people had kept themselves away from the polling stations that they had lost interest in political affairs and that they had no concern for "the sacred aright of suffrage." The Afro-American, born and brought up in the South, was not indifferent to political affairs. It was amply proved by the patterns of behaviour of the Southern migrants to the country's Northern regions where they had more freedom than in the South.

Still, the latent ill-feelings between the two groups had detrimental effects on their changed relationship as explained by Franklin Frazier[54]:

> As in all cases of accommodation or external adjustments between groups with conflicting interests, there was still a latent conflict between the two races which flared up occasionally. The most important of these conflicts occurred in Atlanta in 1906 as a sequel to an election in Georgia where the disenfranchisement of the Negro had been delayed because of the conflict between various industrial and landowning interests.

The "most dramatic series of changes in the status of Negroes," as Blauser and Zengerin had clearly stated, proved the power of non-violence in mitigating injustice as exemplified by Rev. Dr. King in his historic mission to remove oppression and to bring about a sea change in the status of the Afro-Americans. Gandhiji showed Rev. Dr. King the non-violent route, which though was by no means easy to plod, he how could produce more enduring results. One might justly wonder how much darker would have been the step of the emancipation of Afro-Americans but for the judicious application of Gandhian philosophy by Rev. Dr. King in a Herculean task to win for his black brethren an identity those fundamental rights embodied in the great American Constitution. Today every adult Afro-American can walk into a polling station and exercise franchise thanks to Rev. Dr. King's wise leadership and great sacrifice, a development which his forefathers could not have even dreamt of in a million years.

After studying the problem of Afro-American and the political changes it has brought about in our own times, we shall, in the second segment, analyse the genesis of Gandhiji's campaigns of enlightenment in South Africa for the rights and freedoms of the Indian residents who in large number were crippled with restrictive laws, all meant to retard their development as free individuals in the adopted land and reduce them to the status of sub-human beings. Gandhiji correctly diagnosed their problem and prescribed the right remedy Satyagraha rooted in non-violence.

## SUMMARY

1. The Progress that individuals make in any society is often gradual. Afro-Americans stood witness to the gradual change in societal thinking.

2. The important issue of the Afro-American suffrage could only have taken place in the wake of emancipation. Until that time, he had to undergo great ordeals personal oppression and social disabilities, which had tied his hands to bondage. Each generation witnessed some degree of improvement in the socio-economic life.
3. A number of legal and pseudolegal measures were adopted to restrict Afro-American suffrage. The restrictions had their roots in the racist rant of the Southerners who were bent on protecting their supremacy in society.
4. The two chief legal methods devised to limit suffrage in the South had been the poll tax and the primary system. The black Americans strongly objected to both the methods.
5. The Afro-American people did not have the money to pay the poll tax to register to vote while the regulations governing the primary election had prevented them from participating in the elections.
6. The purpose of the primary election held before the general election was to screen and thereby select the most suitable candidates to run for office. This system does not exist in most democratic countries. In the United States, primary election plays an important role.
7. The actual situation regarding the political status of the Afro-American in the South varied not only from state to state but also from one community to another. In any event, it was one of discriminations.
8. The apologists for the virtual disfranchisement of Afro-Americans often argued that the black people did not vote as they had lost interest in politics and that they cared noting for the "sacred right of suffrage." But they ignored the fact that Afro-Americans had consistently demanded suffrage to become equal partners in society.
9. In the fifties there was growing evidence in many parts of the South to indicate that the race issue had lost its old political charm.
10. In the past three or four decades, the Afro-Americans have made considerable progress in professional and educational fields. Much of the progress can be attributed to the non-violent efforts of Rev. Dr. King, Still, they have to overcome many hurdles in American society.
11. The federal courts in the United States have enacted a number of laws meant to remove discriminatory practices common in housing, employment, job promotion and in gaining admission to educational institutions. For years Afro-Americans were denied

permission to enter public places thanks to the non-violent struggle led by Rev. Dr. King the situation has changed considerably.

**Notes and References**

1. During the Civil War, Main, New Hampshire, Vermont, Rhode Island and Wiscosin had made no discrimination in suffage. These states were in the North. Please see Paul Lewinson, *Race, Class and Party: A History of Negro Suffrage and White Politics in the South,* (Oxford University Press, 1932).
2. New York allowed Afro-Americans to vote, but imposed a special property qualification that prevented them from voting since they had failed to satisfy the criterion. It was widely considered another subtle way to ban them from direct participation in the political process. Such attempts have often kept the Afro-Americans backward in society.
3. Laws were enacted in the states of Mississippi in 1890; South Carolina in 1895; Louisiana, 1898; North Carolina, 1900; in Alabama and Virginia, 1901; Gerogia, 1908; and Oklahoma in 1910. It limited the Afro-American suffrage by requiring payment of taxes, the ownership of property or ability to read and understand the Constitution. More details in Rupert T. Brady, *"Poll Tax: Symbol of Oppression,"* (New York: 1957) and *The Crisis,* Vol. W, pp. 192, and 204-206, June, 1941.
4. Gunnar Myrdal, *An American Dilemma: The Negro Problem and Modern Democracy,* 1944.
5. Maurice R. Davie, *Negroes in American Society,* (New York: McGraw Hill Book Company, Inc., 1949), p. 264. Also see article, "Humans in Bondage," Lilian E. Smith, Social Action, Vol. X, pp. 6-34, February 1944. The article explains the inanities the Afro-American society, as a whole, had to endure during the latter half of the nineteenth century. Also by the same writer in *There Are Things To Do,* reprint from South Thy, Winter, 1942-43.
6. The "grandfather clause" had disenfranchised the black America. But it was declared unconstitutional in 1915 in a Supreme Court decision involving the state of Oklahoma. Today, that clause does not exist anywhere in the country as a result of progressive thinking and the need to change the system.
7. Maurice R. Davie, op. cit., p. 265.

8. *Ibid.,* pp. 265-66. In addition to that discriminatory clause, educational and property requirements had worked against the interests of Afro-Americans. More details in "The Southern Politician, 1900-1950." *The Journal of Politics,* XIII (1951),pp. 215-31.
9. H.D. Price, *The Negro and Southern Politics,* (Westport, Connecticut, 1957), p. 35.
10. In "Southern Case Against Desegregation," *Harper's Magazine,* Thomas R. Waring, CCXII, No. 1268 (January 1956), pp. 39-45. The author analyses the widely held view the Southern conservatives had maintained about the black people and the attempts to subjugate them.
11. Maurice R. Davie, op. cit., p. 266. Another version of the same problem is provided in Bernard, *The Negro Before the Supreme Court,* Phylon, Vol. VII, pp. 34-38. First quarter, 1947. Also in Hortense Powdermarker, *Probing Our Prejudice,* (New York: Harper and Brothers, 1944). Social thinkers in the United States have put forward various theories on racial prejudice, not always objective especially from the Afro-American perspective.
12. Thomas Pearce Bailey, *"Race Orthodoxy in the South,"* (New York: The Neale Publishing Company, 1914), p. 243.
13. In the autumn of 1932, handbills were distributed among the residents in the town of Dennison, Texas. They contained a highly disparaging term 'Nigger'. "The white people do not want you to vote Saturday. Do not make the Ku Klux Klan take a hand. (KKK is a racist organisation which has murdered and/or lynched Afro-Americans on numerous occasions). Do you remember what happened two years ago. May 9th? George Hughes was burned to death, the country courthouse destroyed... For good reason." As quoted in KeUy Miller, Ys Race Prejudice Innate or Acquired? *Journal of Applied Sociology,* Vol. II, pp. 516-523, July-August 1949.
14. Maurice Davie, op. cit., p. 266.
15. Four more Southern states later repealed the poll tax laws. They were North Carolina (1921); Louisiana (1934); Florida (1937); and Georgia (1945). The state legislature in Tennessee repealed the poll tax requirement in 1943.
16. In 1943, the legislature in the state of Tennessee repealed the poll tax requirement, but the state Supreme Court (High Court) declared the repealing statute unconstitutional.

17. Most of the laws governing the poll tax were enacted during the period between 1890-1910 when Afro-Americans had been in virtual bondage. Two main factors motivated the law makers to pass the poll tax; first, to eliminate them from any participation in politics; second, to crush the radical agrarian revolution which had swept the southern and western regions of the country in the 1890s. Further details in Frances Saylor, "The Poll Tax Ws Democracy," The Crisis, Vol. XLVI, pp. 106-14, April 1939.
18. William F. Nowlin, *The Negro in American National Politics,* (Boston: The Stratford Company, 1931). p. 197.
19. M.R. Davie, op. cit., p. 267.
20. *Ibid.,* p. 268.
21. In the poll tax states hardly one out of four eligible voters cast a ballot compared with approximately three out of four in the other states in the entire country. In the Senate, members from the states with the poll tax presided over 10 out of 33 standing committees and also had twice their share on other Senate committees.
22. M. Davie, op. cit., p. 268. Also in George C. Stoney, "The Poll Tax," *Survey Graphic,* Vol. XXIX, pp. 5-9, January, 1940.
23. Virginius Dabney, *Below the Potomac,* (New York: Appleton-Century-Crofts, Inc., 1942) p. 115 and "Liberalism in the South," (Chapel Hill, The University of North Carolina Press, 1932). This work is a good historical study on the subject, see especially Chapters 3 and 4.
24. Gunnar Myrdal, *An American Dilemma,* (New York: Harper & Brothers, 1944), p. 456.
25. *Ibid.,* p. 257.
26. Paul Lewinson, *Race, Class and Party: A History of Negro Suffrage and White Politics in the South,* (Oxford University Press, 1932), pp. 168-69.
27. Myrdal, p. 325. The one party system and the general lack of interest in politics on the part of the white masses were the main factors which gave disproportionate power to individuals and groups feeling that their main interests were linked with conservative views on the prevailing social problems.
28. Orro Weberg, (ed.) *Characteristics of the American Negro,* (New York: Harper & Brothers, 1944), p. 214.
29. Direct and indirect primary elections exist in the American democratic system. The direct primary is the most common; a party member who intends to run for office files petitions to have

the name placed on the ballot. The voters then directly vote for the candidates of their choice. On the other hand, in an indirect primary, the party members vote for delegates to party conventions which choose candidates for election.

30. M.R. Davie, op. cit., p. 242.
31. The National Association for the Advancement of Coloured People or NAACP is a highly effective organization striving to improve the social conditions of the black people. The late Rev. Dr. King was its president. In direct contrast to other black organizations, NAACP does not advocate violence. By using peaceful means, it tries to influence the law makers to enact laws to remove discrimination in public accommodation, in hiring practices and job promotion.
32. Henry Lee Moon, *Balance of Power: The Negro Vote.* (Garen City, New York: Doubleday and Company, 1948), p. 107.
33. Virginius Dabney, *Liberalism in the South,* op. cit., p. 254.
34. *Ibid.,* p. 253.
35. *Ibid.,* p. 267. Also in Henry Lee Moon, *Balance of Power: The Negro Vote,* (Garden City, New York: Doubleday and Company, 1948).
36. William G. Carleton, "Ballot Revolution in Dixie," *Negro Digest,* Vol. N, pp. 65-68, August 1946.
37. Tom Watson, *Biennial Report of the Attorney-General, Florida, 1944* (Takhasse: 1945), p. 145.
38. *Ibid.,* p. 149.
39. As quoted by Stetson Kennedy, "The White Primary vs. Democracy," *The Southern Frontier,* VI, No. ii (November 1945). The author gives a detailed account of various aspects of the primary and its role in choosing the official candidates to run for office. He also analyses how the Afro-Americans were barred from the primaries.
40. *Ibid.*
41. Detailed account in Francis P. Locke, *Public Men In and Out of Office,* (Chapel Hill: University of North Carolina Press, 1946), pp. 257-77.
42. H.D. Price, op, cit., p. 27.
43. *Ibid.,* p. 42. In the state of Florida court intervention proved necessary. Legal steps were taken against supervisors of registration in a number of countries. The majority of suits ended at the local court level in favour of Afro-Americans being accepted for registration as Democrats.

44. Blauser and Zengerin, *Civil Rights and the American Negro,* op. cit., p. 469.
45. H.D. Price, op. cit., p. 32. Other viewpoints are provided in *Black Nationalism,* (Chicago: University of Chicago Press, 1962). In several parts of the United States black nationalism had manifested itself in violence. Rev. Dr. King's attempts showed his people the path of non-violence. He said: "The non-violent approach does not immediately change the heart of the oppressor. It first does something to the hearts and souls of those committed to it. It gives them new self-respect ..." Rev. Dr. Martin Luther King, *Stride Toward Freedom,* op. cit., p. 219.
46. M.R. Davie, op. cit., p.277.
47. *Ibid.,* pp. 277-78.
48. *Ibid.,* p. 278. In the Northern communities the Afro-Americans not only exercised franchies in almost the same proportion as the white-skinned people but were holding public offices in large numbers in contrast to the situation in the South. Thus they became a political force in elections.
49. W.G. Carleton, "Ballot Revolution in Dixie," *Negro Digest,* Vol. IV, pp. 65-68, August, 1946.
50. M.R. Davie, op. cit., p. 279. Afro-Americans have been elected to the state legislatures or state assemblies in the following states—California, Illinois, Indiana, Massachusetts, Michigan, New Jersey, New York, Ohio, Pennsylvania, Vermont, West Virginia and Wisconsin.
51. *Ibid.,* p. 279.
52. *Ibid.,* p. 280.
53. *Ibid.,* p. 280.
54. "The Negro in the United States," op. cit., pp. 162-63. Since the main issue of the gubernatorial campaign in Georgia in 1906 was the disfranchisement of the Afro-American, a high degree of racial rivalry was stirred up against the black community. Clark Howell, the representative of the industrialists, supported the disfranchisement of the Afro-Americans, but opposed the idea as he believed that it would also disfranchise some white-skinned people. Thus the stage was set for racial riots. In some counties in Wilmington, North Carolina ("The Race War in North Carolina," *The Forum,* Vol. XXVI, pp. 578-79) with large concentration of Afro-American voters, defeated politicians raised the cry of "Afro-American domination and white-skinned people formed armed

units against them with the participation of lawyers, doctors and merchants. Despite the fact that the Afro-Americans did not vote and the white-skinned people triumphed in the state, the armed men descended on black people on the day following the election destroying the office of the Afro-American daily.

SEGMENT-B

# CHAPTER-IV

# THE FOUNDATIONS OF GANDHIAN SATYAGRAHA

## ARTICLE-1

### (A) Meaning of the Term Satyagraha

The vision of Satyagraha is as old as the Indian civilization with its roots in Sanskrit and like several compound words in Sanskrit, Satyagraha is precisely a compound term of *Satya* and *Graha* meaning *Truth* and *Holding Fast*. Thus in coining the term *Satyagraha,* Gandhiji, more than any other political figure, stressed two highly significant aspects of our being: truth and holding fast to it. The search for truth is one of the strong yearnings of human beings transcending all barriers and Gandhiji, in contrast to other political figures, equated Satyagraha with truth, the ever lasting yearning of Man, his dream. Spiritual reality remains one of the highest forms of truth and non-violent philosophy a true path to reach that goal in life. In a specific sense, the ideology of Satyagraha, as Gandhiji practiced it, is the vindication of truth by means of self-sacrifice, a form of love, without causing pain and suffering to others. The world's great exponent of *ahimsa* said that Satyagraha "is gentle,"[1] adding that "it is the complete opposite of compulsion. It was conceived as a complete substitute for violence."[2] **In the global context, individuals still have to appreciate the power of Gandhian Satyagraha as the true way to resolve conflicts.** The technique of Satyagraha is the pursuit of truth by adopting non-violent methods: etymologically it means truth. Generally, political leaders suppress truth while Gandhiji, the saintly politician, upheld it in Satyagraha.

## (B) Foundation and Ideology

A political or social ideology is known by the principles and objectives that guide it, viz. the foundation on which the ideology is built. In the past, a number of ideologies had radically altered the thinking of mankind in several parts of the world and with that the very history of man. The twentieth century witnessed the birth of some of the most perverted and most violent ideologies known to mankind such as Fascism, Nazism, Communism and Colonialism leaving a long trail of destruction and exploitation from which a great part of the world is still trying to recover, from the pain and destruction caused by them. The ghosts of the violent ideologies are still haunting various continents.

The last century also witnessed the birth of the most non-violent ideology ever recorded in history: Satyagraha, the opposite side of the violent doctrines that came to light, spread hope in the last century. Gandhiji, its father, challenged the conventional wisdom of meeting violence with violence, and aggression with aggression signalling a sharp departure from the extremely violent ideologies of the same century in the form of Nazism and Fascism in Europe. He employed Satyagraha, his most powerful non-violent tool, to end 350 years of the British colonial misrule with its trademark belligerence in India. The importance of employing Satyagraha with its basis in non-violence to fight colonialism, an extremely violent economic and political ideology, may be understood by the fact that during the years, 1876 to 1914, the colonial misrules had illegally seized 22.3 million square kilometres of prime land in the world with a total population of 236.8 million inhabitants.[3] Following the outbreak of the war in 1914, the colonies had accounted for approximately 67 per cent of the world's land mass and 60 per cent of the citizens of the world.

Gandhiji, directing his non-violent Satyagraha against the most violent and unlawful aspects of colonialism in India, set in motion a process of decolonisation in several parts of the world. He won the anti-colonial campaign in India in a most peaceful manner. What are the foundations of the ideology of Satyagraha? What are its teachings? How can they be applied to resolve conflicts? Although Satyagraha has been explained in general terms in the succeeding pages of the study, let us evaluate certain specific aspects of its tenets and objectives.

## (C) Formulation of Satyagraha

The non-violent technique of Satyagraha, born out of the adverse circumstances faced by the Indian residents in South Africa, was Gandhiji's lasting contribution to India and to the rest of the world which, until Gandhiji introduced that non-violent ideology, had lacked an effective non-violent philosophy to resolve conflicts. Anyone who reads the works of Gandhiji would easily understand that the Gandhian technique is erroneously associated with passive resistance or non-violence. During the early days of the development of Satyagraha Gandhiji himself had used the term 'passive resistance', and not the term Satyagraha. The basic reason for this wrong equation of the term was that the technique was in the state of experimentation. In his own words:[4]

> I am myself growing in the knowledge of Satyagraha I have no textbook to consult in time of need ...Satyagraha as conceived by me is a science in the making.

## (D) Evolution of Satyagraha

As early as 1946 Gandhiji coined the term Satyagraha in South Africa during his non-violent resistance to the retrogressive Asiatic Law Amendment Ordinance introduced in the Transvaal Legislative Council. Anti-Indian laws in South Africa were dragging the law-abiding Indian settlers, a vast section of humanity, down a suicidal path after having languished for years in the African nation's political wilderness. Gandhiji did not want the lingering bitterness to continue and first called the movement Passive Resistance expressing moral outrage against the deadly cocktail of such laws. In order to differentiate it from the campaign of the suffragettes in the United Kingdom and South Africa under the banner of passive resistance Gandhiji's sharp intellect found the new term.[5]

A new term, or ideology in unchartered waters requires clarification to have the maximum appeal to and acceptance by the people and in the absence of its clear principles and objective, its followers would fall by the wayside. In order to clear the confusion, as Joan Bondurant points out, the Gandhian doctrine of Satyagraha can be characterized as follows: (i) Gandhian goals (Sarvodaya or common welfare); (ii) Gandhian techniques (truth, ahimsa and the dignity of labour); and (iii) Gandhian methods (Satyagraha, fast and land gift or *bhoodan*). In this connection we only deal with the powerful tool of Satyagraha representing a true Gandhian method of non-violent resistance.

Gandhiji, more than any one in our times, had practiced Satyagraha, which, he admitted, was an evolving science. For, he says: [7]

> For the past thirty years I have been preaching and practicing Satyagraha, as I know it today, constitute a gradual evolution.

Gokhale, Gandhiji's protege, defined the non-violent technique as something "essentially defensive in nature,"[8] pointing out further that it also "fights with moral and spiritual weapons."[9] Gokhale goes on to say:[10]

> A passive resister resists tyranny by undergoing suffering in his own person. He pits soul-force against brute-force; he pits the divine in man against the brute in man; he pits suffering and against oppression.

Gokhale, with his strong influence on Gandhiji's thinking, further characterized Satyagraha as a strong instrument that "pits faith against injustice and right against wrong." The technique permits many phases of winning over an adversary. The first phase emphasizes persuasive methods by appealing to reason and the later stages are characterized by persuasion and personal suffering. The Satyagrahi peacefully tries to draw attention to different issues and to get through to the adversary's unprejudiced judgment and in this attempt he may consciously arrive at a level where the opponent may be persuaded by judgments based on reason.

## (E) The Basic Elements of Satyagraha

Every movement should have certain basic principles to guide its followers to achieve its prescribed objectives and if we were to guide someone to the technique of Satyagraha, the following essentials of Satyagraha deserve special attention:

(i) *Training and methods of the movement.* Training must be made an integral aspect of the campaign with the goal of convincing the novice that it is one of the most effective methods of action for a peaceful resolution of conflicts. Education of the Satyagrahi, the opponent and the participants must go on apace as appropriate methods of attaining the ultimate objectives of the campaign.

(ii) *Self-reliance.* A Satyagrahi should rely on his own convictions that non-violent resistance is much more effective than violent reaction. In his efforts, outside assistance may, under proper conditions, be accepted, but should never be expected all the time.

(iii) *Elimination of weakness.* A Satyagrahi must be mentally strong to resist violence with non-violence. A weak person can never be a valiant Satyagrahi. The greatest advocates of non-violent resistance in history, Gandhiji included, were also history's strongest and the most civilized human beings. A Satyagrahi is a civilized individual and his goal is to adopt civilized methods against the infectious virus of violence and other forms of evil before they damage the fabric of society.

(iv) *Refusal to surrender principles.* A Satyagrahi acts on the principles of non-violence and reconciliation. He is called upon to exclude attempts for compromise which may damage the basic tenets of the noble ideology of Satyagraha or its valid objectives. Satyagrahi's efforts become a model for others to seek a peaceful resolution of the issues and should exercise caution against bargaining or barter in negotiations with the opponent.

(v) *Steadfast search for channels of cooperation.* A Satyagrahi, with his firm faith in the spirit of cooperation with the opponents, should be encouraged to win over the adversary by assisting him in times of need. This cooperative spirit would force the opponent to reconsider his belligerent attitude and adopt a conciliatory attitude. Love is the basis of this approach and Gandhiji adopted such a conciliatory attitude in settling issues with Botha in South Africa. [12]

(vi) *Agreement on fundamentals.* Care must be exercised to reach an agreement on the basic ideals prior to a final settlement.

(vii) *Conciliatory attitude.* A Satyagrahi should always adopt a conciliatory attitude in his negotiations with the opponent, who should not be offended or provoked in the process. Any attempt to insult the adversary is outside the boundaries of the ideology of Satyagraha with its basis in humility, love and cooperation, which would win over the opponent.

## ARTICLE -2

### (A) The Code of Conduct

One hastens to add that Gandhian Satyagrahi should be an individual of exemplary character with the attitudes of a monk or a spiritual leader.

Satyagraha is an aspect of India's spiritualism. In the campaigns in the 1930s[13] Gandhiji promulgated a code of discipline for Satyagrahis requiring great mental discipline on their part. Some of these requirements are:

(i) Harbour no ill-feelings or anger towards the opponent whose assaults should receive no violent response from the volunteers, but only **love and reconciliation in a concentrated form.**
(ii) Refrain from resisting arrests.
(iii) Do not insult or swear at the opponent.
(iv) Refuse to surrender to angry orders although harsh penalty may be the bitter fruit of the refusals for submission.
(v) Even at the point of risking life, protect the adversaries from physical attacks or insults from others.
(vi) If imprisoned, act in an exemplary and civilized manner towards the officials who may have a different attitude. That would change the minds of the adversary.
(vii) As a volunteer of a Satyagraha unit, accept the orders of the Satyagraha leaders, but resign in the event of serious differences of opinion.

Undoubtedly, Gandhiji's code of discipline put Satyagraha on an extremely high level of human conduct rooted in his deep spiritual convictions. The code of discipline of a Satyagrahi with Gandhiji's clear signature on it is the antithesis to the training of a soldier who is trained to destroy his enemies and even, kill innocent women, children and men, raze houses, with rape and loot as common practices among warriors. In contrast, a Satyagrahi is friendly and amiable and aims at the reform of his enemy.

### (B) The Methods of Satyagraha

Satyagraha, as a technique of social action, is used to resolve conflicts without resorting to violent methods and to realize its objectives it uses divergent forms of action, all based on non-violence, even risking ones own life. After Gandhiji inaugurated his non-violent movement to topple the British colonial power, he employed a number of non-violent methods including non-cooperation with the British, non-violent boycotts of British products and mass civil disobedience, which are widely employed today in the fight for justice and equality.[14] Such methods represent the positive side of the campaign causing no injury to the adversary. We shall evaluate them here.

*(i) Boycott*

During India's effective and arduous non-violent struggle for freedom Gandhiji used the peaceful means of boycotting British products, which were ruining India's home industry, driving the artisans into penury. In this non-violent attempt he was striking at the root of British colonialism in the most peaceful manner as the primary goal of the colonizers was to use India as a market for their goods. Gandhiji urged the people of India to boycott British products with a view to bring down the colonial edifice. Peaceful boycott, a form of Satyagraha, is not intended to cause injury to anyone, **but to stage a protest in a highly forceful and non-violent manner against exploration.** We have to understand that Satyagrahis are not boycotting the opponents, but their action is directed against an unethical system.[15]

*(ii) Fasting*

One of the most effective weapons in the Satyagraha movement is fasting with its own form of science,[16] used by Gandhiji on several occasions for just causes. (Gandhiji said: "Most religious people are politicians in disguise while I am a religious man in the guise of a politician.")[17]

*(iii) Who Can Be A Satyagrahi?*

To be a full-fledged Satyagrahi may be as difficult as climbing the Mount Everest. A Satyagrahi requires great self-discipline and self-control and Gandhiji, who fasted for various purposes, called it "a fiery weapon," claiming that "it has its own science."[18] He further pointed out the following in reference to those eligible for fasting as a weapon in the arsenal of Satyagraha.[19]

> A fast may be undertaken by him who is associated with the person against whom he fasts. The latter must be directly connected with the purpose for which the fast is being undertaken.

Gandhiji admitted that no one "has a perfect knowledge of it [fast]"[20] adding that:[21]

> Unscientific experimentation is bound to be harmful to the one who fasts, and it may even harm the cause espoused. No one who has not earned the right to do so should, therefore, use this weapon.

According to this interpretation and the requirements of fasting, an individual should fast as an adjunct to the other forms of Satyagraha in view of the fact that fasting may cause serious damage to an individual's general health and should not be regarded as a mass method of Satyagraha.[22] In "representative Satyagraha" certain volunteers are chosen to represent a group for particular reasons. Realizing the immense spirit of a Satyagrahi, Gandhiji laid down the qualifications for a Satyagrahi in three stages, in 1921, 1930 and 1939.[23]

1. A Satyagrahi should have abiding faith in God, who is his eternal guide.
2. He should lead a chaste life, willing to give up his life and earthly possessions.
3. He should have strong faith in truth and *ahimsa* and belief in the basic goodness of all men hoping to evoke his commitment to truth and love expressed through suffering.
4. He should be a spinner and wear *khadi* as these two require merits were essential for Indian conditions.
5. He should obey with an open heart all the codes of discipline as may be laid down from time to time.
6. He should obey the rules in jags in the event of imprisonment unless such rules are specifically meant to damage his self-respect.
7. He should not use alcohol and other intoxicants to enable him to have a clear vision.[24]

### (C) Fasting as a Forceful Instrument

Gandhiji considered fasting as the last instrument in the arsenal of Satyagraha with a clear[25] distinction between fasting by a Satyagrahi and suicide. Fasting, a voluntary act adopted by an individual dedicated to a cause, is meant to change the mind of the opponent without causing him any harm but to make him reconsider his attitude towards the individual who refrains from eating or even drinking and face a perilous outcome of such a brave act. In this sense a Satyagrahi has to be truly brave in his endeavour to redress injustice done to himself or to an entire society.

**Gandhiji often undertook fasting, moved by LOVE of his fellowmen to remedy social injustice caused by other fellowmen towards whom he harboured no ill-feelings, even bringing his life to the verge of death forcing in an extremely non-violent manner to reconsider the opponents' attitude towards a particular issue, be it political or social or religious in nature. By bringing his life to the jaws of death, he gently touched the soul of the opponent. Is there anything more moving than this selfless action?**

Gandhiji's selfless fasting resulted in grave concern about his health, not to say of criticism of his action and to those who said that fasting was tantamount to suicide under a fast moving train or by leaping from the bridge. He responded to the criticism stating that suicide by abstaining food and water was still better than violence.[26] **Gandhiji globalized the idea of fasting, a powerful non-violent method of a Satyagrahi, and since his time it has been practised in several parts of the world with varying degrees of success. Is it not an effective way to attain a specific objective without causing pain or pangs of hanger in an opponent? If we can change the mind of another individual by a non-violent method like fasting, why raise clenched fists against him! Non-violence would never fail.** Until all individuals become Satyagrahis, violent actions are bound to result in violent responses with their dire consequences for the present generation and the generations to come.

Concerning fasting as a non-violent tool available to the Satyagrahi, Gandhiji, a life-long practitioner of fasting, has made a few important distinctions.

Fasting can be coercive if it is carried out for a selfish objective and as such it is a self-defeating attempt to be avoided at all costs. A Satyagrahi cannot be a selfish human being. Moreover, if the goal of fasting is to usurp money or other valuable possessions from another individual, it would be a coercive attempt[27] foreign to the philosophy of Satyagraha. **Accordingly, a Satyagrahi's fast should be grounded in sheer love.** Gandhiji stated that "if it is greed that my fast sprang from, then it is coercion..."[28] and added:[29]

> It is the implicit and sacred belief of millions of Christians that love of Jesus keeps them from falling and that it does so against themselves ....And if all this love could be regarded as coercion, then the love prompted my fast on several occasions.

Fasting can be divided into three distinct categories, all related to one another and all undertaken with selfless motives. They are: (a) for bodily cleansing; (b) as an act of the spirit's supremacy over the physical; (c) as an aspect of nature cure; and (d) for the purpose of penance.

The satyagrahi's[30] fast is motivated by his firm intention to resist the forces of social and political injustice as well as to change the mind of the opponent by personal suffering[31] until a change in attitude takes place in him. It is only by accepting these basic conditions of fasting, that it is turned into a powerful tool by a Satyagrahi to convert the evil doers before they take another job at society.

## ARTICLE -3

### (A) Self-Sacrifice and Pre-occupation

There is no evidence to indicate that Gandhiji ever undertook fast in his non-violent campaign in South Africa. During his public life in India one of Gandhiji's chief pre-occupations had been to bring about communal harmony and with that clear vision he resorted to fast until death. He undertook the last fast in life in January 1948 to further the cause of unity in the country where communal rivalry was tearing it apart. The deep chasm and the subsequent agitation that erupted in Delhi and in other volatile areas following the partition of India were a great source of mental anguish to Gandhiji compelling him from all directions to fast until death. (The partition of India and the havoc it created have been highly exaggerated in several parts of the world. True, partition of the country was a painful reminder of the infectitious sickness of communal rivalry affecting various levels of the Indian society. The death and destruction it caused were but pale in comparison with the political balkanization and havoc in other continents of the world. Exaggeration of different developments in history can produce dangerous results.) During his fast to create unity in India he had announced that he would fast until the Muslim brethren, could move about freely in New Delhi. The threat of self-sacrifice produced the expected result, as a scientist precisely knew the final result of combining two chemicals in a test tube. **Gandhiji's non-violent step to fast until death touched the hearts of all communities which vowed to give up violence. Peace was restored in the midst of despair and clouds of hopelessness.** At a critical juncture in the history of India Gandhiji's fast, a technique of Satyagraha proved invaluable, proved effective.

### (B) The Role of Personal Suffering

A Satyagrahi should be willing to undergo periods of personal suffering to achieve his goals in society and fully realizing the role of suffering, Gandhiji even considered Satyagraha the law of suffering.[32] A soldier in arms also experiences sufferings in the form of taking refuge in a bunker on rainy days, during the day or at night or during a heavy snow-storm, depending on the region and the climatic condition. But the purpose of a warrior's basic education, fully armed from head to toe, is to meet violence with violence, arrogance with more arrogance, flights of fury with bursts of fury and aggression with more aggression in contrast to a Satyagrahi who is determined to meet aggression with love and non-violence. They constituted two clashing realities. Gandhiji believed that a Satyagrahi is only capable of knowing relative truth and not the absolute truth and in that sense he could not be violent to the adversary to change his attitude. What seems truth to the Satyagrahi may not be so to the opponent. Therefore, he can only attempt to convert the adversary by inflicting violence on himself and in this case by personal suffering and deprivation.[33] Violent means against the opponent would hurt both the evil and the evil-doer with a deterioration in relationship damaging the non-violent ideology. The success and impact of the non-violent principles and their application depended on the individual suffering of a Satyagrahi as Gandhiji perceived. He elaborated:[34]

> Progress is to be measured by the amount of suffering undergone by the sufferer. The purer the suffering, the greater is the progress.

Gandhi was convinced that by operating under this law of suffering it was possible for an individual to resist "an unjust empire."[35] For, he points out:[36]

> Working under this law of our being [suffering] it is possible for a single individual to defy the whole might of an unjust empire, to save his honour, his religion, his soul, and lay the foundation for the empire's fall or its regeneration.

### (C) Civil Disobedience

Satyagraha, like a tree, has several branches and off-shoots one of which is civil disobedience. Gandhiji, who advocated civil disobedience and non-violence against colonial oppression and injustice, derived his inspiration from Count Leo Tolstoy's monumental work, *Essays On Cid Disobedience and Non-violence.* Tolstoy denounced the use of violence and upheld the importance of civil disobedience to attain social objectives.[37] He says:[38]

> It is thus with the law of non-resistance. People know it is wrong to use violence, but they are anxious to continue to live a life secured by 'the strong arm of law,' that instead of devoting their intellects to the elucidation of evils which have flowed, and are still flowing, from admitting that man has a right to use violence to his fellow-men, they prefer to exert their mental powers in defence of that error. *'Fais ce que dois, advienne que pourra'*—'Do what's right, come what may'—is an expression of profound wisdom.

This expression of profound wisdom of doing what is right irrespective of its consequences forms one of the foundations of Gandhian Satyagraha and civil disobedience, with its strong arm of non-violent resistance in Gandhiji's life in South Africa and in his activities and those of countless Satyagrahis in India with Gandhiji as its shipmaster. In India he steered the ship of civil disobedience campaign against the violent storm of colonial oppression, high tide and strong waves, all with the goal of giving Satyagraha a permanent place in history as an acknowledged form of non-violent resistance.

It is common knowledgc that while Thoreau and Tolstoy provided Gandhiji with the theoretical franework of non-violent resistance, Gandhiji converted the theory into a practical formula in the world's civil disobedience campaign in India, the largest exercise in man's history.

Tolstoy and Gandhiji, owed a great deal to Jesus Christ in their denunciation of violent methods, applied under different pretexts. Tolstoy adds:[39]

> It was just this sophistical justification of violence that Christ denounced. When two enemies fight, each may think his own conduct is justified by the circumstances. Excuses can be made for every use of violence, and no infallible standard has ever been discovered by which to measure the worth of those excuses.

The terms Civil Disoledience imply civility in attitude and disobedience in practice. Although the term disobedience means any type of anti-social behaviour, it becomes incumbent on an individual to question immoral laws for the simple reason that non-compliance to such a law is compliance to the higher laws emanating from truth and justice.[40] The word *civil* is opposite to a violent and criminal deed. Gandhiji said that disobedience "must be sincere, respectful."[41] and that it should have other attributes:[41]

> .....it should be respectful, restrained, never defiant, must be based upon some well-understood principle, must not be capricious and above all must have no ill-will or hatred behind it.

In other words, civil disobedience represents the direct contravention of a set of specific laws and the resistance against such regulations for their just implementation may take the forms of non-payment of revenues, boycotting various products or massive peaceful demonstration against the unjust laws of the state.[42] Unjust laws are the trademarks of states. Civil disobedience becomes the ultimate non-violent weapon of the society to rectify unjust laws, as unjust law is a contradiction in terms since the purpose of law is to create justice and order. Unjust law is as inconceivable as a river without water.

Civil disobedience against the unjust law demands self-discipline and the atmosphere surrounding the campaign should be free of violence, acrimony and resistance. Describing the attributes of civil disobedience campaign, Gandhiji pointed out that "one must have a willing and respectful obedience to the state laws."[43] He even conceded the limitation in a huge civil disobedience campaign as a "Himalayan miscalculation."[44] If the campaign has to be civil in nature, in its application and the realization of its objectives, it has to be public and made known to the officials[45] who should not be provoked.

Human beings are products of love. Satyagraha is a product of love, specifically of Gandhiji's love of human beings. Therefore, Satyagraha is extremely humane with the Gandhian emphasis of love of one's rivals.

## ARTICLE-4

### (A) Distinct Categories

A civil disobedience campaign can be divided into two distinct categories which, according to Gandhiji, are "aggressive, assertive or defensive civil disobedience.. ."[46] Gandhiji adds:[47]

> Civil disobedience is wilful disobedience of the laws of the State whose breach does not involve moral turpitude and which is undertaken as a symbol of revolt against the State.

During the peaceful struggle against the British colonial rule, Gandhiji popularised the idea of civil disobedience campaign in India and the rest of the world more than any other individual, later to be adopted by Rev. Dr. King in his struggle for racial justice in the United

States. Today, this well-known Gandhian legacy is practised in several parts of the world including America, Caribbean island nations and Europe for social justice, to oppose escalation of arms race or the part of an island nation being used by another state for mindless target practice for the military.[48] Gandhiji upheld the importance of civil disobedience in reference to the disregard for laws.[49]

> Thus disregard of laws relating to revenue or regulation of personal conduct for the convenience of the State, although such laws in themselves inflict no hardship and do not require to be altered, would be assertive, aggressive or offensive civil disobedience.

If aggressive civil disobedience is a source of intimidation to the opponent, it should be bypassed,[50] lest such a step should deteriorate the situation, something that Satyagrahis should avoid in their conciliatory attempts to convert the opponent into the philosophy of non-violence by setting an example in non-violent practice. Aggressive form of disobedience should be applied only if its practitioners have to face harsh discipline, but it should be avoided if the adversary is in the clasp of a difficult situation.[51] The purpose here is to avoid embarrassing the opponent who should only be converted by the good deeds of the Satyagrahi, guided by a set of higher moral codes.

## (B) Firm Intention

Gandhiji believed that the code of civil disobedience is based on the purest form of social agitation with the strength of the inalienable right of the citizenry.[52] He states:[53]

> Civil disobedience combined with love is the living water of life. For, civil disobedience is a sovereign method of transmitting this undisciplined, life-destroying latent energy into disciplined life-saving energy whose use ensures absolute success.

The theory and practice of civil disobedience by its practitioners presuppose the firm intention of disobedience to the unjust laws of the State without the fear of sanction, as any deviation from that path would seriously erode the effectiveness of the campaign. Based on that assumption individuals can accept it only as a last resort and by a handful of individuals against the authority of the State in the first instance.[54]

The purpose of civil disobedience is to remove the excess of those laws of the State that are not conducive to the general welfare of the citizens by adopting peaceful methods as Gandhiji did in South Africa and India.

Violence and acrimony are alien to the concept of civil disobedient acts as violent methods tear apart the fabric of life. In the words of Tolstoy, "life, based on the principles of violence, has culminated in the negation of the basis on which it was founded."[55] Here the ideology of civil disobedience campaign unmasks the folly of violent means to resolve conflicts at local, national and international levels at a time when the application of violent means is justified to put an end to violence as though pouring fuel on her can stop the rising flames of fire. Referring to this great contradiction in human thinking, Tolstoy again says that "it has often been said that the invention of the terrible military instruments of murder will put an end to war, and that war will exhaust itself..."[56] He elaborates:[57]

> This is not hue. As it is possible to increase the means for killing men, so it is possible to increase the means for subjugating those who hold the social life-conception.

Civil disobedience campaign is directed against laws for subjugating the individuals by the State or against the possible chances of subjugating them at a future time by reshaping the existing laws. In South Africa Gandhiji championed the non-violent struggle against the excesses of the government as reflected in legislating harsh laws against the interests of the Indian settlers. In the same manner, he led civil disobedience movements in India to put an end to the British laws to subjugate the people of India. The British anti-Indian legislative measures in India were often much more harsh than those passed against the Indian settlers in South Africa. It demonstrates the effectiveness of the Gandhian civil disobedience campaign in putting an end to a basically corrupt administrative structure. A soldier in an arm believes in spilling the blood of the opponent to realize his goal by adopting the most violent means while every effort is made to protect his life. A Satyagrahi wants to protect the life of his opponent without spilling a drop of his blood. He is willing to spill his blood. Satyagrahis are honourable individuals Satyagrahis do not shatter the lives of other individuals, by disobeying the laws in the most civilized manner.

### (C) Resisting Unjust Laws

It is the birthright of individuals to disobey an unjust law or even resist the attempts of the legislators to enact an unjust law. It was with this precise goal that Gandhiji inaugurated his Civil Disobedience Campaign in India. In the absence of such a campaign, the British lawmakers' would have callously passed severely restrictive laws in India to tighten their grip on the nation and to prolong their misrule. (The British ruling class had also passed several restrictive laws bordering on autocratic methods against their own subjects in England. After John became King in 1199, he abused his power and demanded more military service from the feudal class than did his predecessors. He sold royal positions to the highest bidders and increased taxes without the consent of the barons or the people who revolted against the King. He was compelled to lighten the burden on the people. In 1215, Magna Carta came into being *engrossed* (written in legal form) guaranteeing certain privileges including religious freedom and less governmental interference. In defiance of individual freedom, the British Parliament adopted stem. Measures against the Catholics and in 1606 imposed severe penalties on them as they did in India two centuries later. More details in notes and references).[58]

Non-violent resistance against unjust laws is an integral aspect of any civil disobedience movement as windows and doors are integral parts of a house. The more mass-oriented the peaceful resistance is, the wider is its effect upon the authority to effect changes in the society. Referring to the importance of such a resistance, K. Santanam makes the following remarks:[59]

> Resistance is the most aggressive form of Satyagraha. It has naturally the greatest appeal to those who are eager for spectacular results. It may take the form of *disobeying the laws which are objectionable in themselves* in order to bring home to the people that the satyagraha is opposed to the government as a whole. (Emphasis added)
>
> It may also take the form of a government or social institution so that it is driven to inflict some kind of suffering on the satyagrahi which will generate moral force necessary to *bring about the necessary change.* (Emphasis added.)

Refusal to comply with the regulation to perform an unlawful obligation imposed by an unjust authority is an aspect of the Gandhian philosophy of civil disobedience. Refusal to pay an unjust tax and to support an unjust law offer examples of this method and the Satyagrahis who question the legitimacy of the laws may have to experience personal suffering in the form of physical abuse or long prison terms. It is the inevitability of personal suffering combined with a high degree of moral conviction that is vital to self-suffering directed against flagrant injustice and political oppression that constitute the dynamic forces of the civil obedience campaign. Throughout his public life Gandhiji went through cycles of personal sufferings which did not matter him much since he was an ardent champion of Satyagraha and its effective arm, the civil disobedience campaign. The study of Satyagraha is the study of India, the discovery of the soul of India. Gandhiji imbued others with the enlightened spirit of Satyagraha and in the process created an army of volunteers in India to resist unjust laws. They were particularly unjust since they were imposed upon Indian people by a alien colonial nation which had passed several laws to strengthen the colonial grip against the common interests of India. The massive Civil Disobedience Campaign which Gandhiji launched against the foreign rule had Gandhiji's magic touch.

## SUMMARY

1. By coining the term Satyagraha, Gandhiji, stressed two important aspects of our existence, viz. truth and clinging fast to truth. While the vast majority of political leaders are known for suppressing the truth, Gandhiji upheld it and elevated Satyagraha, as a philosophy of peaceful resistance, to a higher level. Compared to other ideologies of the last century, the foundation and principles of Satyagraha were the noblest. They were based on love and no-ill feelings towards the opponents.
2. The ideology of Satyagraha was the noblest in the twentieth century. Gandhiji devised the formula for that. Its foundation was in Indian religions and philosophical thinking in addition to the influence of Henry David Thoreau and Leo Tolstoy.
3. A Satyagrahi should be an individual of exemplary character, he should live by certain codes of disciplines as laid down by Gandhiji for the maximum benefits of his/her non-violent endeavour.
4. Accordingly, a Satyagrahi should harbour no ill-feelings towards his opponents, should be willing to give up his worldly possessions, give love utmost priority in all his dealings with the adversary, should be willing to undergo personal suffering and should not resist arrest. These are but few of the important qualifications to be a true Satyagrahi.

5. The training a Satyagrahi receives and that a common soldier receives are like north and south poles. They are two clashing realities. While the actions of Satyagrahi are based on **love and non-violence** with the opponent, those of a soldier are based on the extreme opposites of hatred and violence meant to kill the opponent, cripple him or spill his blood in a field, on a street comer or in a river.
6. The training of Satyagrahi and that of a soldier in arms are markedly different. A Satyagrahi believes in nurturing human values while a soldier believes in torturing others. Nurturing is far better than torturing.
7. According to Gandhiji, the code of civil disobedience is based on the purest form of individual behaviour elevating it to a higher plain of social response, the response being non-violent and free of rancour.
8. Fasting was an important tool of Gandhian non-violent resistance. He fasted for a variety of reasons, all with good intentions. On a number of occasions the fasting, a form of self-sacrifice, brought him to the brink of death. His abstinence from food often changed the minds of those who otherwise would have not changed their attitudes towards others.
9. Fasting was not meant for everyone. The Satyagrahis who undertook fasting had to meet certain qualifications as laid down by Gandhiji.
10. Fasting can be a coercive exercise if it is carried out for a selfish reason and a Statyagrahi cannot be a selfish human being. For instance, Gandhiji always fasted for common political or social objectives setting examples for others in the society by his own actions.
11. It is the birth right of every individual to resist unjust laws. Several prevailing laws are unjust and it is incumbent on the citizenry to oppose them. Gandhiji opposed unjust laws in South Africa and India and urged others to do the same in the most peaceful manner.
12. Gandhiji said that British rule in India "is evil". He opposed the evil system in the most non-violent manner by organizing civil disobedience campaigns

in the form of Salt Satyagraha, peaceful marches, and mass demonstrations, but asking the people to be non-violent and conciliatory.

13. True to the ideals of Satyagraha campaign, Gandhiji never resisted arrest by the law enforcement officials proving the higher level of the code of the entire Satyagraha movement.
14. Love is the foundation of Gandhian *ahimsa.* Nay it means pure love for him during his public life in his dedication to the cause of the Indian settlers in South Africa and in all his activities in India. He defined love as the capacity to love those who hated you. Accordingly, one who subscribes to the Gandhian doctrine of Satyagraha there is no room of enmity, but plenty of morn for amity.

**Notes and References**

1. Harijan, April 15, 1933, p. 8.
2. *Ibid.,* p. 8.
3. Following the outbreak of the war in Europe in 1914, the colonies and independent territories had accounted for approximately 67 per cent of the world's entire land area and 69 per cent of its citizens. Employing **non-violence** as the most effective instrument Gandhiji launched the history's greatest movement to expose the evil face of colonial aggrandizement and to eliminate colonial rule in India. No foreign colonial ruler had any right to imprison Gandhiji in his own land of birth **as the twentieth century's greatest champion of human rights and the most influential crusader of peaceful means.**
4. *Harijan,* September 24, 1938, p. 266.
5. *Young India,* March 23, 1961, pp. 89-91.
6. J.V. Bondurant, *Conquest of Violence,* (Bombay, 1959), p. 6.
7. *Young India,* March 23, 192 1, p. 5.
8. S. Radhakrishnan, (ed.), *Mahatma Gandhi's Essays and Reflections,* p. 214.
9. *Ibid.*
10. *Ibid.,* One of Gandhiji's important contributions to India and the rest of the world was the non-violent tool of Satyagraha

which is based on supreme human values that would outlive the violent ideologies of Nazism, Fascism and Communism. These ideologies of the last century are dead or are slowly dying while the values of the Gandhian Satyagraha remain with us. A detailed assessment of Satyagraha is provided *in Gandhi the Man,* Eknath Easwaran, (Bombay, Delhi: Jaico Publishing Company, 1997). (Esp. Chapters 2, and 5 to 8).

11. *Ibid.*
12. The case in point was the strike by workers in South Africa. The Indian settlers were involved in the strike. In a conciliatory manner Gandhiji asked the Indian labourers to call off the strike to avoid embarrassing the government. Later Prime Minister Botha had nothing put praise for Gandhiji's initiative to prevent the deterioration of the labour situation in South Africa. Gandhiji's humane attitude won him popularity as a man of goodwill and willing to make peace with opponents, a prerequisite of a Satyagrahi.
13. R.N. Bose, *Gandhian Technique and Tradition in Industrial Relations* (Calcutta: All India Institute of Social Welfare and Business Management, 1956). pp. 34-49. Satyagraha is a highly disciplined technique of social action characterized by dedicating oneself to truth by relying on behaviour which is non-violent and which includes self-suffering. While violent agitation also involves suffering, its purpose is to cause violence to the opponent. In Satyagraha the issue of causing harm to another person is completely foreign. Further details can be found in Richard B. Gregg, *The Power of Non-violence,* (rev. ed., London: George Routledge and Sons Ltd., 1938) The author gives an objective account of the application and effectiveness of the non-violent means as a more powerful force than violent means. He grew up when Gandhiji was practicing non-violent methods in South Africa and India and was familiar with the Gandhian techniques. Also in *Conquest of Violence: The Gandhian Philosophy of Conflict,* J.V. Bondurant, (Berkely and Los Angeles: University of California Press, 1956) Chapters 3 and 5.
14. It is a well-known fact that based on the effectiveness of the history's largest civil disobedience campaign in India, the non-violent technique has been used by Afro-Americans in the United States and by several groups of people in that

country and in Canada, especially by teachers and trade unions. Recently, Alejandro Toledo, the opposition leader in Peru, pledged to emulate the non-violent resistance of the late Rev. Dr. King against the Peruvian Government and its internationally condemned election procedures. "I don't want to compare myself with Martin Luther King, with Curazon Aquino in the Philippines," Toledo said. "I don't want to compare myself with Gandhi. But there are democratic forces, which, collectively, are going to unite to reconstruct democracy in Peru." *The Montreal Gazette,* May 28, 2000, p. A7. Gandhiji's message of civil disobedience has spread to different comers of the world. In Peru, Toledo promised to lead non-violent protests across the South American country and seek further international condemnation of the Peruvian authorities for their alleged illegal actions.

15. *Harijan,* February 18, 1933, p. 4.
16. *Ibid.,* October 13, 1940.
17. *Harijan,* October 13, 1940. Please see *Gandhian Thought and Contemporary Society,* Ed. by J.S. Mathur, (Bombay: Bharatiya Vidya Bhavan, 1974). The authors explain different techniques of Satyagraha and their positive results for the society to remedy conflict situations.
18. *Ibid.,* p. 15.
19. *Ibid.*
20. *Ibid.*
21. *Ibid.* The relationship between the forces of Satyagraha and state is explained in *Satyagraha and the State,* K. Santanam, (New York: Asia Publishing House, 1960).
22. *Ibid.* One's true education to Satyagraha is important for the performance and ultimate success of Satyagraha. Gandhiji had often cautioned against the indiscriminate use of the fast. He also knew that "there is much violence behind such fasting." *Harijan,* March 11, 1939. Still, he firmly believed that fasting, and act of great self—can be a potent weapon to convert the opponent with the recognition that the different aspects of its application should be carefully weighed.
23. These qualities are paraphrased from *The Political Philosophy of Mahatma Gandhi,* Gopinath Dhawan.
24. *Harijan,* March 25, 1939, pp. 64-65.

25. One can eliminate simple fasting, strike or simple protest march as they are far from fulfilling the essential attributes for a campaign qualifying as Satyagraha. Satyagraha at best may be employed during some phase of a non-violent movement and Gandhiji did precisely that.
26. *Harijan,* October 30, 1940. p. 323.
27. *Ibid.,* May 6, 1933, p. 1.
28. *Ibid.*
29. *Ibid.*
30. *Ibid.,* October 13, 1940, p. 322. Gandhiji, more than any political figure in India, approached the people of India with the basic principles and the teachings of the Vedas, with reminders from Upanishads, with quotations from the *Gita* as well as exhortations familiar from the age of Manu. The Indian people, with the great traditions behind them, responded to an appeal reflected in the currency of the Jain, Buddhist and Hindu religious principles, which found its way into the philosophy of Satyagraha. Please see *The Ethics of the Hindus,* Maitra, Sushil Kumar, (Calcutta: University Press, 1925).
31. *Ibid.,* Personal suffering is an important part of Satyagraha and without the willingness to undergo individual hardships no Satyagraha campaign can succeed in realizing its objectives.
32. *Young India,* August 11, 1920, p. 3.
33. M.K. Gandhi, *Hind Swaraj or Indian Home Rule,* p. 79.
34. *Young India,* June 16, 1920, p. 3.
35. *Ibid.,* August 11, 1920, p. 3.
36. *Ibid.,* June 16, 1920., p. 4.
37. *Tolstoy's Writings on Civil Disobedience and Non-Violence,* Leo Tolstoy. (New York: Signet Books, New American Library, 1968).This is a book that influenced the entire thinking of Gandhiji in his formulation of India's massive civil disobedience campaign against political oppression and injustice perpetuated by the colonial alien rule.
38. *Ibid.,* p. 188. Throughout the book Tolstoy explains his views on religion, violence as he saw around him in Europe and the urgent need to uphold justice by adopting peaceful methods of social change.
39. *Ibid.,* p. 189.

40. *Young India,* January 5, 1922, p. 5.
41. *Ibid.*
42. *Ibid.,* March 24, 1920, p. 4. Civil disobedience represents contravention of specific laws that are unjust and against the basic interests of the citizens. The steps adopted to eliminate such laws, may include refusal to pay taxes, peaceful protests and going to jail without resorting to violent demonstration. More details in *Conquest of Violence: The Gandhian Conquest of Conflict.* J.V. Bondurant, op cit. pp. 36-45.
43. *Autobiography,* M.K. Gandhi, pp. 357-58. In this brief assessment of Gandhiji's attitude toward established institutions and traditional approaches, notably with respect to religion and ownership, unorthodoxly emerged as a significant aspect. Gandhiji's Satyagraha and civil disobedience movement led to revolutionary social changes. The case in point here is the Champaran working class people and their struggle against the established system in the indigo fields of Bihar resulting in a revision of remarkable proportions. The Gandhian system of non-violent strikes upset the traditional patterns, which had assured a submissive labour force. In the same manner, the well-known Satyagraha of Vaikom for the right of low class to gain access to temple road radically altered the entrenched authority wielded by the members of the upper class. Related details in *Studies In Gandhism,* Nirmal Kumar Bose, 2nd ed. (Calcutta: India Associated Publishing Company, 1947) and *The Political Philosophy of Mahatma Gandhi,* G.N. Dhawan with a foreword by Dr. S. Radhakrishnan (Bombay: The Popular Book Depot, 1946).
44. *Ibid.,* pp. 357-58.
45. *Harijan,* April 1, 1939, p. 72.
46. *Young India,* February 9, 1922, p. 85.
47. *Ibid.,* p. 85.
48. For instance, the people of the Caribbean island nation of Puerto Rico recently staged a non-violent demonstration against their island being used for the explosion of weapons of mass destruction by the U.S. military as part of an experiment. The non-violent demonstrators did not resist arrest by the police, but vowed to return to protest against

further testing of the deadly weapons in their backyard. The fact that no demonstrator resisted arrest indicated his/her commitment to the non-violent principles of Satyagraha.

49. *Young India,* February 9, 1922, p. 85.
50. According to Gandhiji, civil disobedience is reluctant non-violent and non-compliance of unlawful governmental regulations which can be found in different societies in the world. There would be no change in such laws if they are not defied, and the defiance should be peaceful. The formation of teams of volunteers for non-violent demonstrations or holding public ralleys still adhering to peaceful methods "no contemplating or inciting to violence in spite of prohibitory orders, is defensive civil disobedience." (*Young India,* February 9, 1922, p. 85). In his memorable work, *On Civil Disobedience and Non-violence,* Leo Tolstoy has expressed similar views in his arguments against unjust laws. If the law makers heed the call of individuals like David Thoreau, Leo Tolstoy and Gandhiji many of the harsh realities of unjust laws could be prevented for common good and make the people bring closer to the administrators who often ignore the interests of the people creating the need for non-violent resistance. By any definition, a Satyam is a man striving for lasting peace and he would not go about starting quarrels or preparing blueprints for confrontation in advance against unjust laws or unjust social systems.
51. As a dedicated Satyagrahi, Gandhiji cooperated with South African officials when they faced difficult situations such as strikes by various pups of individuals and won the goodwill of the authorities.
52. *Young India,* January 5, 1922, p. 3.
53. *Ibid.,* March 27, 1930, pp. 107-08.
54. *Ibid.,* March 23, 1921, p. 90.
55. *On Civil Disobedience and Non-violence,* Tolstoy, *Ibid.,* p. 259.
56. *Ibid.* p. 231.
57. *Ibid.*
58. England, more than any region in the world, established its so-called reputation on the number of colonial possession, which it acquired by means of pefidy and violent aggression. Different parts of the globe that it colonized were poorer when it left their shores then when it first landed on the new

shores and beach-heads to launch further aggression. The authorities in England had hardly resorted to violent means that they had not taken in their land to quell popular riots against the autocratic rule of its kings and barons. In many ways they were colonial attitudes against their own subjects.

59. *Satyagraha and the State,* K. Santanam (New York: Asia Publishing House, 1960) p. 17. With preface by S.P. Sinha, Chief Justice, The Supreme Court of India.

# CHAPTER-V

# MAHATMA GANDHI IN SOUTH AFRICA (Satyagraha: Background and First Phase)

## ARTICLE -I

### (A) Forceful Instrument

No objective evaluation of Gandhiji's strong influence on the civil rights movement launched by Rev. Dr. King in the United States would be complete without closely examining Gandhiji's early life, the influence of Indian philosophy and his attempts in South Africa. If the twentieth century was a sad witness to the outbreak of two cataclysmic wars, both erupted in Europe,[1] it has also found the limitless capacity of non-violence advocated by Gandhiji as a trenchant instrument to attain equality and individual freedom. When Adolf Hitler and Benito Mussolini, 'the immediate relatives of Attila the Hun and Genghis Khan,' were sowing the seeds of violence all over Europe toiled by aggressive policies with the predetermined harvest of destruction and human blight, Gandhiji single-handedly was extolling the virtues of *ahimsa* as the most sensible and humane way to seek solutions to political problems. In a jolting book, *The Crazy Ape,* Albert Szent-Gyorgyi, the Nobel laureate in medicine, took serious note of Gandhiji's non-violent triumph.[2]

> Between the two world wars, at the heyday of Colonialism, force reigned supreme. It had suggestive power, and it was natural for the weaker to lie down before the stronger.
>
> Then came Gandhi chasing out of his country, almost single-handed the greatest military power on earth. He taught the world that there are higher

> things than force, higher than life itself, he proved that force had lost its suggestive power.

The British Empire, built on the application of brute military dint and perfidy, may have been the greatest in the twentieth century. **Gandhiji, the greatest apostle of non-violence and truth of the same century, toppled it in India where the emph had found immense wealth**. Empires were not built on legal and moral grounds, nor were they built to enhance the economic or social conditions of the people who lived in its different regions. Referring to the fundamental stimulus of the British in India alone, Lord Brentford, with a touch of arrogance, said in 1930[3]:

> We did not conquer India for the benefit of the Indians. We conquered India as the outlet for the goods of Great Britain. We conquered India by the sword and also by the sword we should hold it.

But the sword proved powerless in holding the empire or giving it long a life span as Gandhiji had denounced the use of sword in defeating an empire that had raised swords indiscriminately using them to perpetuate its rule in several parts of the globe. Gandhiji' initial efforts and experiments in *ahimsa* in South Africa had proved inestimable in his non-violent struggle in India and its paramount triumph over the forces of colonialism. Viewing Gandhiji's victorious non-violent campaigns in India, Albert Einstein stated: "Generations to come, it may be, will scarce believe that such a one as this ever in flesh and blood walked on this earth." Viscount Lord Mountbaten had this in mind: "Mahatma Gandhi will go down in history on a par with Buddha and Jesus Christ."

October 2, 1869 was a propitious day. Mohandas Karamchand Gandhi, to be universally known as Mahatma or Gandhiji, was born on the auspicious day into a traditional Bania family at Porbandar in Kathiawar peninsula. Since the days of Uttamchand Gandhi, his grandfather, the Gandhis had ruled as Diwans in a number of princely states in Kathiawar under the suzerainty of the British rule.

Born into a deeply religious and orthodox family, the young Gandhi was under the hex of his father, who had been unquestionably truthful and brave, the qualities which had filtered down into the life and activities of the while he was attending school. His father, being a ruler himself, wanted his son to be a ruler while his mother wanted him to be a *sanyasi*. The sacred message of Lord Krishna, contained in *Bhagavad Gita,* had left an indelible mark on the young Gandhi's perceptible mind and in little wonder in later life he became a saint among politicians and a politician among saints. His father did not care to accumulate wealth or material possessions. His mother, Putlibai, was highly religious in addition to being a symbol of distinctive qualities, which she transmitted to the rare personality of her son. Most of the sublime qualities of Gandhiji could be traced to his parents. Gandhiji learned the power of fasting from his mother (Appendix-1). Since Mohandas Gandhi grew up in a highly religious environment, he explored the basic tenets of different religions and his character became a rich amalgam of the best in every religion, besides being wholly free from bigotry and fanaticism.

Having studied law in England, he returned home and set up practice, which coincided with an offer from Muslim merchants to represent them in legal proceedings in South Africa. A prominent merchant in Porbandar had business dealings in South Africa requiring the services of a lawyer to defend his business interests. Gandhiji seized the opportunity and went to South Africa in April 1893.

## (B) The Three Gunas

Hinduism fully acknowledges the diversity in the disposition of individuals and their interests. Many Hindu traditions account for this diversity by their reference to the three basic qualities or *gunas* which determine the nature of all creation—human beings, animals and plants.[5] We shall briefly analyze the three *gunas* and their effects on human behaviour to understand their impact on Gandhiji's life and career.

The three *gunas* are *sattva* (the nature of pleasure and light); *rajas* (the principle of motion and activity); and *tamas* (heavy and passive). The presence of these *gunas* in different degrees and their permutation determines the atypical temperaments in human beings and Gandhiji[6] had shared one or more than one quality in his life and career. When *sattva* predominates, for instance, an individual may be drawn to a life of scholarship and spirituality as in the case of Gandhiji. When *rajas* is the prevailing *guna*, one, may aspire to political or social leadership.[7] The specific nature of an individual is referred to in Sanskrit by the term *svabhava* and the nature in which this mien finds its proper expression is one's *svadharma* or duty; ideally one's work should be an expression—a mirror image—of one's distinct nature. Gandhiji exemplifies the message in *Bhagavad Gita* (6:32; 13:27-28) as *Gita* asks us to see all beings with the eyes of equality by discerning God's presence everywhere, seeing the indestructible One in the variety of the many is Truth, for it is through the One that the many are united and seen as equal. In other words, there is abiding unity in diversity. This perception may be said to be the core of Gandhiji's moral and intellectual framework. Thus Gandhiji is a product of Indian heritage.

In our study we will notice that while Gandhiji lived in South Africa from 1893 to 1914, he put to test the concept of non-violence on different occasions **and to his utmost satisfaction he found it to be a powerful device to meet any challenge in life.** He perfected it into a scientific level with highly predictable results blending truth, love and non-violence harmoniously into one mould; **The victory of Gandhian Satyagraha was the victory of the essential goodness in man.** Gandhiji proved beyond a trace of doubt that non-violence was no wishful thinking, but an effectual and pragmatic remedy to eradicate injustice in South Africa or anywhere else.

Analyzing the onerous situation Indians were facing in South Africa, S.K. Mukherji says:[8]

> If the nineteenth century was an unhappy one for the Indian community in South Africa, the twentieth century has been even more so. It has been characterized by increasingly shrewd, determined and also well-thought-out onslaughts on the Indian's rights to live as honourable citizens of their land of adoption, the land which owes its prosperity as much, if not more, to them as to any other section of its population.

His future attempts to free India from the iron clasp of alien control and to lay the foundation of a democratic structure would have been seriously tarnished if his campaign had not been non-violent and free of rancour towards the arrogant foreign rulers. It was certainly the non-violent aspect eschewing bitterness and its ultimate success that provided goad to Rev. Dr. King in his struggle for justice in the United States.

In the struggle for justice in South Africa Gandhiji himself had become a victim of violence as he had approached the registration office after Smuts had released him from jail. Gandhiji, the absolute peacemaker, should never have been in a jail. Later he recalled the agonizing experience.[9]

> My upper lip was cut on one side. I have a bruise above the left eye and a wound on the forehead. In addition, there were minor injuries on my right hand and left knee. I do not remember the manner of the assaults, but people say I fell unconscious with the first blow which was delivered with a stick.
>
> Then my assailants struck me with an iron. Thinking me dead, they stopped. I only remember having been beaten up. I have an impression

> that, as the blows started, I uttered the words: 'He Rama'. As I came to, I got up with a smile. **In my mind, there was not the slightest anger or hatred towards the assailants.**

Gandhiji, seriously mauled with blood dripping from the open wounds, caused by his assailants took more than ten days to recover and to gain enough strength to resume his normal activities. He became a victim of violence for his faith in non-violence and it was not to be the last attempt on his life, for he became unpopular with many who resented his work to improve the conditions of the Indian people. Let us study the historical background of the problem.

The people of Indian ancestry first arrived in Natal in 1860 constituting the largest and the earliest group of Indian settlers in the entire Africa, and the largest Asian community at that time. According to the Minority Rights Group, the Indian settlers "differ in their composition and in their status within the host society from both the East African Asians and from the East Indians of the Caribbean."[10] During the early days of their arrival, hailing from Calcutta, the overwhelming majority of the people from India had been from a fairly large area that included Uttar Pradesh, Orissa, Bihar, parts of West Bengal and Madhya Pradesh. When the authorities had realized the need for additional manpower, an agency had been set up in Chennai with the result that in the succeeding years an increasing number of Tamil and Telugu-speaking people came to South Africa.[11] A number of developments which had occurred before the dawn of the 19th century witnessed a shift in the exodus of the Indian settlers. The report elaborates:[12]

> Before the 19th century there had been no voluntary emigration of the labour from India. Still, between one and two million Indian labourers had gone ovarseas in the forty years. British capitalism meted the demand for labour and the economic conditions in India compelled labour to migrate.

## (C) The Oceanic Route

Besides South Africa, Indians are said to have established commercial ties with the east coast of Africa for a long time, but the trade links were certainly established in 1848 following the discovery of the vast oceanic route from Europe to the subcontinent by Vasco-da-gama. Hamerton, the first British Consul at Zanzibar found in 1891 that the number of Indian people in the island or residing in the coastal towns within the Said's dominion in East Africa was sizeable[13] after embarking mostly from parts of western India, viz. Kutch and the surrounding districts of Surat, Porbander, Jamnagar and Bombay. Kauleshwar Rao makes the following observation about the condition of the Indians who had lived in the area:[14]

> Among the leading Indian merchants in Zanzibar during the 19th century, mention should be made of Jairam Sewji. In 1835, he acquired control of the important post of customs collector and his firm gained considerable advantages and making rapid progress in business in East Africa.

One of the notable aspects of the British colonial policy in East Africa, as elsewhere, had been the cynical exploitation of labour, including that of the Indian settlers, to build networks of railways, and to state the capitalistic appetite. In order to realize that dominant goal the colonial merchants were willing to adopt various measures irrespective of their legal or moral implications, "In May 1987," according to Rao, "Grindlay Groom & Co. at Calcutta was appointed to act as the Railway's agents there and to recruit labour from Bengal and the eastern districts of the North-Western Provinces."[15] In retrospect, it was providential that Gandhiji came to South Africa rather than to any African country with large Indian migration, to start the non-violent campaign and to strengthen the Satyagraha movement always holding the moral compass in hand for Indians and others.

In the same manner, Indians who had also set sail to the Caribbean in the distant Atlantic Ocean, hailing from the same regions of the country (Bihar, Calcutta, Madhya Pradesh, Chennai and Uttar Pradesh), were akin to those who migrated to South Africa during the same period. In the field research in the West Indies, the researcher found that in Trinidad, where the Indian settlers had first landed in 1845, they did not encounter the same problems as their distant cousins in South Africa where the problems a were created by the political structure colliding with the vested interests of the settlers from Europe. Such interests were apparently absent in the distant Caribbean islands where settlers from Africa had been residing before the arrival of the Indians. Yet, there were frequent murmurs against what the British had called the indenture system which Gandhiji did not spare in his non-violent resistance. L. Rajni, pertaining to this aspect, says that the storm which was to sweep away "the indenture system [in the Caribbean island] was started by Mahatma Gandhi in South Africa," arguing further that:[18]

> Having aroused awareness of the adverse conditions for indentures there (South Africa), he took the campaign to India. The flames of protest

> were further fuelled by the Sanderson Commission, McNeil Report, the Gokhale motion and by leading Indian political figures.
>
> For Instance, D.S.C. Banerji, President of the Uttar Pradesh Congress said of indentureship: Till few years back, Indians were the outcasts of the Empire, and today they are the outcasts of the world.

On March 21, 1916, Pandit Madan Mohan Malaviya spoke in the Indian Legislative Council of the negative side of the indentureship in the West Indies.[19]

> Indentureship system is an evil system in the trade of human beings. India lost two million of its young, able-bodied citizens to South Africa, Natal, Mauritius, Fiji, Seychelles and West Indies. The Indian public was in a state of ignorance about the conditions to which indentured Indians until 1890s **when Mahatma Gandhi started to expose its evils.** The voyage was often long and dangerous poor housing and health care, low wages, long working hours and severe punishment were characteristic of the system. (Emphasis added).

After making the public declaration, the Indian political leader introduced the following resolution affirming his strong determination to root out the system and to strengthen the needed harmonious links among the Indian people. He appealed to high ranking officials:[20]

> That this council recommend to the Governor General in the Council that early steps be taken for the abolition of the system of Indian indentured labour.

The problem had drawn the special attention of Rabindranath Tagore, who expressed his feelings in the following lines:[21]

> *For dreams fade, hopes farl, but*
> *They gathered the fruit of the day.*
> *But I am the eternal Truth,*
> *And you shall meet me again and again,*
> *In your journey of life from shore to shore.*

Lord Hardinge proposed to accept the resolution further stating that the "labourers had no real reason"[22] to travel thousands of miles from India over the rough sea and to settle in a "strange country and to place themselves for a long period in conditions of adversity"[23] when they "can find work in the jute mills of Bengal."[24] Later, a letter of support was sent by the Anti-Slavery Society to Pandit Malaviya and his associates and the system met with its inevitable and on January 1, 1917 triggering off an unrehearsed euphoria on the streets of Delhi.[25]

## ARTICLE -2

### (A) Political and Economic Control

The influx of European settlers into South Africa, a large number of them to improve the economic standards not found in their own lands of birth, began two centuries before the arrival of the Indian people. Admittedly the Natal settlement was relatively nascent. During the initial phase of the Indian immigration, two groups of settlers from Europe had been locked in conflicts as can be expected even by babies with each other to gain economic and political power. The situation had its definite impact on the Indian settlers who faced challenges, perhaps more than in any other part of the world at that time. Surveying the emerging trend, the Minority Rights Report, points out:[26]

*One of the three Maxham daguerreotype portraits of Thoreau (Courtesy Concord Free Public Library)*

Soon after, imperial powers, in particular Britain, began casting covetous eyes upon the rich mineral discoveries in the whole region. Until the

> establishment of the Union of South Africa, the general position of Indians in Transvaal was determined by the conflicting as well as the overriding interests of Afrikaaners, the British settlers, the mining as well as the financial concerns of the Imperial policy and for all of whom the situation faced by the Indian settlers was incidental.

During the twenty years of his stay in South Africa, with its gaping legal loopholes, the racial discrimination in open and subtle forms, its poisonous effects on the Indians and the one which Gandhiji himself had experienced, were a key ingredient for his non-violent resistance. In the process Gandhiji loomed as an enduring symbol of justice. It may be noted for a seemly awareness of the racist attitude that racism was not channeled against just the Indians residing in the Transvaal or Pretoria pursuing their interests in a just and peaceful manner. There was little doubt that European people in many parts of Africa had resented other European traders and had competed against one another like avaricious sales agents for political control in a fierce manner pitting one group against another. In South Africa, the native citizens also had been the victims of discrimination by the Dutch and English settlers. The report by the Minority Groups Committee stated that in order "to ensure British supremacy in South Africa, the Indians could not be given equality,"[27] chiefly to protect their turf. Britain viewed the situation from a different angle as a amplified in the report:[28]

> ... but to maintain control and placate the nationalists in India, they (the Indians) had been allocated a place above that of the indigenous African people. Though satisfying the British enonomic interests, such a 'solution' was not entirely acceptable to the white settlers who wanted to maintain their own position.

South Africa's racial policy towards Indians was no more than a reflection of the country's general attitude. Even in our times, as did during the time of Gandhiji in South Africa, racist feelings exist in countries in Europe towards their neighbours who have past wounds to heal requiring large bottles of medicine. (During the early days of American history immigrants from certain regions in Europe had faced brick walls of discrimination from their brethren in the same continent).

The situation in South Africa, as Gandhiji had viewed and interpreted it, compelled the young attorney, based on his own legal background, to argue their case even subordinating his own highly promising legal career to public service. Gandhiji did not resort to violence. Violence as a means to end was unthinkable as Gandhiji envisioned a just and peaceful society based on compassionate will to combat a system based on racist attitude towards the Indian settlers. His emphasis on the decentralization of power and an egalitarian society was born out of the Indian philosophy and the reading of Tolstoy who rejected the utility of the state, pleading for the creation of a non-institutional and non-violent society. Ever since Gandhiji had set foot in South Africa, he was fully aware of the unlit side of injustice since the Indian residents were vilified and were not allowed to travel without a valid permit or to move about after 9 p.m. as though they were hardened criminals. They were innocent. They were good citizens. The harsh laws severed their veins. S.B. Sitaramayya states:[29]

> Transvaal, how we were denied admission in the first and second classes on the railways, driven out of the tramcars, and pushed off foot-paths, kept out of hotels, and refused the benefit of public parks, and how **we were spat upon, hissed, cursed, abused and often subjected to a variety of other indignities which no human being could patiently bear.**

The law-abiding and the extremely gentle looking Indian residents were dragged down for no reason in South Africa. Realising the magnitude of the problems faced by the Indian settlers, public meetings in India had expressed deep concern over such widespread indignities as *Kesari*, a Marathi newspaper, published a caustic editorial:[30]

> When any coloured people venture to set their foot in a white man's nation the white wolves manage to make their lives unbearable to them. Among these persecuted races, **the lot of the Indians is the worst while their own nation is freely exploited by the whites;** they receive nothing but insults and indignities whenever they go off to a white man's country.

*Kesari,* a prominent publication, sufficiently echoed the prevailing Indian sentiments on the glaring injustice inflicted on the Indian settlers and Gandhiji's non-violent attempts to remedy the situation in a peaceful manner. The scales of balance were tipped against the peace loving with a dismal prediction:[31]

> The Transvaalers had been treating us worse than slaves and all our appeals for protection to the Imperial Government had hitherto proved futile ... The present brutal and insulting treatment of the Indian settlers in the British Colonies is surely one day to prove **one of the principal causes of the downfall of the British Empire.**

**San Fernando, Trinidad, West Indies**

Gandhiji, a great communicator, had believed in the power of communicating with people from all walks of life in order to galvanize them for the cause of justice. He strongly felt that a journal could play a decisive role in uniting the community by publishing its common aspirations and grievances. In 1904, Gandhiji started the journal,

*The Indian Opinion* with the sole objective of realizing the broad objectives and the popular journal, had been a clear signal of the swift current of changes taking place in the development of Gandhiji's philosophy. The Indian Opinion soon grew into an effective medium to propagate his non-violent philosophy and the aims of Satyagraha while his own work titled, *Hind Swaraj* articulated its basic principles. During his sojourn in South Africa, Gandhiji was wedded to Satyagraha as nail to door and non-violence as a means to attain justice. In South Africa Gandhiji's ingenuous commitment to non-violence and Satyagraha, the lasting symbols of his political adroitness and intellectual brilliance, had assumed a new dimension in a society that turned to many paths to expurgate the Indians for no good reason.

Gandhiji had identified himself with the problems of the Indians, as he was also a victim of the dismal practices prevailing in the country. He was thrown out of the first class coach of the train; he was forbidden to wear turban in the court. He was determined to remove the ugly shadows of injustice and devised appropriate instruments for combating it. Racism is a narcissitic attempt to project an individual's presumed superiority when it actually does not exist. In Gandhian rhetoric we require the tools for *sarvodaya*, not resentment and the weapons of destruction. The following diagram would illustrate the problems faced by the Indian settlers and the goals of Satyagraha.

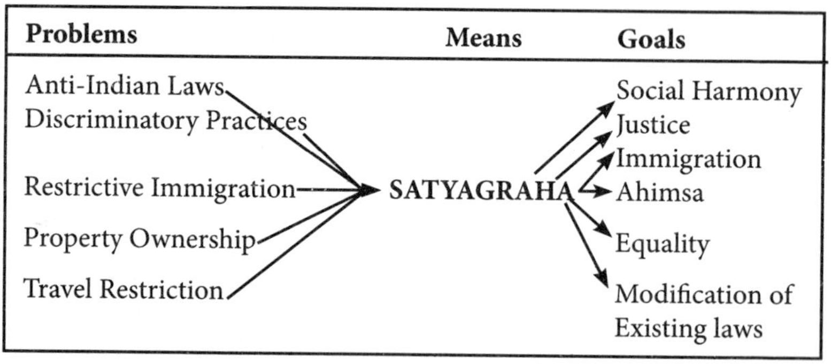


The Indian residents, with a passion for justice burning in their collective soul, showed readiness to rally around the Indian leader who believed in the fairness of the means as in the righteousness of the end. Gandhiji had many friends and supporters outside the Indian community. Gandhiji and H. Kallenbach, a German architect and close associate, purchased a farm, about 1,100 acres, and offered its use free of charge[32] to the Indian residents. Named after Count Tolstoy, the farm was used mainly to promulgate the ideals of Satyagraha, which was unquestionably a new phenomenon in the struggle for justice anywhere in the world. The Gandhian philosophy since it proved beyond doubt that individuals could realize their social and political objectives by applying non-violent means. Satyagraha's multifarious facets included search for truth and non-violence. It was far from a theoretical proposition but an absolutely pragmatic approach capable of sweeping out evils engrained in the body politic: S.B. Mukhe ji says.[33]

**Integration—Birmingham Train Station. Afro-Americans were once digied-access to public facilities before Rev. Dr. King's campaigns.**

> The idea of satyagraha was born in the crucibles of the sufferings and humiliations of the Indians in South Africa. Satyagraha, generally translated as 'passive resistance,' and regarded as a 'weapon of the weak' is, according to Gandhi, a true 'expression of soul force.'

Referring to the significant role Satyagraha played in South Africa and later in India, William L. Shirer makes the important comment:[34]

> **It was Gandhi's genius, to be sure, that had inspired the Indian masses given them [including the South African Indians] the technique of Satyagraha with which to stage a non-violent revolution.**

P. Moon argues that "non-violence and the avoidance of hurt to another were the essence of Satyagraha as he [Gandhiji] conceived it."[35] The Tolstoy Farm,[36] honouring Alexei Tolstoy, was used as a laboratory to carry out the uniquely Gandhian experiments in manual labour, self-control, educational facilities, vegetarian diet, *ahimsa,* simple life and nature cure. Gandhiji had no interest in accumulating wealth, but showed profound concern for the poor. In South Africa he had led a simple life, which helped him identify himself with the problems of the marginalized everywhere in the world. In Satyagraha the past is alive in the present.

## (B) Resistance Against Unjust Laws

Gandhiji was determined to improve the social and political conditions of the Indians in South Africa. It was an irony that the European settlers in South Africa were discriminating against the native citizens and the Indian settlers. As an important part of the non-violent campaign, Gandhiji inaugurated the now famous signature campaign to dramatize opposition to the highly discriminatory disenfranchising bill.[37] in 1894, following the imposition of the annual tax of £25[38] by the National Government on the Indian settlers, he spearheaded a campaign against the tax and much pressure was brought to bear on the officials. The Government was forced to lower the rate though Gandhiji was not completely satisfied with the outcome of the bill.

One of the draconian bills introduced in the National Legislative Assembly was calculated to work against the interests of the Indian merchants while another was aimed at imposing stringent control on their commercial interests. Mindful of the serious consequences of the new legislation Gandhiji stepped up his non-violent struggle, arousing public sentiments against the regulation, consolidating, Indian opinion against them in South Africa.

In South Africa Gandhiji combined his political activities with humanitarian service in the interests of his fellowmen since he strongly felt that political work could not be isolated from humanitarian obligation. His altruism had raised him high above the communal level. P. Moon says:[39]

> One of Gandhi's lifelong avocations was nursing the sick, and an outbreak of plague in an Indian 'location' near Johannesburg not long after had settled in that city afforded him an opportunity of practicing it. His service at this time and his public castigation of the municipality for its negligence aroused great interest among Europeans as well as Indians and was the direct cause of his acquaintances with Mr. West and Mr. Polak, seeking much closer association with him.

Ample evidence of his sympathy for the sick and the needy was demonstrated in his decision. Gandhiji had to offer himself as a male nurse in a hospital, which had been built with the charities of Parsi Rustomji and was running under the management of Dr. Booth. Gandhiji stressed the need of preventive steps and nature cure. His dedication to social work was so strong that later in India, he wanted to turn the Indian National Congress into a social organization to look after the poor and the downtrodden.

Gandhiji resorted to Satyagraha to demonstrate his vigorous opposition to South Africa's registration law, which had precluded the Indian people from attaining equal status. He was chiefly responsible for effectively organizing a non-violent campaign with the direct outcome that many who had participated in the non-violent struggle had been imprisoned without a day's trial as South Africa had become synonymous with racist vendetta. In January 1918, Gandhiji, the chief architect of the campaign, was imprisoned and was kept in jail in Pretoria. His imprisonment did not dampen his non-violent spirit, nor did it dilute his resolve to obtain justice by destroying the myth of violence as a means to resolve differences among individuals.

Gandhiji, was handed down a nine-month jail sentence for his key role in organizing the non-violent campaign for justice. During the second trial at Volstrust, he was given a three-month term imprisonment. He had instructed the volunteers **"not be threaten anyone, nor to use force."**[40] The authorities were oblivious that each acrid step provided **an extra dose of fervour to his firm belief that non-violence was the only avenue open to him and to his fellow countrymen to attain justice in South Africa, and later in India.**

Gandhiji refused to give up his method of action in South Africa even after he had found himself at the centre of opposition and in many instances he and his political cohorts, E. Kallenbach and Polak, were unconditionally set free even before they had completed their jail sentences. The harsh penalties the authorities imposed on them widened the scope of the campaign as an appropriate political option. Mukherji speaks of the development of Satyagraha:[41]

> The volunteers had been instructed not to threaten anybody, nor to use violence. They were to persuade, not to coerce. If the police intervened, they were not to resist. The volunteers of the Passive Resistance Association helped in creating an enlightened public opinion in South Africa.

In January 1914, as a result of a round of negotiation conducted with General Smuts, a common ground was found and according to the terms of the agreement, the £3 levy on the Indian residents was abolished. The Indian marriages were declared valid. The successful outcome of the campaign was indeed a loud proclamation of the efficacy of non-violence. The campaign was temporarily suspended with the implementation of the historic Indian Relief Bill.

### (C) Decisive Impact

Throughout the campaign, Gandhiji and his followers never preached violence. On the other hand, they had denounced it as a means to realize their objectives besides, in the attempt, proving its effectiveness on a mass scale. This had far-reaching consequences and Rev. Dr. King embarked upon an equally great mission in the United States taking inspiration from the Mahatma who elevated non-violence to the plane of a universal panacea for all evils in society. Rev. Dr. King goes on:[42]

> ......the method which seeks to implement the just law by appealing to the conscience of the great decent majority who through blindness, fear, pride or irrationality have allowed their consciences to sleep. In the years to come, non-violence would win tens of thousands of adherents.

"Gandhi's philosophy," he continued, "was equally assertive in the moral sense. It surpassed the pragmatic pacifism of Thoreau, one of Gandhi's original inspirations ..."[43] Rev. Dr. King had studied Gandhiji's life and activities in South Africa and India, much more than any individual outside the country;[44] the Gandhian ideals filtered into his mind especially after the non-violent struggle led by Gandhiji gained greater momentum to rid India of colonial rule as the streets became surging rivers of men who willingly participated in the struggle.[45]

The concept of Satyagraha was unique since no leader before Gandhiji had embarked on a non-violent struggle on a large scale. In the eighteenth and nineteenth centuries countless individuals and communities were being discriminated against in several parts of the world, mostly in their own lands of origin, by colonial agents. The world was in the throes of history's two major wars, when Gandhiji became the history's greatest apostle of non-violence. During his political career in South Africa Gandhiji found that several pieces of legislation enacted by lawmakers were directed against free men and women in any region of the world as they undermined human dignity. The rulers in several parts of Europe had passed harsh legislative measures against the basic interests of their own people and to preserve the special status of the ruling elite and, from that perspective, the Indian settlers were not the only individuals to be crippled by a web of unnecessary regulations. The vast powers granted to the police in South Africa could, without doubt, be employed to harass Indians, even to the point of stifling their ardent desire to be prosperous in the adopted land or to make them leave the country. In Gandhiji's mind such laws were designed to strike at the very root of (Indian) existence in South Africa where they wanted to live in harmony. Social indignation and jealousy had much to do with the implementation of laws. The Indian merchants owned assets worth thousands of pounds, which many settlers from Europe lacked. They were facing deportation and complete in under the weight of the ordinance which had kept them away from the gates of justice.

Gandhiji had frequently reminded his non-violent troops of the importance of maintaining order and self-discipline in their ranks. His commitment to discipline became apparent when he had decided to march on foot protesting against the imposition of tax, from New Castle to the Transvaal-Natal border thirty-five miles away while some strikers took their wives and children with them. Those who were weak for the lengthy trek would proceed by train to their destination. The owners of the Natal collieries, largely impressed and a little unnerved at the same time, perhaps by the discipline and orderliness among the ranks of the Indian workers, invited Gandhiji to meet them at Durban. Gandhiji frankly told the colliery-owners that he did not intend to call off the strike until the workers had realized their objectives of the repeal of £3 tax and equal treatment before the eyes of the law (Appendix-2).

It was an agreeable surprise for the father of Satyagraha to discover on his return to New Castle from Durban that the non-violent nature and orderliness of the striking workers had disarmed the initial belligerence of the mine officials at New Castle, some even wishing the workers success in their non-violent endeavour. If the authorities promised to abolish the tax, Gandhiji would stop the march while the reply was swift, "Gen. Smuts will have nothing to do with you. You may do just as you please." Gandhiji was the first to cross into the Transvaal, followed by a party of Satyagrahis while the mounted police at the border had no intention to interfere. The non-violent demonstrators. reached Volksrust, the first Transvaal village on the road map. Then came the glad news, perhaps to the surprise of everyone that the tax was repealed, another feather on the cap of Gandhian Satyagraha, a model for the non-violent progression of societal forces.

Although Gandhiji had spent two decades of his life in South Africa, 1893-1914, practicing non-violence, he kept himself in constant touch with the other architects of India's freedom Gopal Krishna Gokhale, Lokamanya Bal Gangadhar Tilak, Sir Feroze Shah Mehta, Justice Ranade, and Bahruddin Tyabji, and Dr. Ambedkar. Gokhale, needless to say, was Gandhiji's protege.

## ARTICLE-3

### (A) A Dominant Role

After Gandhiji had launched the Satyagraha movement in South Africa, hardly anyone could surmise that the campaign was destined to play a dominant role in yet another effective and national movement to bring down the British administration in India. The problems of the Indian settlers and South Africa's political circumstances gradually became a strong engine for the lengthy campaign to gain speed on all four cylinders for justice for the Indians in that country. Its notorious system of inequality, reprehensible from any point of view, became the perfect breeding ground of their struggle. General Smuts declared his appalling rationale for such a policy in the following manner:[46]

> The whole basis of our particular system in South Africa rests on inequality.... It is the bedrock of our constitution ... You cannot deal with the Indians apart from the whole position in South Africa: you cannot give political rights to the Indians which you deny, to the rest of the colored citizens of South Africa.

The acknowledged British policy was to put a heavy lid on the entry of the Indian immigrant groups into the Transvaal region while Britain was illegally occupying African and Asian countries. A lacuna had always existed between the British legal theory and its general practice. The South African authorities strictly enforced an archaic registration scheme meant to prevent the newcomers from slipping into the country by pretending to be someone else by circumventing the law. The stifling legalism that each Indian resident had to carry a permit issued by the British officials, bearing his signature or thumb-print appeared quite inadequate for the official purpose of verification and strict control of the flow of settlers. In the light of this development the Indian residents were required to carry new permits or cards under the provision of the so-called Peace Preservation Ordinance with a photograph and other pertinent details. Although the Indian residents objected to the regulation, they were persuaded to register and carry the permits. The new regulation was to become the well-spring of Gandhiji's Satyagraha movement, a great catalyst to publicize his fellow-countrymen's just cause rooted in the classic wisdom of the Roman law *audiature et altern pars* (Let the other side be heard).

When the Government had realized that his fellow countrymen were willing to comply with the order it decided to move a step further. Even though the registration was completed in 1906, officials reached the unanimous conclusion that the laws did not, in fact, put an end to the 'surreptitious' entry of the Indian residents into the Transvaal, nor did they provide for deporting unauthorized residents. They were forced to shut off the remaining loopholes. After Gandhiji had been released from his ambulance service, the Transvaal Government Gazette published a draft called the Asiatic Law Amendment Ordinance. He travelled to Johannesburg and expressed grave concern over the implications of the new regulation stating that it would spell absolute ruin for the Indian residents in South Africa. Under the terms of the new ordinance, every Asiatic man, woman and child over eight years of age would have to surrender the old permit entitled to reside in the Transvaal and receive a new certificate of registration. Any individual, who failed to comply with the regulation, would forfeit the right of residence and surrender himself to jail sentence or immediate deportation from the country.

The Indian residents argued that the stringent regulation was unnecessary, that it was discriminatory as there was no law to control, let alone regulate, the number of immigrants from Europe. The ambivalence was the exodus of people from that continent searching for a better way of life, away from the pockets of poverty and its dictatorial regimes, being considered legal migration. (The case in point is mass migration from Europe to North America in violation of the 'agreements' entered into with the Red Indians or Native American Indians). After they settled down in other countries, largely by resorting to illegal and violent means, they imposed their unjust laws on others, or attempted to prevent others from entering the country. Gandhiji had studied the wide range of problems faced by the Indian residents and Referring to his deep concern, Dr. S.H. Patil makes the following observation:[47]

> After his [Gandhiji's] arrival in South Africa, he found the, racial discrimination had in different forms against the Indians who had settled there. He decided to take up their just cause and subordinate his

legal practice to public service, The Natal Indian Congress was formed in eighteen hundred and ninety four to voice the many grievances of the South African Indians.

## (B) The Twists and Turns

The twists and turns of the key issues faced by the Indian settlers were serious. Gandhiji with sufficient reason argued that no such discriminatory laws existed in other parts of the world and that police were given the power to harass Indians to the point of forcing them out of the country. He believed that the new law was born out of jealousy and greed and its real intent was to drive the Indian residents out of the Union. An Indian businessman, with assets worth thousands of pounds, was on the verge of being deported under the cacophonous law. On the other hand settlers from Europe with no assets worth mentioning did not face the same dilemma. There was mounting resentment against the Indian merchants who had made steady progress despite a labyrinth of discriminatory laws and until Gandhiji started his campaign in South Africa, the Indian residents had lacked effective leadership.

Indian family in South Africa (1897). Anguish carved into the faces. (*Source*: The Minority Rights Report, London, 1954).

Gandhiji strongly felt that the regulation intended "to strike at the very root" of the existence of the Indians in South Africa and if the law had been judicially applied, it would have had an effect on the European immigration. Some people believed that Gandhiji's concern regarding the general political climate in South Africa was highly exaggerated, arguing, for instance, that any Indian resident in possession of a legitimate permit, faced no special problem in South Africa in pursuing his interests. The authorities who had implemented the regulations had devised various methods—and this is true in our own times—to limit the entry of immigrants.

Gandhiji felt that the regulation to carry valid cards was fulsome to his compatriots, particularly when they were prepared to accept the regulation without public protest. He thought that the fellow-Indians were being treated as criminals, a situation which he refused to recognize and decided to take firm action against the measure. Although many Indian settlers did not feel so keenly about the situation, there was consensus that the condition to re-register was a serious issue and that they had the right to express deep indignation over the regulation of *purdah* for women. Gandhiji's leadership rekindled the fire of protest and resentment in the heart of the Indian Community in South Africa.

At a meeting of prominent Indian residents, including many businessmen, Gandhiji viewed the situation from a larger perspective asserting that the ordinance had been a source of humiliation not only to the Indian residents in South Africa but to India also. Those who attended a subsequent meeting held on September 11, 1906, solemnly declared their intention to defy what they had termed the "Black Ordinance" if it was declared law and to face any penalties resulting from their defiance. Gandhiji supported Satyagraha and the response he had received from the Indian residents was encouraging. The highly encouraging reaction had been the result of his close association with the Indian residents and his genuine identification with their problems. We had already built up a strong base for Satyagraha at the Phoenix settlement and the Tolstoy farm, the laboratories for experimenting with the principles and objectives of his philosophy. Dr. S.H. Patil points out that the "Phoenix settlement and Tolstoy farm were his centres for experimenting with his philosophy of public life,"[48] adding that:[49]

> Gandhiji had also identified himself with the South African Indians in their sufferings and trials and organized them against racial discrimination and other social injustices. Gandhi himself had experienced humiliation

of racial discrimination on many occasions in the early part of his stay in South Africa.

In the past, the acknowledged British policy or that of other sponsoring agents of colonialism was not much different from the general attitudes they had adopted in their own countries. There was growing discrimination by one group of people in England against another and severe exploitation of Labour. Many individuals were not permitted to take membership in organizations patronized by those belonging to the upper echelons of the society in France and England while the people of Irish origin faced discrimination in housing and employment in London and Manchester.

Although conditions in South Africa were undoubtedly serious, there was no compelling reason to resort to extreme measures. The Black Ordinance had yet to become the recognized law of the land while the Indian residents, under the banner of the Gandhian Satyagraha, had reached the decision to exhaust every constitutional and legal method to prevent it from becoming the law. S.H. Patil states the bill "was calculated to affect the Indian traders adversely. Another intention was to impose stringent restrictions on Indian immigration."[50] Such harsh regulations did not bind the members of other communities, which strengthened Gandhiji's fundamental assertion that the regulation had been highly discriminatory in character and in its actual intent.

As a result of a number of complaints registered with the local Government and several deputations, it was agreed that the regulations would not be applied to the Indian women and the ordinance was issued without much alteration. The officials claimed that the women were exempted out of magnanimity with no external pressure. The Indian residents were convinced that the decision to exempt women was the fruit of their protest and so they were all the more encouraged by the move. The assumption of the officials that their actions would have little repercussions was belied while Gandhiji was encouraged as his non-violent activism began to show visible signs of effectiveness. Until then the Indian community was like a nut held between the jaws of a pincer, the pincer of South Africa's intense racist mentality.

In 1906, the Transvaal, still under the cloud of the racist colonial rule, lacked a responsible Government requiring royal assent to its legislative measures. The royal assent was far from a mere formality, but might be withheld. In view of such a legal requirement, constitutional remedy was not altogether exhausted in terms of the legitimate aspirations of the Indian people and the manner by which the problems could be remedied. Gandhiji and a prominent Muslim leader, H.O. Ali, went to England to voice their concern met the Secretary of State for the Colonies and urged that approval of the ordinance be withheld.

Gandhiji, carrying a pledge signed by South Africa's Indian residents, also met Lord Elgin, the former Viceroy of India, who had already served as Secretary of State for the Colonies, Lord Morely, Secretary of State for India and a number of Parliamentarians. The response was on the whole favourable, but Lord Elgin, far from making any commitment, only advised the King to withhold his formal assent to the ordinance in South Africa.

Gandhiji and the Indian residents in South Africa were to discover that the refusal to give assent to the discriminatory regulation was a ruse, typical of the policy of the colonial agents. The Transvaal had ceased to be a Crown colony when it was granted the status of responsible Government on January 1, 1907, a move, which had serious implications for South Africa. The move granted ample power to the authorities in the Transvaal to implement a piece of legislation, which, *ipso facto,* did not require the royal assent. That was yet another sinister loophole in the colonial administrative machinery to side-track resistances and to facilitate the imposition of the crude will of the colonisers on the gullible victims of oppression.

### (C) Abrogation of Legislation

Now, Lord Elgin advised the officials in the Transvaal that if the newly constituted legislative body enacted a new bill in its original form, he would no longer be legally bound to request the King to withhold his assent. A new bill was introduced in March 1907, quickly ramming it through the legislative halls at a single sitting. The alacrity at which it was completed disregarding the established parliamentary procedure was a typical example of the audacity of the colonial rulers to introduce laws to further their interests or even totally to abrogate the existing legislation as they pleased. The Black Ordinance became the Black Act requiring the Indian residents to register by July 31, but the stem instructions and injunction did not dissuade Gandhiji to forswear his non-violent ideology. He was determined more than ever to adhere strictly to his avowed philosophy of Satyagraha with no intention of abjuring it.

No true leader is discouraged by withering setbacks or no leader is born by accepting obeisance to periodic challenges. An individual's philosophy on life is the aggregate of his early upbringing, the influence of family and society and the nature of his social contacts over a long period of time. Brought up from the early days of his life by parents who had held deep orthodox religious beliefs and influenced by the basic principles of the world's religions, Gandhiji had boundless faith in the spirit of non-violence. He unambiguously stated, "I have advised my countrymen at all costs to resist the Act (Asiatic Law Amendment Act) in the most peaceful, and shall I add, Christian manner."[51] *Ahimsa* as well as the need to avoid harm to another human being—even to animals—had been the cardinal principle of Gandhian philosophy (Gandhiji once said: "The greatness of a nation and its moral progress can be judged by the way its animals are treated.")

In South Africa, the Indians coordinated plans to cany out the pledge against submitting to the tart regulations while a large number of Indians had already signed the petition, which Gandhiji had taken with him to England as an indication of their strong feelings. During the early stage of protest Gandhiji described the campaign as "passive resistance," but was not fully satisfied with that description believing that an Indian movement, essentially in its spirit and orientation, should not be given an Anglo sounding terminology for psychological as well as political reasons. Passive resistance, moreover, carried a somewhat negative connotation for a political movement of historic proportions. What was Gandhiji's final formula? How did he cany it out? Was it successful in South Africa?

In *Indian Opinion* a prize had been offered for the most appropriate name for the South Afiican campaign and in the end the most effective term, Satyagraha, had been chosen by the will of the majority. Today it has become part and parcel of the international vocabulary—a revolutionary, but a peaceful term. Although the term has been defined in various ways, its meaning essentially remains the same and Gandhiji defines it:[52]

> Truth (*Satya*) implies love, and firmness, (*Agraha*) engenders and therefore, serves as a synonym for force. I thus began to call the Indian moement 'Satyagraha' that is to say, **the force which is born of Truth and Love and Non-violence.**

Satyagraha was born out of Gandhijis intense love of fellowmen. He wished none of his fellowmen would resort to violence to remove social inequality and injustice to which they had been subjected. Satyagraha was born out of the acrid political and social realities, which Gandhiji had faced in South Africa. Satyagraha was conceived of Gandhiji's religious fervour as the most viable answer to an evil system, which required eradication like a contagious disease. Only India and a great individual like Gandhiji, with his immutable faith in God buttressed by the teachings of the world's religions could have given birth, final shape and form to Satyagraha encompassing all noble ideals—the quintessential embodiment of Gandhism.

A brief survey of the political changes, which had occurred in the Transvaal and the Orange River Colony during the post Anglo-Boer war period would help gain a proper understanding of Gandhism and the Indian problem in South Africa. We shall analyze the problem.

After officially signing the peace accord, the Afrikaaners kept themselves aloof from power politics turning their backs on the opportunities that presented themselves before them. Concerning this important point, Robert A. Huttenback observes:[53]

> Botha and Smuts both claimed in 1903, that the time was not still ripe for the establishment of representative institutions in the Travansaal, and they consequently had refused the seats they were offered in the legislative council as well as the labor commission.

Political uncertainty at home and the emotions created by the Chinese labour problem had convinced the British officials that the time was not yet propitious for the increased involvement by the colonists in the conduct of their own affairs[54] and in the shadow of such serious issues "the issue of the Indian settlers became incidental."[55]

Inasmuch as the Indian settlers constituted a minority within an oppressed majority, it is relevant to consider their situation to measure the disabilities in relation to the problems of the indigenous African majority. The situation presented serious problems in terms of the struggle by the Indian community for justice, which Gandhiji had placed at the very centre of his non-violent campaign: Satyagraha. Gandhiji's uninterrupted stay in South Africa sign died a revolution, revealing the rekindling of India's soul. It was a remarkable exhibition in which an unarmed community could overcome various hurdles in an alien land for justice by peaceful means. That Gandhiji filled South Africa with the echoes of the best in Indian heritage and civilization, that he proved himself, by his example, an asset to the country, that he was able to harmonize different forces of the Indian residents, that he made himself responsible for transforming the Indian community, that he instilled into India's heart a lasting spirit of reconciliation and that he dispelled an air of intense gloom with hopes have gone down in history in letters of gold.

Devoid of a 'homeland,' and hopes, the Indian community had been forbidden to reside in one of the four provinces in South Africa, besides being illegally confined to the segregated areas in the other three. Furthermore, they were deprived of an equitable share of their labour which the colonisers exploited for their own interests. Satyagraha, an enlightened form of protest, offered the Indian community a new stepladder in the struggle for justice. Soon Gandhiji came to be regarded as a synonym for Satyagraha and Satyagraha was Gandhiji.

He used the non-violent tool to seek amiable solutions to a multitude of problems the Indian settlers had faced in Natal and in other areas. Commenting on the special nature of the relationship between the Indian community and the Government, Dr. S. Radhakrishnan said that often their was justice in the working of history, further adding:[56]

> India, though not of its own volition, had given to South Africa one of its most difficult problems. South Africa in its turn, likewise not of its own volition gave to India the idea of civil disobedience.

With all credits to the singular contribution Gandhiji's religious upbringing and unyielding principles had made to the idea of Satyagraha and its increasing influence in his struggle in South Africa, the Indian residents also deserved accolade for their support of the novel invention since it demanded great courage and conviction as never before. This device had never been tested with success anywhere in the world. Satyagraha was an amalgam of the true Gandhian spirit, the severity of the problems the Indian settlers had to overcome and the heavy price they had to pay to the society. There is no evidence that the Indian settlers, true to their heritage, had any plan to unleash a violent campaign as the basis of the struggle for justice, Gandhiji non-violently championed their cause undaunted by the harsh retaliation unleased on the Satyagrahis imprisonment, starvation and physical assault. *The Rand Daily Mail*[57] for instance, published a statement by one J. Veeramuthoo, a volunteer, regarding the fatal incident of Nagappan who, Veeramuthoo claimed, had been struck "a fearful blow" by a jail warden that rendered him unable to eat food for two days. When the main warden had been told of the serious incident his curt reply was, "Let him die." Later, Nagappan was forced to pick a shovel and work. He passed away soon after being released from the prison. The official explanation for Nagappan's tragic demise was listed as double pneumonia and heart attack. Dr. W. Godfrey had stated that the cause of the Indian settler's death was ill treatment and physical abuse in prison by the police and that his body had bruises and blood stains all over. Gandhiji wanted to save the Indian community from social and political paralysis.

## SUMMARY

1. October 2, 1869 was an auspicious day. Mohandas Karamchand Gandhi, to be universally known as Mahatma Gandhi or Gandhiji was born on that important day into a Bania family.
2. In June 1891, Gandhiji completed his legal studies and was admitted to the bar. The event also marked the end of his preparations to become a barister. He had contacts with Theosophists in England and conducted experiments with vegetarianism.
3. Gandhiji's initial work at Rajkot coincided with an offer from some Muslim merchants, who persuaded him to go to South Africa to carry out legal work on their behalf.
4. In Rajkot he had set up for his legal office and drafted documents, which included memorial and applications for his large clientele.
5. In South Africa Gandhiji became a victim of an extreme form of discrimination. The Indian settlers were living in the shadow of racist prejudices and Gandhiji could identify himself with their problems.
6. Gandhiji asked the Indian people to apply non-violent methods to redress injustice. Renunciation of violence was the basis of his philosophy of life.
7. South Africa was the cradle of Satyagraha and the Indian settlers were true to Indian heritage.
8. Gradually, Gandhiji resisted injustice and discrimination in an extraordinarily peaceful manner. He gave the world Satyagraha, a revolutionary principle which no individual on earth had advocated for social and political objectives. Gandhiji and Satyagraha became synonymous. He instructed volunteers to use persuasion rather than coercion.
9. Gandhiji did not feel the slightest anger or hatred for the assailant who had seriously injured him. It took him ten days to recover from the assault.
10. Gandhiji was imprisoned in South Africa for his role in the struggle for justice and equality for the Indian settlers. The harsh nature of the legal system did not deter him from his commitment to Satyagraha. Defying unjust laws Gandhiji continued his non-violent approach in the interests of the

Indian people whom he had treated as members of his own family.

11. In South Africa Gandhiji led a non-violent campaign to protest against registration law.
12. The whole history of the Indian settlers is in part a case study in imperial futility and moral vacuum. Gandhiji's activities brought the problem into sharp focus. His work helped resolve many problems faced by the Indian residents living in the Transvaal and other parts of the country. Gandhiji and his Satyagraha movement made the outside world aware of the problems faced by the Indian community and the power of non-violence at large.

## Notes and References

1. An analysis of the war waged in 1914 is given in H.L. Balsford, *The War of Steel and Gold,* (London; 1941) and K. Liebknecht, *Militarism,* (New York: 1917). For the main causes of the war started in 1939, see A.J.P. Taylor, *Origins of the Second World War,* (London: Hamilton Company, 1961) and Guy Wint and Peter Calvocoressi, *Total War: The Story of World War II*, (Brattleboro, Wars Vermont, 1972). Both Wars declared in Europe were the outcome of a perverted social philosophy, which had glorified war. Friedrich Nietzsche (1844-1900) praised war. Pacts and alliances which were meant to avert war collapsed in the face of intense national spirit and bitter rivalry among the countries in Europe.
2. As quoted in *Gandhi A Memoir,* William L. Shirer (New York: Simon and Shuster, 1979), p. 12.
3. William L. Shirer, *Gandhiji: A Memoir,* (New York: Simon and Shuster, 1979). Shirer gives extreme credit to Gandhiji for giving the world the great non-violent instrument of Satyagraha. He also said: "He (Churchill) instructed the Viceroy (Linlithgow) to let Gandhi starve to death" at Yeravda prison in Poona, p. 213. Churchill also cried out: "Gandhiji, and all he stands for, must ultimately be grappled with, and finally crushed." p. 211. After he assumed office as wartime Prime Minister of England, he attempted to do just that—and failed. "He would ultimately triumph over him—and gain 'all he stood for.' p. 211. Today the world pays rich homage to Gandhiji.

4. Gandhiji kept silence on Fridays for self-discipline. Lord Mount Batten wanted to have talk with him and the great apostle of non-violence sent him a note saying that he could not talk on that day. It happened to be Friday. Mount Batten later said that it was "the most important note" that he had received in his life. Also, Gandhiji tried to lead a simple life of dates imported from Arabia and mineral water from Vichy, France. Sarojini Naidu once told him, "Mr. Gandhi, it takes a lot of money to keep you in poverty."
5. *Trinidad Guardian,* February 28, 1998, p. 10.
6. *Ibid.*
7. *Ibid.*
8. S.B. Mukherji, *Indian Minority in South Africa,* (Delhi: New Age Printing House, 1959). p. 45.
9. "Works," VII, pp. 93-94. Also in Swami Bhawani Dayal, *Satyagraha in South Africa,* (Calcutta: 1946). the author describes various stages of Satyagraha after Gandhiji inaugurated the non-violent movement. For a study of the Indian residents in other African countries, please see F. Doston and L.O. Dotson, *The Indian Minority of Zambia, Natal, Rhodesia and Malawi,* (New Haven: Yale University Press, 1968).
10. "Indians in South Africa", *The Minority Rights Group, Report no. 34,* (London: 1954), p. 5. The report contains valuable information on the background of the Indian settlers in South Africa.
11. When the recruiting of labour from India was halted in 1911, two-thirds of the total number of 142,670 of the settlers were Tamil and Telugu speaking people from the Madras Presidency, a predominance which continued in South Africa for a considerable period of time.
12. "The Indians in South Africa," *The Minority Rights Group, supra.* p. 7.
13. Kauleshwar Rao, *Indians and British Colonialism in East Africa, 1883-1939,* (Patna: Associated Book Agency, 1979), p. 5. when Captain Smee visited Zanzibar in 1811 representing the East India Company, the total value of the imports into the island nation was estimated at 1,300,000. The chief imports were dungaree clothes from Kutch, Surat clothes, rice, sugar and iron from Bombay and adjacent areas.
14. *Ibid.*, p. 10.
15. *Ibid.*, p. 21. The Indians also faced injustice. As time passed by, they became politically more aware and voiced their grievances against

the unfair treatment to which they had been subjected. They made representations to the Colonial Office or the Foreign Office. European settlers finding the educated and industrious Indian traders and workers a threat to them in South Africa, confined them to Natal.

16. After the discovery of precious minerals in South Africa, Britain was chiefly concerned with protecting its supremacy. the English and the Dutch were in strong competition while the Interests of the Indians, out of resentment, like those of the Africans were sacrificed in the process.
17. *Trinidad Express*. Port of Spain, Trinidad, West Indies, May 25, 1998. p. 12.
18. *Ibid.*
19. *Ibid.*, the Indian settlers, who first arrived in Trinidad in 1845, added yet another dimension to the religious and cultural life of the village called Tacarigua in the island nation in the Atlantic. The intention of the British colonial agents in bringing the Indians was to replace the Africans and lower their wages since the African people who, after years of slavery, had refused to toil in the sugar fields at wages below the subsistence level. Initially, the Indian people were brought to work for five years and return to their homeland. Approximately 14 per cent returned to India. After their arrival in the adopted land they, like thousands of immigrants anywhere in the world, had lived in the shadow of deprivation and misery. Today, the direct descendants of the early Indian immigrants, after having gained considerable upward social and economic mobility, work as federal cabinet ministers, lawyers, doctors, successful businessmen, entrepreneurs, bankers and owners of the nation's largest jewellery stores. More details about the early Indian settlers are given in "Tacarigua: A Village in Trinidad", Dr. Selwyn R. Cudjoe (Wellesley, Massachusetts, 1995).
20. *Trinidad Express*, op. cit., p. 7.
21. *Collected Works*, Rabindranath Tagore, (Calcutta: 1934).
22. *Trinidad Express*, op. cit., p. 8.
23. *Ibid.*
24. *Ibid.*, M.P. Alladin wrote about the Indian immigrants that in the 1920s "there were eighty-five to ninety houses in the village (Tacarigua) with a population of between 450 to 500. Of this number, some 50 were Negroes and the rest, East Indians. Of this number some 30 were Muslims and the rest Hindus of whom no

more than two dozen were of the upper castes (Brahmins and Chatries). On the whole, everyone was had working and religious and lived well with one another. Social and racial mobility was the order of the day and intermarriage was uncommon." *A Village in Trinidad,* (Maravel: M.P. Alladin, 1970, p.1).

25. Other details are given in *The East Indian Indenture in Trinidad,* Rio Pedras (University of Puerto Rico, Institute of Caribbean Studies, 1968) and *Aboriginal and Spanish Colonial Trinidad: A Study in Culture Contact.* (Londorx Academic Press, 1976).
26. *Minority Rights Report,* op. cit., p. 5. The most glaring aspect was related to the fact when white-skinned workers began to see Indian labour as a threat to their interests and towards the end of the 19th century, systemic efforts were taken to introduce indentured labour for semi-skilled occupations as indentured work was cheap to be exploited to a degree that white labour was not. In 1897, there were demonstrations against Indian traders, most of the demonstrators being white-skinned workers. Having received a threat from cheap labour, the workers used their political power to secure protection for their jobs from Indian settlers and even from the native African workers. The adherence to the colour bar was strengthened in the name of safeguarding 'civilized standards' and eventually to giving priority to the use of 'civilized labour' in a most callous manner. As a result of deliberate attempts, legislation discriminated against African and Indian labour in varying degrees, with African workers having no right at all. Gandhiji was faced with massive problem. Yet, he advocated non-violence to resolve the Indian problem "with malice towards none".
27. *Ibid.*, p. 7. Also in C.F. Andrews, *The History of the Congress,* Vol. I, p. 47.
28. B. Pattabhi Sitaramayya, *The history of the Congress,* Vol. I, p. 47.
29. *Kesari,* Bombay, February 4, 1908. In the same manner, *Nyak*, a Bengali weekly, expressed indignation at the oppression of Indians in South Africa since their compatriots at home had no power to render them assistance, but they expressed solidarity with their common objective.
30. This information is from *Kesari, Ibid.*
31. *Ibid.*, A strong argument for eschewing violence is the central theme in Tolstoy's *War and Peace.* He considered the rulers and generals as 'history's slaves.' His reflections on the outbreak of the war of 1812 are worth mentioning. "Millions of men renouncing

their human feelings, had to go from West to East to slay many of their fellows ...It was an extraordinary occurrence. The actions of Napoleon and Alexander were as little voluntary as the action of any soldier who had been drawn into the campaign by lot or by conscription." Tolstoy's views had considerable influence on Gandhiji.

32. S.B. Mukherji, op. cit., p. 53.
33. *Ibid.*, Also In *Gandhiji: A Memoir,* William L. Shrier, op. cit. p.128. William Shrier provides an objective and detailed account of the life and work of Gandhiji. Also see, L. Fisher, *The Life of Mahatma Gandhi,* (New York: Collier, 1966).
34. L. Shrier, *Ibid.*, p. 7. Related views in P. Moon, *Gandhiji and Modern India,* op. cit., p. 53.
35. Moon, op. cit., p. 53.
36. Kallenbach, a German architect living in Johannesburg and a great admirer of Gandhiji, owned a large farm, 20 miles from Johannesburg. He placed the property at the disposal of Gandhiji who called it the Tolstoy Farm where Satyagrahis and members of their families lived in harmony under his guidance "each playing his appropriate role in the maintenance and communal living each offering service in a noble cause." At the height of the Satyagraha campaign in South Africa, Gandhiji had invited volunteers from the Tolstoy Farm, including, women, to serve as Saytyagrahis. The volunteers, men and women, were harshly treated in jail. Additional details are provided in P. Moon, *Gandhi and Modem India,* op. cit., pp. 64-67, H. Kuiper, Indian People in Natal, (Pietermaritzburg: Natal University Press, 1960) and Benjamin Sacks, *South Africa: An Imperial Dilemma,* (Albuquerque: University of New Mexico Press, 1938).
37. In the eighteenth and nineteenth centuries, several steps were taken to disenfranchise Afro-Americans in the United States of America as well. Such steps were mainly to protect the interests of the rest of the society. Later, the restrictions were removed. Further details can be found in Maurice R. Davie, *Negroes in American Society,* (New York: McGraw Hill Book Company, 1949).
38. Like many Indian settlers who were brought to African countries to build railways, the Chinese were brought to Canada in the nineteenth century to lay railway lines. They were expected to pay head-tax which the Chinese labours had considered highly discriminatory. But they were not allowed to bring members

of their families from China to Canada and even today the descendants of the Chinese living in Canada have clear memories of the discriminatory practices in the past.

39. P. Moon, *Gandhi and Modern India,* op. cit., p. 45. Moon also said: "A further opportunity for nursing came with the outbreak of the Zulu rebellion... this time the Governor of Natal promptly accepted the offer. Gandhi was given the temporarily the rauk of sergeant major and, with a staff of twenty-four, was on active service for over a month." pp. 45-46.
40. *Ibid.*
41. S.B. Mukherji, *Indian Minority in South Africa,* op. cit., p.53. Also in Ashe, G., *Gandhi,* (New York: Stein and Day, 1968). Especially chapters 3 and 7. and Dr. S.H. Patil, *Gandhi and Swaraj,* (New Delhi: Deep and Deep Publications, 1983).
42. D.L. Lewis, *King: A Critical Biography,* (New York: Praeger Publishers, 1970), p. 106.
43. *Ibid.*, p. 85.
44. *Ibid.*, p.214. The author says: "Viewed clinically, the origins of the philosophy of non-violence are traceable to the numerically determined and irreversible social fact that the American black cannot utilize violence on a collective scale for more than brief and infrequent periods, without jeopardizing his existence as a member of American society, no matter how marginal that existence may be alleged to be ... Martin's deep Christian concern with the brotherhood of man and his abiding faith (until late in his career, at least) in the fundamental decency of his fellowmen directed his philosophical speculation far more than old realism could have." p. 86.
45. *Ibid.*
46. Quoted in S.H. Patil, op. cit., pp. 13-14.
47. *Ibid.*, p. 14. Further details can be found in M.K. Gandhi, *The Collected Works of Mahatma Gandhi,* Vol. 20, April-August, 1921, (New Delhi. The Publications Division, The Ministry of Information and Broadcasting, The Government of India, 1966) pp. 507-10.
48. *Ibid.*, p. 15.
49. S.H. Patil, op.cit., p. 16.
50. *Ibid.*, p. 16. Patil says that Gandhiji's "two weapons which were based on truth and non-violence are: (1) satyagragha and (2) constructive programme. Satyagraha with its techniques like

non-cooperation, civil disobedience and picketing are to be used to redress injustice." *Ibid.*, p. 43.

51. Robert A. Huttenback, *Gandhi in South Africa,* (Ithaca: Cornell University Press, 1984). p. 171.
52. Further details can be found in M.K. Gandhi, *Satyagraha in South Africa,* (Ahmedabad: Navajivan, 1928), and *The Story of My Experiments with Truth,* (Boston: Beacon Press, 1957).
53. Robert A. Huttenback, op. cit, p. 175.
54. As far back as April 1904, Alfred Lyttleton had told Milner that the authorities will be confronted with "dishonest and insincere utterances about the Chinese labour by the ignorant and sincere of their fellows and I am convinced that they will extricate themselves from a painful dilemma by granting self-government to the new colonies..." A.P. Thornton, *The Habit of Authority,* (Toronto, 1966).
55. "Indian South Africans," *Minority Rights Report,* op. cit., p. 7. The report analyses the historical background of the conflicts between the British and the Boers. It also makes frequent references to the economic conditions of the Indians in South Africa.
56. For this information, I owe S.B. Mukherji, "Indian Minority in South Africa," op. cit., p. 45.
57. *Rand Daily Mail,* February 6, 1904. In the absence of 'homeland' South African Indians were forbidden to live where they pleased, but were confined to segregated areas in one province. The situation was offensive to Gandhiji and his fellow countrymen, the heirs to a great civilization. The Indian settlers were denied the right to equal treatment in the political, economic or social life of the country, nor did they receive an equitable reward for their labour in the adopted country. They could not take part in making the decision that government of South Africa besides being denied the freedoms of expression or association. Before the dawn of the 19th century, there had been no voluntary emigration of labour from India, but British capitalism forced the labour to migrate.

# CHAPTER-VI

# SATYAGRAHA AND ITS PROGRESS (The Second Phase)

## ARTICLE -1

### (A) Major Demands

Gandhiji's non-violent campaigns for the restoration of the fundamental human rights began to show positive signs on November 4 when officials in the Transvaal expressed for the first time their willingness to meet some of the major demands of the Indian community. Permission was granted to a number of professional Indian residents who were not qualified to enter the colony or even to register in accordance with the ordinary regulations. The officials had intended to introduce a change in the regulations providing for the issue of temporary certificates requiring periodic rend. Selbourne's formal letter of December 12 forwarded to Botha states:[1]

> The British Indians' demand that the right of free immigration under the general Immigration Act of the Colony be conceded now to six highly educated Indians yearly in order to minister to the spiritual and intellectual needs of the people ...

Concessions or not, the Indian community had kept up the pressure on the officials as a result of the protest was quite apparent. When an affluent and highly educated Parsi from Charlestown, Natal, volunteered himself to enter the Transvaal, the government decided to act with utmost circumspection while the officials did not challenge Sorabji Shapurji Adajamia. Instead, he was permitted into the colony,[2] but deported him later for his refusal to register during the period permitted under the law.

Undaunted, the Indian settlers inundated the officials in Britain and the Transvaal to eradicate the law with petitions demanding justice. Selborn's letter to Botha was rejected without hesitation and it was followed by the unacceptable recommendation of the Transvaal Government "that temporary permits be granted to the priests, professional men and teachers." Anti-Indian laws were unnecessary and prejudicial.

Gandhiji put forward three recommendations, which Crewe felt, as key to remedy some of the perplexing problems created by a set of unjust laws. The proposals were: (i) the repeal of Act 2 of 1907; (ii) the elimination from the immigration act of existing differential bar to the entrance of Asiatic people as such; and (iii) the exclusion of the Asiatics, with the exception of a minority to be duly exempted, by administrative decision alone.[3] The Secretary of State said that "the exclusion of such immigrants shall not be provided for in a manner which caused subjects unnecessary humiliation."[4]

The controversy centred around the registration of educated Indian immigrants admitted into the Union in accordance with the terms of the special exemption. Smuts, then minister of the interior in the Union Government, informed Gandhiji that such immigrants were free to enter the Union and reside in any province without having to register. When Gandhiji had indicated that such an assurance was not included in the actual text of the bill,[5] Smuts offered the assurance to introduce an amendment to exempt the future immigrants from registration under the terms of the Transvaal Act 36 of 1908. Throughout the campaign, the Indians had insisted on *sine qua non*; for, their recognition of any immigration bill ought to be on the basis of the absence of the vestiges of ethnic classification in the wording of the law. In a telegram to Smuts, Gandhiji demanded that the Indian residents who had entered the Union should have the inherent right to reside permanently in any province. A just demand it was.

All through his South African campaign, Gandhiji had absolute faith in the essential goodness and rectitude of man and this unerring insight into human nature was the fundamental basis of the unqualified success of his ventures. He mobilized public resentment and challenged the three-pound tax. P. Moon makes the following observation on it:[16]

> The demand for the repeal of the three-pond tax had a considerable appeal to the many thousands of Indians of the labouring class who had to pay it, and this opened a wide area of recruitment to the Gandhi's 'army'. He had always befriended these poor people—he had helped them as a lawyer for little or no reward; he had voluntarily worked as a dispenser in their

hospital; he was widely known to be sympathetic to them, and so there was every chance that they would follow his leadership.

The effectiveness of his campaign was indisputable when Indians were organized into burning the special certificates and picketing various government offices in the most peaceful manner imaginable. The coal miners were made to play an important role in the campaign. **"As if unseen by anyone," Gandhiji wrote, "God was preparing the ingredients for the Indians' victory."** Victory was lurking in the corner when Gandhiji tried to stop the hemorrhaging of the industrious Indian community.

In March 1913, the Supreme Court in Cape rendered the judgment invalidating Indian marriages in South Africa not officiated according to Christian rites. The judgment, in effect, was meant to bastardise the Indian children whose parents had been married in the country according to the traditional Hindu, Muslim or Zoroastrian religious rites. Gandhiji appealed to the authorities to have the court decision set aside on appeal or to amend it at least to recognize the validity of the Indian marriages. The Government wanted to enter the bedrooms of the Indian people. The problem was of considerable importance to Indians regardless of their religious persuasion since a great deal had depended upon the legal recognition of their offspring. Gandhiji's requests were reasonable, but the Government adopted a hostile attitude, declining to take the steps necessary to remove the legal impediments from the absurd world of South Africa's regulations (Appendices 7 and 8).

The problem of the legal recognition of the Indian marriages did have a decisive impact upon the course of Satyagraha in the sense that until the judgment, Gandhiji had refrained from inviting women to become partners in the campaign. The court decision impelled him to cast away the inhibition and the women's participation provided great momentum to the movement.[8] Satyagraha had remained somnolent for a while. A select group of twelve Indian women from the renowned Tolstoy Farm was arrested in the Transvaal for hawking without licence, but later released. Later they were sent to Newcastle, a large coal mining region in Natal, to stir up the Indian miners to declare strike until the removal of the three pound tax while another group of sixteen women, including Kasturba and Gandhiji's close relatives, had gone to the Transvaal. They crossed the border but refused to disclose their identity.[9]

## (B) Imprisonment and Harsh Treatment

The non-violent steps taken by Gandhiji had positive outcome as the ladies added charm to non-violence. The white establishment could not resist the charm. The women's imprisonment, Gandhiji felt, "worked like a charm upon the labourers in the mines near Newcastle"[10] and we have the following incisive description of the manner by which the women were treated by a system which claimed great virtuosity: [11]

> The women Satyagrahis were lodged in Marittzburg prison. They were treated quite harshly. The food given to them was poor in quality and indeed inadequate in quantity. Moreover, they had to work as washer-women. Their health began to deteriorate. One of them, Bhalimaya, a young girl of eighteen, came out with fever to which she later succumbed.

Gandhiji's Satyagraha proved effective in arousing public opinion against the excess of the system and the imprisonment of men and women, particularly that of women, and the treatment to which they were subjected in jail, had a magical spell on the protest as Gandhiji had foreseen. The serious repercussions of life behind the bars spread like wild fie beyond the borders of the Union of South Africa, reaching as far as India. A prominent Indian political figure, Sir Pheroze Shah Mehta, who had remained detached to the Satyagraha movement in South Africa, declared that his,[12]

> ...blood started to boil at the thought of these women, lying in jails herded with other ordinary criminals, and India, as a whole, could not sleep over the matter any longer. It is time that someone opposed this.

Gandhiji opposed. He took control of the volatile situation even though he did not have a clear picture of the magnitude of the problem he was about to encounter. Referring to the Satyagraha campaign, S.B. Mukherji said that the "final phase of the struggle was about to open,"[13] arguing:[14]

> ...Gandhiji was faced with the problem the magnitude and difficulties of which he had not clearly foreseen. Strikers in thousands had flocked thither from the mining districts around. The ill-treatment by the mine owners—flogging of the strikers, still in their barracks, permanent cutting off electricity and water, forcible removal of the strikers' belongings by the mines' officials and the like had made it increasingly difficult for the strikers to live in the barracks. That was also Gandhiji's advice. The advice was promptly acted upon.

Gandhji, as the propounder of Satyagraha and the unquestionable leader of the army of Satyagrahis found himself faced with the moral responsibility of feeding as well as accommodating thousands of striking workers and, at the same time, maintaining order.

Gandhiji, decided to resolve the problem by marching the cavalcade of Satyagrahis into the Transvaal region under the firm assumption that they would also be imprisoned forthwith as the Phoenix party on a previous occasion for stepping inside the territory without valid certificates. The Satyagrahis set out for the border at Charlestown, some thirty-six miles from New Castle. Gandhiji, with his commitment to Satyagraha, instructed the Indians not to resist arrest if the police decided to handcuff them. He also announced the names of those Satyagrahis who would successively lead the volunteers in their place. They took a minimum of clothes, sugar, loaves of bread and *dal.*[15] Mr. Kallenbach had built mud huts for the Satyagrahis and after offering prayers, the Satyagrahis with dauntless spirit set out on the march crossing the border on November 6.

Gandhiji was arrested that evening and was released the next morning. He was again arrested on November 8 along with his chief lieutenants. He was freed on bail. On November 9, Gandhiji was handcuffed again. On November 11, the father of Satyagraha was sentenced to nine month's imprisonment for the love of fellow men.

All that resulted in a non-judgmental acceptance of Satyagraha. On the tenth day, Satyagrahis, under Mr. Folak's leadership, were rounded up, put on trains to be returned to Natal. They were imprisoned and were soon sent to work in the mines as prisoners. P.C. Joshi describes:[16]

> **The struggle showed that victory was the fruit of firmness, patience and peace.... It had evoked heartfelt sympathy in India and the deepest indignation against the oppressors in South Africa. Lord Harding, the Viceroy espoused the Indian cause in South Africa, and made a momentous speech openly supporting the passive resistance against the invidious and unjust laws, which had undoubtedly created an Empire-wide sensation.**

What caused such a sensation? What was the role of Gandhiji's Satyagraha in creating a favourable opinion of the struggle? What positive response did Satyagraha create outside South Africa? Lord Hardinge's letter to Gandhiji might answer them. The letter explicitly stated that Gandhiji's compatriots in South Africa had taken matters into their hands"[17] and also by organizing 'passive resistance.'"[18] The letter goes on:[19]

> They [the Indian settlers] have the sympathy of India—deep and burning—and not only of India, but of all those who, like myself, without being Indians themselves, have great feelings of sympathy of the people of this country.

## (C) The Intermediary

The Government had expressed consternation at the rising wave of the Indian campaign while General Smuts who had refused to have a dialogue with Gandhiji, softened his attitude opening up doors to further talks through Albert Cartwright, an intermediary. As Gandhiji's personal friend and the editor of the *Transvaal Times,* Cartwright had established considerable rapport with the Indians as a well-wisher of their collective aspirations and on his own initiative, he met Smuts after Gandhiji had been jailed. Cartwright seemed the perfect candidate for negotiations. Smuts welcomed his timely offer as an intermediary while the Indian leaders, still at large, informed Cartwright they would reach a definitive decision only after they had received advice from Gandhiji. Cartwright carried with him the general framework of the settlement the terms of which can be summarised as follows:[20]

(i) that the Indians ought to register on their volition rather than under the terms of Act 11, 1907.

(ii) that the information to be duly provided in the certificate of registration should be decided after prior consultation between the Government and the Indian community.

(iii) that provided the majority of the Indians had voluntarily registered Act 11, 1907 would be removed and that the Government would adopt necessary steps with the objective of legalising the voluntary registration system.

On January 30, 1908, exactly four decades before Gandhiji was assassinated, he held an interview with Smuts after he had returned from Johannesburg to Pretoria and both the leaders held discussions with the focus on the implications of the original draft and the amendment to the Act.[21] As the discussions had ended, Gandhiji was under the assumption that Smuts had accepted the proposed amendment to the original draft to repeal Act 11, 1907 after the Indian settlers had been voluntarily registered. When Gandhiji explained the situation to the Indians at a public meeting in the Transvaal, the Indian residents greatly disturbed by the general attitude of the officials, remained sceptical of the actual intentions of Smuts' proposals. "The Black Act cannot be enforced," some expressed concern, "but it would always hang over our heads like Damocles' sword."[22] The Indian settlers had entertained misgivings on the nature of the overall developments as well as the bits and pieces of the legislation while they gasped for social justice.[23]

> If, in the meanwhile, we had registered voluntarily, we would have knowingly played into the adversary's hands, and surrendered the most powerful weapon in our possession for resisting the Act.

The Indians wanted that the "Act should be repealed first, and then they should be called upon to register voluntarily."[24] The voice of opposition from a segment of the Indian community had been symptomatic of the prevailing atmosphere as Gandhiji had mentioned in his work, *Satyagraha in South Africa,* that the Indian black sheep living in the Transvaal objected to the conciliatory posture of the Satyagrahis towards the Government. The opposition did not change the final decision taken by the assembly which, in unison endorsed the compromise.

Gandhiji was obtuse to the obstacles being faced by Smuts who had to deal with formidable pressure from a number of parliamentarians from the Free State. He intended to safeguard the so-called sanctity of their borders against the Indians who had intended to enter their citadels of power.[25] It appeared that the outstanding issues would be resolved by introducing changes to the bill. Important amendments were introduced to permit the minor children and the wives of legal immigrants to enter the Union and to exempt the Indian settlers by administrative directives from registration.[26] The Government was in favour of introducing the changes to section 5[27] to protect the domiciliary rights of the individuals born in the Union, their wives and offsprings. The Governor-General gave strong assurance to the Indian settlers that section 25 would be generously administered.[28]

In order to assuage the fears of the Indians in South Africa and the Government of India, the Union pointed out that twelve "will not be arbitrarily regarded as the limit"[29] of the number of permanent admissions, but that "cases will be considered on their merits"[30] in the future. Concerning the status of the Orange Free State, Smuts made the following comments:[31]

> With regard to the Orange Free State, I do not think it gets adopted by Parliament and amendment the effect of which would be the free entry, without the permission of the Governor-General, of these Indians into that province, and on that point I, therefore, propose to leave the present Bill before us unaltered.

At the India Office, Lord Crewe was pleased with the changes which the Union Government had introduced,[32] but naturally, the changes did not satisfy Gandhiji. They were short of meeting the demands of the Indian community, and he sent the following message to the South African India Committee amplifying his position on the issue:[33]

> As passive resisters in South Africa fighting against the racial bar, struggle must continue if the Government goes back upon the thrice repeated assurances and introduce the racial bar.
>
> Resisters fight in purely national honour and defending the British Constitution.

Gandhiji saw the prospects of an equitable settlement on the horizon, arid yet out of reach—a predicament that could cause concern to any one and Satyagraha, the core of Gandhism, was the moral equivalent of the humane struggle of the Indians to attain their fundamental objectives. The campaign had lasted for about five years and while some had fallen on the wayside, other stalwarts had courted arrest to rekindle the flames of the struggle. Satyagraha Association provided their families with strong support as it was also a critical moment for Gandhiji who, since 1906, was too preoccupied with the well-being of his fellow-men. His dedication to that cause had brought his once highly lucrative legal career to a grinding halt. Gandhiji, under such arduous conditions, could no longer provide financial support when the campaign required cash to manage the office in Johannesburg, and London and to keep the press rolling to print *Indian Opinion*. Then the Sun shone. In 1910, a substantial sum of Rs. 25,000 from Sir Ratan Tata, the eminent industrialist, proved invaluable at that critical phase of the movement. Besides, Gandhiji took immediate steps to cut down the expenditure in every possible manner. In times of need he could rely on Indians in South Africa or India and the campaign overcame its greatest financial crisis.[34] In times of need human beings find solutions.

## ARTICLE -2

### (A) Gandhiji's Enlivening Influence

Gandhiji's Satyagraha campaign, as we have already observed, had taken long roots in South Africa in the form of strikes and pickets. Messrs. E. Gitsham and J.F. Trembath had provided an estimable portrayal of his enlivening influence on Indians and on many others who only had a modicum of knowledge of the peaceful agitation:[35]

> One of the highly remarkable industrial upheavals this country has witnessed took place in Natal in November—generally referred to as the Indian strike and also there were at the time some 20,000 labourers working, under indenture in the tea plantations and sugar farms, the collieries, railways and other significant industries.
>
> Mr. Gokhale, the great Indian leader, had some time previously secured a sort of half promise from the Botha Government that the tax could be repealed.

Gandhiji, in frequent consultations with the Indians[36] residing in the Natal, "was apparently not satisfied with the slow progress the Govemment was making..."[37] The authors continue:[38]

> Gandhlji accordingly inaugurated a policy of 'passive resistance' among the Indian workers the first condition of which was a suspension from the toil; the Government had made a definite promise to repeal the tax during the ensuing session of the Parliament.

In order to find an amicable solution to the problems faced by the Indians in the Transvaal, Gandhiji, according to R. Huttenback, was "haunting the corridors of Whitehall on behalf of the Transvaal Indians and a delegation of Indians from Natal was in London on a similar mission."[39] A number of Indian employees in the Durban hotels went on a holiday leaving the hotel guests to carry on as best as they could while the Indian tailors, printers' assistants and saddlers had been missing from their workshops resulting in trepidation among those who had greatly depended on their vital services. Referring to the strength of Satyagraha, Gitsham and Trembath make the following comments[40] (Appendix-3):

> Of course, the strike did not last long; however, it was a pretty effective demonstration; while it had lasted. Gandhi and his fellow-conspirators were sentenced to imprisonment for nine months; but they were soon released to provide evidence before the special commission of enquiry set up by the Government to which, by the way, they declined to attend. The three-pound tax on the indentured Indian was speedily abolished as a result of the publicity given to the question by this unorthodox method of propaganda.

On April 19, General Smuts had held further talks with Gandhiji and in a most amiable and ingratiating manner Smuts informed Gandhiji:[41]

> **You belong to a civilization that is thousands of years old. However, ours, as you will know, is just an experiment.** Who knows but that the entire damned thing will perish before long. But you say why we do not want Asians here. But as I point out the Natal difficulty being out of the way, I shall cope with the problems here. But I want a little more time. I shall meet the Free Staters. But you should not be aggressive. The whole question, as you well know, will be discussed before the Imperial Conference soon.

Smuts' request could not change Gandhiji's stance. The General was caught on the horns of the dilemma of the unbending Indian attitude and the obdurate refusal by the members of the Orange Free State to modify their position. By that time, H.L. Harcourt had taken over the duties of Lord Crewe at the Colonial Office and Prime Minister Gladstone informed him that the passage of the bill was laborious and argued that "the Jews are hostile. A section of the Unionists do not like it because they fear ulterior use of it by the Dutch Ministers against the British."[42] (The Jewish community in South Africa did not particularly appreciate the presence of the Indian merchants. The Jewish community did not openly show resentment towards Indians, but remained aloof from the issue).[43] Gladstone's telegram to Harcourt further said:[44]

> The Australian method of excluding is generally unpopular. More serious is the fact the repeal of the Cape Colony Immigration Act would allow entrance into Cape of Good Hope of Natal Indians.

Although the objections of the members of the Free State had rendered any step towards progress impossible, the policy adopted by the Government of India had considerably weakened the bill:[45]

> ... J.C. Smuts believes best course is to drop the Bill and endeavour to bring in a more acceptable measure next year ... and that he could arrange a truce with Gandhi till a fresh bill was introduced.

## (B) Winning the Battle

The Secretary of State believed that Smuts was "satisfied that he can prevent a renewal of agitation by Gandhi,"[46] and pointed out the following:[47]

> ... and there is no likelihood of Smut's action in dropping the Bill in deference to Gandhi's opposition, and leading to greater trouble in the future by enhancing Gandhi's prestige. I doubt whether, in the present stage of public opinion, my Government could have gone any further than they have actually gone to meet my representations.

While Botha and the Government had won the battle in this case, they could not gather the fruits of their apparent victory as Botha had to drop the Bill altogether denying any serious consideration in the Parliament, unable to pass it into law. 1912 marked a milestone following the arrival of Gopal Krishna Gokhale, India's exalted political figure, and without doubt, Gandhiji's political mentor. Gokhale had kept in constant touch with Gandhiji and the problems of the Indian residents for more than fifteen years.[48] Beyond doubt he was the most important Indian leader ever to set foot in the southern part of Africa carrying a message with the blessings of the Indian and British Governments.[49] Smuts made every attempt to pamper Gokhale, treated him as a state guest showering him with adulation and flattery, besides providing him with a private railway car. Red carpets were rolled, wherever he visited in South Africa until there were no carpets left in the South African carpet stores.

The great Indian leader was determined to see the repeal of the three-pound tax in Natal, meeting all the prominent members of the Government during his epoch-making South African visit. After Gokhale had reached Bombay, with a large dose of optimism, he informed a gathering at the dock when rumours started to swirl in the city of a just resolution of the problem:[50]

> The actual working of the immigration Law will, I expect, become milder and more and more considerate. Then that outrageous imposition, the three-pound licence tax, will, 1 fully expect, go in the course of the year. In the matter of education also, the position will materially improve ...

The question whether Gokhale had been assured of the elimination of the three-pound tax was of considerable importance and in March 1913, the authorities had argued that the Government had planned to "give consideration to the questions raised by him[51] (Gokhale), concerning the imposition of the tax on the Natal Indians. Still, he had assured that the Government was aware of the problem of inequality and that in strict economic terms the proceeds from the levy were peripheral at best. According to Gokhale: [52]

> I was told that it was quite necessary for the Ministers to mention the matter immediately to Natal members, and I should, therefore, merely announce in general terms that the Ministers had promised their most favourable consideration to my representations in the matter and that I had every confidence that the tax would be repealed in the new session of the Parliament.

Meanwhile, Gandhiji had arrived at the conclusion that the promise had been made, but that the Government was reneging on its own pledge by not repealing the dreaded tax. Gokhale was given the promise to repeal Act 2 of 1907 and that it was a foregone conclusion that the Government had similarly made its commitment to abolish the three-pound tax in Natal and if the Government backed off on its word, the Indians would have to renew Satyagraha campaign. Gandhiji conceded:[53]

> If the Satyagrtaha struggle had closed with the repeal of the Black Act. A fresh fight would have been necessary against the three-pound tax, and not only would the Indians have come in for endless trouble, but it is doubtful whether they would have been ready so soon for a new as well as an arduous campaign.

All the signs had indicated that the peaceful Satyagraha campaign was looming and that Gandhiji had set the stage to galvanize the Indians as the old familiar problems—the same issues of deep contention—had come to the fore. The twin foci of the renewed Satyagraha were (1) polygamous marriage and (2) the critical issue of the infamous three-pound tax. Three £ tax, as the Indians had called it, had been a thorn on their side. Gandhiji regarded it as a rallying point to call a general strike by the Indian coal miners at the Newcastle coal mines and, to demonstrate the great power of Satyagraha as a potent socio-political instrument to combat injustice while the Government was yet to make its intentions known. Rev. C.F. Andrews arrived in South Africa in January 1914 to support the Indian cause and asked Gandhiji whether his position was not just a matter of South African Indians' honour. "Yes", Gandhiji firmly replied, "That is it, that is it. That is the real point at issue."[54] Honour is the crux of an individual's existence. Dishonour is deadly.

The Satyagraha campaign for justice and honour had not crumbled like pieces of rusty metal. When Gandhiji, accompanied by C.F. Andrews, travelled to Pretoria to meet Mr. Smuts on January 9, 1914, the nation was on the brink of a mammoth railway strike. Gandhiji, with true commitment to peace and social harmony, was in no mood to capitalize on the restive labour situation confronting the Government, nor was he out to embarrass the officials. **In contrast to the decisions by countless political figures in identical situations, Gandhiji promised to call off Satyagraha until the strike by the railway employees came to an end. His decision was an illustration of the spirit of brotherhood and compassion typical of the great man despite the prevalent strenuous situation. The civilized conduct had a certain impact apparently**

**echoing in Smuts' tone.** "I do not like your people," he said, "and do not care to assist them at all."[55] But his further query was the definite outcome of Gandhiji's eleemosynary attitude:[56]

> But what can I do? **You help us in our days of need? How can we lay hands upon you?** I often do wish you took to violence like the English strikers, and then we would know at once how to deal with you.

The hardened General found himself thoroughly disarmed and lamented:[57]

> **But you will not injure even the enemies. You desire victory by self-suffering alone and never transgress your self-imposed limit of courtesy and chivalry. And that is what reduces us to sheer helplessness.**

## (C) The Common Ground

**The genuine Gandhian ideal again prevailed.** On and after January 16, Gandhiji, along with C.F. Andrews, held negotiations with Smuts and it was evident that there was a meeting of the mind. A common ground was reached as Smuts asked Gandhiji if he would be content with the abolition of the three-pound tax, with the licence retained. Gandhiji felt that the compromise would be welcome under the circumstances, for the licence should not be required after a three-year domicile in Natal and regarding the problem of marriage, Gandhiji would be satisfied provided the statutory recognition was accorded to "*de facto* monogamous wives." He did not press for new legislative measures concerning the entrance of the Indians from another province into the Cape. He was in favour of an assurance that the law would not be so implemented that the educational test would not be made applicable stressing that the laws of the Union be applied to Indians in a just manner and that in the absence of fairness the situation would be loaded with problems.[58]

In April 1914, the final report of the Indian Enquiry Commission dealing with the problem came to light. It centred around the developments leading up to the Satyagraha campaign including an assessment of the events which had taken place during the general strike. The report contained the proposed changes in terms of law and in actual administrative practice. The report merits our close attention:[59]

(i) Instructions should be given to the immigration officials to open centres in each province for the registration by Indians residing in South Africa for a period of three years or longer and who presently have or have had more than one wife living in the country. They are free to travel to and from India along with their minor children as long as the husbands continue to reside in South Africa.

(ii) Section 5(G) of the Immigration Regulation Act of 1913 should be changed to bring it into conformity with the practice of the immigration department which was to allow one wife and the minor children by her of an Indian entitled to live in any province, or who may be permitted to enter the Union at a future time.

(iii) Legislative measures should be introduced in Act 16 of 1860 of the Cape Colony. Their purpose should be to make provisions to appoint marriage officers chosen from the Indian priests belonging to various religious persuasions in order to officiate marriages in conformity with the recognized religious rites and practices.

(iv) Legislative measures are required for the purpose of validation by means of registration of the prevailing *de facto* monogamous marital relationships. These are understood to be marital unions of one man with one woman according to a system which recognized the husband's right to wed one ar more than one wife.

(v) Section 6 of the Natal Act 17 of 1895, viz., the three-pound tax should be abolished.

(vi) An interpreter on a full-time basis should be appointed at the immigration department in Cape Town to facilitate its work.

(vii) Certificates issued in accordance with the regulations of Act 1913 should remain in force for a period of three years.

(viii) A clerk should be available to fill in the application forms for immigrants who wish him to do so to facilitate its work.

(ix) The one-pound charge for a temporary certificate or the identification permit should be reduced charging no fee for its extension.

(x) The general practice in Cape Town, in some cases, the ten finger-prints rather than the mere thumb-prints should be ended.

(xi) The general practice of a particular immigration officer in one province communicating with his counterpart in another when an Indian applied for a certificate should be stopped.

The Commission's proposals were introduced in the Parliament as Act 22 of 1914 with the chief aim of making ample "provisions for the redress of certain grievances and the removal of certain disabilities"[60] in the Union. The outstanding problems, which were dealt with in the Bill, were to be resolved by means of administrative steps based on the agreements reached between Gandhiji and Smuts in their correspondence. The licence would be issued to the Indians after they had completed their terms of service. The Government would create no roadblocks regarding the entrance into the Union of the existing plural wives of domiciled Indians. The officials would not use the previous convictions against the *bona fide* passive resisters in the future, thereby erasing the legal impediments that stood in the way of the elemental interests of the Indians.

Having satisfied with the significant changes in the legal structure in South Africa *vis-à-vis* the Indian community, Gandhiji finally began to feel that his mission was nearly fulfilled and that he could positively respond to Gokhale's repeated appeals to return to India. It is a matter of any one's conjuncture what Gandhiji, and for that matter India, would have been but for the 'South African experience'. All the sufferings and the needless legal hurdles the Indians had to endure with no valid reasons paved the way for the emergence of the enlightened Gandhian legacy of Satyagraha. Gandhiji alone, with his love for his fellow-men, strong faith in *ahimsa* and his religious and social background could invent this miraculous remedy. The world owes Gandhiji (and those who stood by him during one of the world's greatest experiments) homage of the highest order as his contributions will be remembered as long as man will aspire to scale great heights.

## ARTICLE -3

### (A) Sincere Dedication

Gandhiji had reached Natal as the junior counsel for a commercial firm to represent an Indian merchant, on an annual salary of £105, but within a short span of time he was earning from his practice a whopping annual income of £5,000. He readily spent it all for a cause in which he had deep-seated faith—the faith that shaped Satyagraha. Operating in a sphere where he did not have real opponents, Gandhiji, by means of selfless service and genuine commitment to peaceful reforms, found himself in a position to change the uncertain climate. He strove for the common good of the South African Indians who were subjected to disabilities in an alien land. In Gandhiji we read yet another story. A timid, bashful lawyer who put up a most pathetic show at his first appearance in court emerged as an advocate of outstanding stature, indeed a true lawyer who advocated the cause of the oppressed and the down-trodden everywhere in the world. It is certainly beyond the scope of a dissertation of a limited length as this to describe all the dazzling and dynamic qualities of the Mahatma. As Gandhiji bade farewell to South Africa in July 1914, his followers showered upon him the highest tributes at an elaborate farewell banquet. But it went to the true greatness of this wonderful man that even his former opponents had nothing but good things to speak of him. The Star noted:[62]

> But with this intense pride in his people has 'marched' a feeling for Imperial considerations without which a proper solution might never have been found, and without which future guiders of Indian opinion in this country would find future policy almost impossible to direct.

In an anthology,[63] *Gandhi's Political Methods,* published thirty-five years later, Smuts again made the following significant tribute to Gandhiji:[64]—

> I must frankly admit that his activities at that time were quite inbiguing to me. It was my fate to be the main antagonist of **a man for whom even then I had the highest respect.**

In addition to the serious Indian problem, General Smuts had to deal with a number of other African leaders in search of solutions to various important issues one of which was the unification of the colonies. Gandhi's Satyagraha, from the beginning to the very end as a novel experiment in the affairs of men had complicated the problem. A vindictive ideology, alien to Gandhian ideals, would have precipitated a crisis pregnant with gruesome results.[65]

> Together with other South African leaders I was busily engaged in the task of wielding the old Colonies into a big unified State. ... It was a colossal work which took up every moment of my time. Suddenly in the midst of all those engrossing preoccupations, Gandhi had raised a troublesome issue. We discovered a skeleton in our cupboard.

It might be too easy to muddle over Gandhiji's avowed mission in South Africa. His unique stature as the chief engineer of a new and utilitarian philosophy of non-violent dissension was grounded in mutual love for the realignment of the acknowledged imperial policy. That policy always leaned to an unlawful side like the Tower of Pisa. The Indians were without the franchise. Institutionalised abuses were common as trees in a forest. **If it were not for Satyagraha with its attendant humane vision, the Indians' plight would have been doomed beyond words could adequately describe** as the unjust laws in the book had severed the blood veins of the Indian settlers. Gandhiji's Satyagraha campaign, their life-line, prevented their both hands from being cut off. The laws were not directed to establish justice but to perpetuate chauvinism and bigotry of a kind without parallel in history. No wonder the Indians in South Africa as well as the natives were groaning under the burden of injustice and

THE GANDHIAN PHILOSOPHY

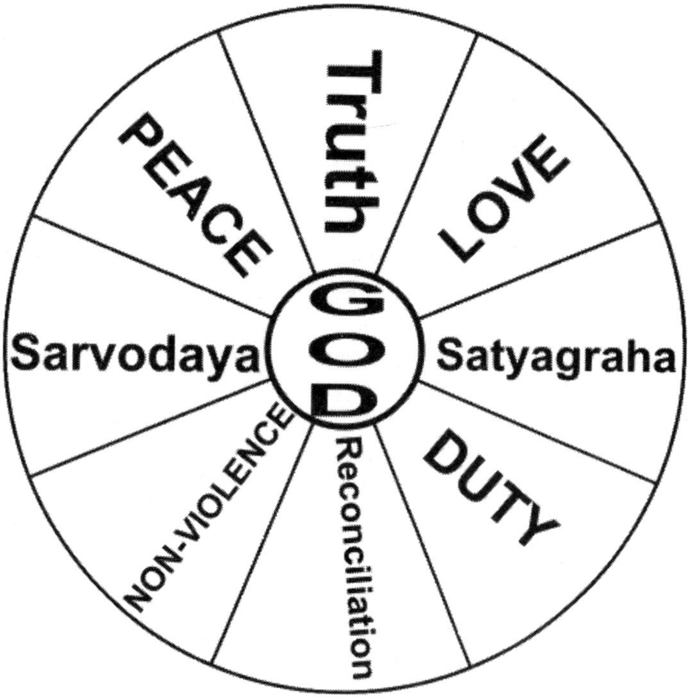


**BUILDING BLOCKS**

humiliation which Gandhiji considered the core of the African Indian problem. Today, the descendants of the large army of Indian settlers can turn the wheels of history backward and feel elated over what their ancestors had accomplished for them in the warm sunlight of the benign philosophy of Satyagraha.

### (B) An Acknowledged Defender

The treatment the Indian residents had to experience in jail and outside was the outcome of a system based on the white supremacy claimed by certain individuals of whom General Smuts was one of the acknowledged defenders. Gandhiji firmly believed, and for valid reasons, that Britain should treat all the subjects of the Crown on an equal basis. A wide gulf had existed between the British theory of equality before the law and its accepted practice in several parts of the world. The frequent encounter between Gandhiji and Smuts was "a prologue to two careers".[66] Gandhiji's public career was based on a non-violent campaign for social justice while that of Smuts was founded on the ideas of supremacy and in that broad sense the encounter had certain elements of inevitability. (Smuts had served as the attorney-general of the South African Republic and was a British General in the Boer War). There was no doubt that Gandhiji, much more than Smuts, was greatly enamoured of the British Constitution and the principles it stood for. As Gandhiji himself had stated he had also grafted "Sense of Equity" from *Bhagavad Gita.*[67]

We have already noted the haste in which the Asiatic law amendment was passed to restrict immigration from the Asian countries, a development which was joyously greeted throughout the Transvaal. The member representing Barberton (Loveday) echoed the strong views maintained not only by his constituents but also by all the colonists when he considered the legislative step as:[68]

> ...the first step to prevent what may mean the extinction of the white races in this country by immigration from the East. It has also been rightly stated ....that this measure should appeal to every individual in this country.

While the colonists had been ecstatic over the legislative step, the Indian settlers were obviously distraught and Gandhiji, in great despair, wrote bitterly about the underhand attempts by Lord Elgin, deeply felt that Lord Elgin had misled him and the entire Indian community. Gandhiji declared:[69]

> In Johannesburg the whole topic of conversation was the trick played upon us by both Lord Elgin and the Imperial Government. Our disappointment in South Africa was deep.

Gandhiji's accusations in relation to Lord Elgin's underhand manoeuvre when the situation developed into a serious problem were not without substance. When he compared the Asiatic Law Amendment with Ordinance 29, the Secretary of State pointed out:[70]

> The Act which is now submitted has behind it a very different kind of weight of authority. It has been introduced by the first responsible Ministry of the Colony and has been passed unanimously by both Houses of the new Legislature.

Recalling his imperial obligations, Lord Elgin felt constrained to state that it was his duty to make it clear "that His Majesty's Government do not consider the position of the Asiatics lawfully resident in the Transvaal, as settled by this to be satisfactory."[71] He argued:[72]

> ...that they adhere to the varied opinions which have been expressed by successive Secretaries of State as to the desirability of relaxing the restrictions to which Asiatics are at present subject; and that they commend this opinion to the Transvaal Government in the firm hope that it may be carefully considered how far practical can it be given to.

## (C) The Measure of Victory

After having his duties as the enunciator of the imperial order fulfilled, the Secretary of State felt a sense of relief at the reduced scale of responsibilities. For, he wrote to Selbourne:[73]

> They (the British Government) would not he justified in offering resistance to the general will of the Colony clearly expressed by its first elected representatives; and I am accordingly to inform you that His Majesty will not be advised to exercise his powers of disallowance with respect to the Act.

In 1906, the Indian settlers tasted some measure of victory by the peaceful protest against the provisions of Ordinance 29, but in the light of their previous experience they were not to acquiesce silently to the implementation of almost the same regulation in a new garb in 1907. Until Gandhiji's arrival and the dawn of the Satyagraha movement, the Indian settlers were resigned to accept the prevalent condition beset with inequality and injustice.[74] All the same, a weather change was visible on the horizon.

The apparent sign of the changing situation was a mass protest meeting organised by the Indian people on March 29 and held in Johannesburg as the Indians did not so much oppose the idea of registration as they did to the regulation that the issuing of the new certificates and the ten-digit finger-printing were to be compulsory. In a spirit of reconciliation, the British Indian Association dispatched a telegram on April 7 to the Secretary of State expressing the willingness to cooperate in a programme of voluntary registration. During the early phase of its new life, the colony had given its endorsement to Immigration Registration Act which, to a degree, had replaced South Africa's Peace Preservation Ordinance of 1903.[75]

The serious problems which the Indian residents faced in South Africa were lingering on as section 2, sub-section 1, had attempted a new formula which excluded the Indian residents without specifically mentioning them. But the language requirement, another form of discrimination against the Indian settlers, made it virtually impossible for them to be qualified. According to the existing stipulation, an individual should write the application in the character of European language:[76]

> Any person who when asked about whether within or outside this Colony by a duly authorised official shall be unable through deficient education to write out (either from dictation or otherwise) and sign in the character of a European language an application for the permission to enter the Colony or such other documents as such officer may require ... would be treated as a prohibited immigrant having stripped of any identity.

Both the Asiatic Law Amendment Act and Immigrants Restriction Act, which followed it, had been designed to supplement each other with the specific objective of restricting the flow of Indian immigration. Against this background a group of Punjabis and Pathans, almost all of them veterans, wrote to the Secretary of State stating that:[77]

> ...as men and British Indian soldiers, who are proud to have risked their lives in the cause of the Empire and have braved privations of war, to be spared the degradation of imprisonment or deportation ...

The letter, one of the several which were sent to the Secretary of State, also emotionally said that they had to face many hardships even though they had served "their King-Emperor as well as the British Empire."[78] The situation had forced the Indian settlers to seek the protection of justice as they had found the new regulation yet another form of the denial of justice. Even in such difficult circumstances they, under the influence of Gandhiji, did not turn violent, as Satyagraha had become the basis of their struggle.

Gandhiji, as part of the struggle committed groups of volunteers to picket the registration offices. They had been previously instructed that the picketing was to be peaceful, free of ill temper and that the use of foul language was forbidden at all times. Only less than 5 per cent of the Indian residents, submitted to "bond of slavery" forcing the authorities to extend the time limit of registration several times in the expectation that there would be a change in the attitude of the Indian community. Gandhiji poignantly stated **"Indians in the Transvaal will stagger humanity without shedding a drop of blood."** The *Indian Opinion* called those who had complied with the regulation as "black-legs" and

the "piano players" who were weak and cowardly to stand up for their basic rights while Gandhi appealed to all Indian settlers in the following words in the true spirit of non-violence. "I consider myself to be a lover of the Empire for what I have learned to be its beauties,"[79] but expressed serious reservations about the 'beauties." For, he remarked:[80]

> ... rightly or wrongly, in the Asiatic Law Amendment Acts are also seeds of danger to it. I have advised my countrymen at all costs to resist the Act in the most peaceful, and shall I add, Christian manner.

Admittedly, both Acts had been closely connected, as links in a chain, while the Indian objection to both tended to focus first on the cumbersome problem created by the Asiatic Law Amendment Act, but specifically on the mandatory registration clause, not to mention the stringent administrative requirement of all ten finger-prints. The agitation on the second point caused much surprise among the officials followed by a statement by Selbourne that his ministers were willing to be flexible on the situation and that "Indians will raise the same objections to five finger-prints as to ten, as their objection is more to the spirit than to its details."[81] Nevertheless, the key problem of mandatory registration and finger-printing were so interconnected that it was difficult to find a solution satisfactory to one without, in reality, remedying the other. In 1908, Winston Churchill, then Under Secretary in the Colonial Office, supported Botha and "his government most strongly on the Indian question" as "I thoroughly understand the views of white South Africa."[82]

### (D) Serious Misgivings

Reacting to the Indian problem. *The Times* eloquently argued that "as a nation we have little reason to be proud of the treatment being meted out to our fellow subjects in the Transvaal."[83] Other individuals such as Sir Richard Solomon, who had been the Transvaal's Agent-General in London and Agent J.X. Merriman, obviously no friend of the Indian residents, were also perturbed by the situation that a certain number of Indians residing in South Africa should be unnecessarily persecuted. Sir. Solomon informed Smuts:[84]

> If you persist, as you are entitled to do, you will succeed, but I much fear that you will also alienate the bulk of the liberal opinion in England, and you will give the Imperial Government the most serious blow in her most vital part: India.

The letter further cautioned Smuts against providing "a pretext for a great deal of mischievous interference in the native matters."[85] *The Times* also expressed serious misgivings on the treatment of the Indian residents:[86]

> And the worst of it is that their (the Indians') grievances will be just. Nor can we wash our hands off the business merely by casting the responsibility on the Colonial Government, for Mr. Harold Cox points out with undeniable force that His Majesty's Minister, especially had reserved the right of the Imperial Government to deal with the question of this nature.

*The Times* concluded its remarks by stating that "the wrongs of the Transvaal Indian community will soon be known and brooded over.... and will be used for all they are worth by the agitators against our rule."[87] The Transvaal Government relented a bit and was ready to accept the signatures of educated Indians rather than finger-prints provided that they would register.

All the while, the determined Indian residents were in no mood to give up their non-violent struggle under Gandhiji's competent leadership. As the official date for registration had expired, the recalcitrant Indian settlers were summarily tried for their non-compliance with what the Indians called the "Black Act". They were jailed. They were imprisoned for their non-violent agitation aimed at obtaining justice and equality denied under the euphemisms of 'colour' and racial superiority. The law which had been in existence was contrary to the very nature and goal of the legal structure: justice. Consequently, the actions taken by the legal establishment against the Indian settlers were illegal and the steps adopted by the Indians were just particularly when the steps were non-violent, based on the principles of Gandhian Satyagraha.

The will of the people is the law of the land. But the social attitude can be seriously rusted requiring frequent and thorough overhauling and Gandhiji, sought to recondition the system in South Africa. Alluding to the illegality of the situation, P. Moon emphasises Gandhiji's viewpoints:[88]

> **Gandhi said that he had never known legislation of this nature being directed against free men in any part of the world. This may have been so....** The power given to the police could, of course, be used to harass the Indians, even to the extent of making them leave the country and Gandhi certainly thought that this was the true goal of the law.

Gandhiji said that an Indian merchant with assets worth thousands of pounds, would face deportation and ruin under the harsh terms of the law.[89] He was equally concerned about the general welfare of the South African Indians irrespective of their economic status. (South Africa was considered the richest nation in the entire continent with vast natural resources including valuable minerals. Although the Indians were, on the whole financially well-off, several lived below the poverty line as did a large number of indigenous South African people.)[90] Satyagraha had galvanized them for a cause in which they all had serious stakes and the Indian community rallied around Gandhiji for a peaceful campaign to undo the effects of "Black Act".

When the Indian agitation started to accelerate, an exasperated Selborne wrote to Smuts conveying his sentiments on Gandhiji's non-violent crusade: "Mr. Gandhi ardently desires such a thing, one's natural instinct is to give it to him," Gandhiji for his role in Satyagraha was tried in the presence of a huge audience on January 10.

### Gandhiji Pleaded guilty

**Such a startling reaction was the most eloquent expression of his truthfulness symbolising his deep faith in the goodness of the human spirit, the corner-stone of his philosophy. His action reflected complete absence of hatred as even an iota of abhorrence or malice towards the perpetrators of a system which had unquestionably denied him the light of justice or even a faint hope of equality.** Many in his place could not have done what he did and would have gone ahead challenging the allegations, creating in the process strong under currents of hostility and animosity.

## ARTICLE -4

### (A) The Apostle of Ahimsa: Maximum Sentence

Astonishingly, Gandhiji, the greatest protagonist of non-violence in the last millennium, asked the court for the maximum sentence of six months at hard labour and a £500 fine. The magistrate, perhaps a bit unnerved by the amazingly strange conduct, chose to limit the punishment two months' imprisonment at hard labour. On January 28, Gandhiji, Thambi Naidoo, his compatriot, and Leung Quinn, who had been his close collaborator and a leader of the Transvaal Chinese community, put forward a compromise proposal to General Smuts, the then colonial secretary in the Transvaal Government.

According to the proposal, the Indian residents would voluntarily register and not out of any compulsion. Gandhiji was willing to permit all ten fingers to be printed and told the Indian settlers:[91]

> My own view of the matter is that all of us should give digit impressions without the least hesitation. But those who have conscious objection to giving them, or believe it to be derogatory to their self-respect will not be obligated to give those impressions.

The new recipe was far from placating the entire Indian community as some settlers considered it a serious setback in their struggle for justice—or even a defeat. Agreements and accords cannot always meet the divergent needs of an entire society. As soon as Gandhiji was freed from the jail, he explained the terms of the compromise at a meeting of the Indian residents at Johannesburg. He was criticized, even heckled, for the agreement, which, they believed, had been counterproductive. Gandhiji attempted to allay their fears with a tranquil explanation:[92]

> To die by the hand of a brother, rather than by disease or in such other way, cannot be for me a matter of sorrow. That is how I feel about the present situation facing us.

The resolution of the controversy hovering around the registration left a few unresolved problems in limbo. The India Office was seriously concerned with the failure of the Act to provide for the visitors' permits and its intention of excluding even the highly educated Indian settlers from the Transvaal. The India Office contended that the result of Section 2(4) in the current bill as formally recognized will be:[93]

> ...to exclude perpetually from a portion of his Majesty's Dominions all British Indian subjects, however high their social status or educational attainments, who have not already acquired domiciliary rights.

The Secretary of State had focused on the educational test, while Lord Morley, the Secretary of State for India, was further concerned that the Indian residents who had established domicile in the colony before 1902 and who had temporarily absented themselves may be forbidden to enter the Transvaal in the future as prohibited immigrants.[94] Although the Colonial Office was in agreement with the India Office, it was less vehement in its objection to it, regretted the language requirement,[95] and supported the admission of distinguished Indians and ranking public officials of Asian origin into the colony as visitors.[96] As a result of the pressure brought to bear on the Transvaal Government, it agreed without much resistance to accept the Home Department's stipulations.[97]

The South African Indian residents in the Transvaal were not completely satisfied with the results of the compromise,[98] and a number of other problems continued to obtrude themselves upon the scene, particularly following the introduction of a draft municipal bylaw. It imposed curfew limits, footpath regulations and restrictions on the use of public trains and trams. Botha admitted that some regulations had been rather preposterous and claimed that others were hardly enforced. "Respectable and well-conducted Asiatics and even South African natives," he argued, "can be seen daily walking on the sidewalks of Johannesburg and Pretoria and no one objects."[99] He continued:[100]

> The whole question of the use of side-walks by coloured persons is one which is in itself not important so long as the *status quo* is maintained,

> but any effort to legalise the prevailing practice of tolerance will arouse bitterest opposition and ferment anti-colour prejudice among various members of the European community in South Africa.

Had the existing law been applied only to the so-called lower class Indian settlers, the viceroy would have been greatly satisfied,[101] but the Government of India had limited itself to complaining against the failure of the mining bill to make the distinction among different levels of the Indian community.[102]

The Transvaal Act 32 (1908), widely known as the Shop Hours Act, had been a disguised attack on the Indian merchant community. Lengthy debates on the legal manoeuvering had proved that the regulation was aimed at the various trading practices of hawkers, peddlers and retail businessmen, who worked hard for long hours. They had been competing successfully with European traders. In many instances the tide of resentment against the successful Indian merchants triggered off the hue and cry for introducing laws against the residents from India.

## (B) The Steady Erosion of Rights

The Government of India expressed apprehension over what Lord Minto, the Viceroy, had correctly interpreted as the steady erosion of the fundamental rights of the Indian settlers residing in the Transvaal. Lord Elgin was alert to the limitations relating to the new regulations while the Colonial Office expressed the obvious:[103]

> Lord Elgin is fully dive to the disabilities unconnected with both the Asiatic Law Amendment and Immigrants Restrictions Act, to which Asiatics in the Transvaal are still subjected ... and in Lord Elgin's judgment it would be just useless at the present time to secure further concessions for resident Asiatics.

A general climate of enduring peace and goodwill, which the compromise was thought to have ushered in, was yet to be found and in such a bleak atmosphere a crisis was looming, ready to erupt in the Transvaal. In order to avoid further deterioration of the situation Gandhiji asked General Smuts to take immediate steps to dispel the rumour that the Asiatics, who had been outside the colony at the time of agreement, were required to register in accordance with the provisions of the Asiatics Law Amendment Act.[104]

At that critical time E.F.C. Lane, Smuts' private secretary, sent a letter to Gandhiji. The letter, among other things stated:[105]

> Indians who may come in now must apply for registration. General Smuts does not agree with your interpretation of the terms of the accord. General Smuts hopes, therefore, that you will use your influence to persuade the fresh Indians to apply for registration.

The dye was cast to step up the Satyagraha campaign as the Indian residents were in no mood either to comply with the order or to register as the conditions for both were unjustable. General Smuts put forward the rationale that "certain class of the population here should not be in a state outside the law."[106] (The authorities had often put forward this argument to whitewash their sinister motives.). Smuts said:[107]

> All I could add was that, pending the meeting of Parliament, there should be an interim state of affairs, and that as soon as Parliament met, it should deal with the situation. It was impossible for me to promise that at such a future date Asiatics coming into this country should be left to register as they wished.

Smuts resolutely repeated his refusal of the claim made by Gandhiji in mitigating the situation. The series of letters exchanged between the two leaders bore out his contention. Gandhiji countered by rendering his version of the dialogue when he quoted the colonial secretary as stating that:[108]

> I have consulted general Botha and I can assure you that I will repeal the Asiatic Act as soon as most of you have undergone voluntary registration. I wish to respect the feelings of your people.

General Smuts had conceded that out of a total population of ten to twelve thousand Indian residents, 9,158 had applied for voluntary registration[109] and that some 70 residents were unwilling to be finger-printed.[110] The Indian community objected to certain provisions contained in Act 36 despite certain improvements it had made. Indians argued that its terms deprived those residing outside the Transvaal with domiciliary status of their rights to return.

On August 6, the Indian community, inaugurated the non-violent struggle. Gandhiji had chosen Hamidia Mosque as the most appropriate venue for that very purpose. A large gathering of some 3,000 Indian settlers from all over the Transvaal had assembled outside the mosque in Johannesburg to hear their leaders speak out against the unfair aspects of the law; the leaders included Gandhiji, Essop Ismail Mea, Chairman of the British Indian Association and Leung Quim, the leader of the Chinese community. It proved to be a momentous occasion for the Asiatics, to voice their strong opposition to the unfair provisions of the Act. It was also a test case of the Gandhian Satyagraha since it was soon to prove a landmark in the non-violent struggle. It was a singular experience in mankind's struggle using peaceful means to resolve disputes. The Transvaal Leader carried the following account of the incident:[111]

> A three-legged pot was filled with the registration certificates, about 1,000 in all, and about 500 trading licences. Then parafin was poured in and the certificates set on fire amid a scene of wildest enthusiasm.

Gandhiji inspired the crowd into something short of frenzy by burning his own card into ashes. The paper went on:[112]

> The crowd hurrahed and shouted themselves hoarse; hats were thrown in the air and whistles blown. One Indian walked on to the platform and setting alight his certificate held it aloft. For a considerable time, it was quite impossible for the leaders on the platform to make themselves heard.

### (C) A New Plateau

Gandhiji's Satyagraha campaign had reached a height with no parallel in the history of peaceful struggle, which was centred around the fundamental problems of immigration and the unfair system of registration. Both issues had been inextricably connected. Although the Indian community made an urgent appeal to the Colonial Office explaining the serious situation, the officials remained silent while Lord Morley attempted to "point out that the Transvaal Government is entirely responsible for the vexation caused".[113] He made it clear:[114]

> ...that [Act 36 of 1908] ...if adequately represented in the very brief summary which is before him...makes substantial concessions to the Indian community in the Colony.

Selbourne tried to exert considerable pressure on the British Government for the quick recognition of the terms of Act 36. He wrote that it was difficult, "to resist the conclusion that Mr. Gandhi and his friends were not very anxious to arrive at a settlement,"[115] and that "if the passive resistance movement continued,"[116] he had been informed that there was "ground for concluding that the rank and file Asiatic community do not entirely share the views of their leaders",[117] and that, in the absence of "reasonable justification for it,"[118] the agitation "will die a natural death before long."[119]

There was little doubt that the Governor was under an illusion thoroughly ignorant of the stark realities down on earth. The Indians were determined to vitalise the non-violent campaign in South Africa as the Indian residents from all walks of life were united in their common objectives. Their historic non-violent movement had received considerable attention and approval in several parts of the world, particularly in the British Empire with the focus on (a) Gandhiji and (b) the force of Satyagraha. The situation had forced the viceroy to dispatch a telegram to the India Office stating that a number of protests had erupted in many parts of India against the mistreatment of the Indian residents in South Africa.[120]

> It is most desirable in my opinion that some settlement of the question in dispute should be arrived at without delay as in present circumstances we consider as a very serious matter the political effect in this country of the measures taken to enforce the law.

Meanwhile, Lord Crewe had stressed the unfortunate outcome of the problem of the Transvaal Indians in India and Britain, but argued that he "was unable to find sufficient reason for a refusal on the part of the Indians to accept the Act of 1908,"[121] adding that he found "no promise to repeal the Act of 1907."[122] He then elaborated his position in the following manner:[123]

> It is not denied that in the subsequent negotiations as to the best method of giving the legal sanction to the compromise, the Transvaal Colonial Secretary did consider whether the Act of 1907 might not be repealed. But it is clear that this was only discussed as one of several possible courses, and now it seems to me impossible to base a demand for repeal on this fact or to make it the ground for any breach of faith against the Colonial Secretary or the government on whose behalf he was negotiating.

Gandhiji had supported the right of the Indian residents to immigrate into the Transvaal on the basis of equality given to other British subjects, but he was pragmatic enough to understand that true parity, under the circumstances, was but a distant dream. He felt what resulted from the administrative practice was a source of concern recognizing that some broad objectives would be met if the Transvaal Government in its infinite wisdom admitted six educated Indians every year. The proposal seemed quite reasonable to Crewe, who believed that the "Ministers would not object to give an assurance of this kind with a view to facilitate the final settlement."[124]

**Gandhiji was arrested on October 7, on the ground he had refused to produce the registration certificate when he returned from Natal,** subsequently charged before a magistrate at Volksrust with violating section 9 of the regulation passed under Act 36 of 1908. Gandhiji was fined £25 and sentenced to two-month prison term with hard labour. We have the following account:[125]

> We in court as a witness he did not appear in prison clothes. He was brought from Voksrust as a witness in a case being set down for hearing in Johannesberg on 27th October; escort was provided from Johannesberg gaol, and he was brought up from Volksrust under orderly conditions in his prison kit; arrival after dark, at 6 p.m. and was conducted from station to fort in prison kit without handcuffs.

Regarding the hard labour, Gandhiji was not engaged in scavenging work, but he worked on Agricultural Show Grounds digging up 'holes for trees and weeding in municipal plantation."[126] It should be admitted that the hardship and humiliation that awaited him in India in the course of India's struggle for independence, was far more excruciating. Words cannot amply describe India's enormous debt of gratitude to Gandhiji who cleansed the whole universe by the purity of his mind, his intense penance, profound wisdom, abnegation and ultimately by his renunciation of brute force in favour of the unique talisman of Satyagraha, ennobling even his worst opponents.

If one of the principal objectives of Satyagraha was to draw the public attention to a specific issue, the instrument proved beyond doubt an unqualified success. Though Satyagraha with all its ramifications was applied and perfected in the protracted fight for India's independence, the fact remained that the unique device was moulded in the anvil of the persistent but patient non-violent campaign in South Africa. It was successfully tested in the indomitable will of South African Indians to fight for justice and equality.

Whenever Gandhiji was hauled and beaten up in the streets of South Africa, thousands of his countrymen rushed to him from every direction to share his misery and humiliation. When he was inside the jail a large army of Satyagrahis volunteered to take up the cause, held protest meetings, picketed factories and public places without resorting to violence of any kind whatsoever. They accepted without grumble, torture and oppression let loose on them by an army of insane colonial agents. Author P.C. Joshi says:[127]

> **Mahatma Gandhi put new life into the passive resistance movement which won great admiration on all sides for heroic resistance, selfless struggle for elementary civil rights. It brought funds from India of thousands of rupees.**

The settlers from India in the vacuum created by the absence of effective leadership, had to overcome a multitude of problems,[128] when Gandhiji changed the social climate by setting himself up against the unlawful regulations incessantly imposed upon them. "Mahatma Gandhi," Joshi says "has been the saviour of South African Indians,"[129] a fact that is carved into the history of the struggle for justice by the South African Indians and, for that matter, of all those who aspired to free themselves of all iniquities. The unique aspect about Gandhiji's method of resistance was that he avoided hurting the enemy even when he was struck. He won the war even when he lost the battle. In South Africa he gave the World Satyagraha.

### (D) The Final Days

Gandhiji did farewell to South Africa feeling optimistic about the future of the Indians, while the official pronouncements made by statesmen and savants alike continued to espouse an imperial ideology bent on preserving the system of exploitation. The intention was evident in the views expressed by Sir West Ridgeway, a former provincial governor and erstwhile chairman of a committee, sent to the Transvaal in 1906 to handle the problems of franchise and electoral system. *The Times* quoted him:[130]

> ... academic imperialists at home who dream of a Utopian Empire where all citizens enjoy equal rights. This dream can never be realised; at least not for many generations to come. If the Government were to make any attempt to enforce this policy, or even to support it by argument the break-up of our Empire would follow.

The whole history of the Indians, for one thing, bore witness in part to a case study in moral predicament and an exercise in imperial futility. In unambiguous terms one could argue that South Africa's main intention in bringing the Indians into the country had been to profit from the sorely needed cheap Indian labour and, not to countenance them as full citizens in a land under the control of settlers from Europe. In retrospect, the Indians should have been recognized as immigrants, rather than as indentured labourers, besides being accorded the rights of immigrants. The term indentured labour had carried with it a stigma. Social stigmas are numerous all over the world. In the absence of Gandhiji's leadership the Indians would have sunk like the Titanic in South Africa's bottomless ocean of racism. **But for Satyagraha, an integral part of the new equation, the voice of Indian residents would also have remained a**

**faint echo drowned in the uproar of and the opposition by the ruling hierarchy, which had little patience for compromise based on justice.** Who would hear it? Maybe, none.

The British Government was in an untenable position—and most likely did not intend—to exert pressure on South Africa as it might jeopardise its interests. It was also unrealistic to hope for any change without precipitating a crisis, for which Satyagraha became the only lasting solution.

South Africa has built numerous memorials to honour Gandhiji as living monuments of the triumph of non-violence over violence. He did not indulge in ferreting out ill-judgements on others. He was a man with the soul of a saint and his life convinces us of the ultimate victory of good over evil. Despite darkness, light persists; in spite of hatred, love persists; in spite of death, life persists. Smuts, who had to deal with Gandhiji on numerous occasions, clearly relieved at his exit. **"The Saint has left our shores," he said with a deep sigh, "I sincerely hope for ever."[130] After an eventful life of more than twenty years, Gandhiji finally made up his mind to set sail from South African shores to his motherland. He wrote sitting in the ship as it disappeared into the distant horizon:[131]**

> **I have been so often prevented from reaching India that it seems hardly real that I am now sitting in a ship bound for India. And having reached that what shall I do with myself? However, "Lead Kindly Light, amid the encircling gloom. Lead thou me on." That thought is my solace.**

We have now concluded the first two segments of the present study. The next segment would focus on the influence of the Gandhian philosophy of non-violent resistance on Rev. Dr. King's campaign in the United States for civil rights for the Afro-Americans. The following chapter will discuss the bus boycott in Montgomery led by the American champion to win equality for the black people.

## SUMMARY

1. One of the principal goals of the Satyagraha movement was to redress injustice suffered by the Indians and to focus public attention on their problems.
2. On November 4, the Transvaal Government showed willingness to meet the demands made by the Indian community. Officials were in favour of permitting certain number of Indian professionals who were not previously eligible to enter the colony.

3. The Secretary of State attempted many strategies to evade the problems faced by the Indians.
4. Less than 12,000 Indians had resided in the Transvaal, yet they could stun the colonial Government and to draw the attention of the empire to their problems.
5. The transvaal ministers tried to delude themselves into believing that the unrest was abating. Gandhiji and the Satyagrahis pressed on with their just demands. They eschewed violence.
6. After Gandhiji was arrested and handcuffed, he was asked to draw his sleeves and to carry a book to conceal the handcuffs.
7. In jail the Indians were subjected to the same harsh treatment as convicted settlers from Europe. Indians were but peace-loving Satyagrahis.
8. The final report of the Indian Enquiry Commission appeared in April 1914. A great part of it was concerned with various developments leading up to the Satyagraha movement.
9. Gandhiji felt that he could at last obey Gokhale's advice to return to India. General Smuts said with an obvious sense of relief. **"The saint has left our shores,"** of course a complement from his worst enemy.

## Notes and References

1. TA, December 12, 1908. Gov. to prime minister. After three days, Botha sent a reply to Selbourne to the effect that the admission of six educated Indians by right would not, in view of the intense animosity in the country, be in public interest.
2. After this development, and during the succeeding months, Sorabji was to offer himself for several tests of the Transvaal Asiatic laws which, he was convinced, had been flagrantly discriminatory. His action heightened the morale of the Indians in defying the unjust laws. Further details in Benjamin Sacks, *South Africa: An Imperial Dilemma.* (Albuquerque: University of New Mexico Press, 1967), pp. 135-169.
3. TA, December 12, 1908, op. cit.
4. CO, 551/4, Secretary of State to Governor General. October 7, 1910. For the economic conditions of the Indians in Natal, please see C.A. Woods, *The Indian Community of Natal: Their Economic Problem,* (Natal Regional Survey No. 9). (Cape Town: Oxford University Press, 1954). South African Indians constituted 2.8 per

cent of the total population of the country. In Natal, many lived below the poverty line. Please see "Indian South Africans," The Minority Rights Group. Report. No. 34 (London: 1980).

5. "Works," op. cit., XI, 100.
6. P. Moon., op. cit., pp. 71-72. The situation faced by the Indians were such that they were forbidden to live in one of the four provinces in South Africa. They were also deprived of the freedom of organization.
7. *Ibid.*, p. 135.
8. The ground for issuing the licences was the nature of the certificate of registration in accordance with the terms of the Black Act. They had to be produced on demand by the police any time. Indians were harshly treated in jails. The European criminals also received similar treatment.
9. These moves were completely successful. The Satyagrahis of the Phoenix party were arrested in September 1913. They were sentenced to three months' imprisonment with hard labour. In October, the Tolstoy party, which had induced the Indian miners to stop working, was given the same sentence.
10. As quoted in P. Moon, op. cit., p. 69. Also in M.K. Gandhi, *Collected Works*, (Delhi. Government of India, 1958) and L.H. Kuper and R. Davies, *Durban: A Racial Ecology*, (London: Jonathan Cape, 1958).
11. S.B. Mukherji, *Indian Minority in South Africa*, op. cit., p. 73.
12. Gandhiji proceeded to Newcastle taking over the leadership of the miners. Water and electricity were cut off from their houses and he advised them to leave their homes and "fare forth like pilgrims." About five thousand men, women and children heeded Gandhiji's call and gathered in a camp. They were fed rice and *dal* which the Indian traders had willingly provided.
13. S.B. Mukherji, op. cit., pp. 73-74.
14. *Ibid.*, p. 73. After the facilities were cut, life in the barracks for Satryagrahis became increasingly arduous leaving with the only option of altogether leaving the barracks. As the chief architect of the Satyagraha movement, Gandhiji found himself faced with the unavoidable responsibility of feeding them. Other Indians came to the rescue with the generous offer of money and foodstuffs.
15. P. Moon, op. cit., p. 70. At that juncture, Gandhiji put through a last-minute phone call to the secretary to General Smuts. Gandhiji informed him that he would end the march into the Transvaal if Smuts promised to remove the three-pound tax, but he was told

that Smuts would have nothing to do with his decision and that he could act as he wished. The following day, November 6, Gandhiji offered prayers, set out on his march and crossed the border in a peaceful manner.

16. P.S. Joshi, *The Tyranny of Colour,* cf., p. 73.
17. *Ibid.*, p. 75.
18. *Ibid.*, p. 73. The Indian workers residing in towns also staged demonstrations in order to show their support and solidarity with their compatriots. For another version of the same problem, please see G.B. Pyrah, *Imperial Policy and South Africa, 1902-1910.* (Oxford: Oxford University Press, 1955).
19. P.S. Joshi., op. cit., p. 73.
20. The terms concerning the repeal of the Black Act were somewhat ambiguous. Seeking clarification, Gandhiji proposed an amendment. Cartright expressed reluctance saying that Smuts considered the draft final. After consulting his colleagues in jail, Gandhiji insisted on amendment. Later, the proposed alteration was accepted and Cartwright agreed to present it to Smuts for his due consideration as well as formal consent.
21. M.K. Gandhi, *Satyagraha in South Africa,* op. cit., p. 242.
22. *Ibid.*, p. 244.
23. *Ibid.*, pp. 245-46.
24. *Ibid.*, Gandhiji and the rest of the Satyagrahis were freed from prison soon after the Gandhiji-Smuts meeting. Gandhiiji kept everyone abreast of the latest developments immediately after his release and they were in agreement with what had been done.
25. Indeed, the Natal representatives endorsed the views of the Free State members in addition to the liberal opinions from the Cape and of the former prime minister J.X. Meniman. "Do not let them follow their example," he said, "and do not let them trample on the weak. He did not love the Asiatics, and did not want to see them in South Africa, but if they came, let us give them fair and honest treatment. (cheers)" "Union Hansard," February 28, 1911.
26. CO, 551/10, Governor General to Secretary of State, March 23, 1911.
27. CO, 551120. Paraphrase of tel., from Secretary of State to Viceroy, March 30, 1911.
28. *Ibid.*
29. *Ibid.*, It was a war of attrition and there were financial constraints. Hermann Kallenbach came to the rescue by offering Gandhiji the

huge 1,100-acre farm about twenty-one miles from Johannesburg without rent for the use of the Satyagrahis. Gandhiji and Kallenbach helped erect a cluster of corrugated buildings for their accommodation.

30. *Ibid.*
31. CO, 551/10. Statement by Smuts, March 15, 1911.
32. CO, 551120. India Office to Colonial Office., March 31, 1911.
33. CO, 551121. Telegramme from Gandhiji to South Africa British India Committee, March 24, 1911.
34. On the Tolstoy Farm the residents included men, women and children. The residents were expected to do their share in the running of the establishment. Gandhiji said: "The work before us was to make the Farm a bee-hive of industry, thus to save money and in the end to make the families self-supporting."
35. E. Gitsham and J.F. Trembath, *A First Encounter of Labour Organization in South Africa,* (Boston: 1943), p. 214.
36. *Ibid.*, p. 147. By 1904, 8,489 Indians resided in the Cape. The figure was not much different from that in the Transvaal. Nonetheless, the problem was less acute in the Cape because of its liberal policies.
37. *Ibid.*, p. 215.
38. *Ibid.*, p. 149. One of the disabilities which had created discontent among Indian workers was a provision contained in Act 17 of 1895 on Natal that the workers who declined to renew their contracts of employment were forced to pay a Government tax of three pounds annually in order to continue to live in the colony.
39. Gandhiji had kept in constant contact with the lives and activities of his many confreres while he was sailing, for theirs had been the ever familiar story of governmental harassment and the steady erosion of the Indian rights in South Africa.
40. E. Gitsham and J.F. Trembath, op. cit., p. 73. The Satyagraha movement and the sufferings of Indians evoked sympathy throughout India and strong indignation against the South African Government. Gandhiji's peaceful agitation had a great deal to do with such strong favourable attitude in India.
41. B.R. Nanda, *Mahatma Gandhi* (London: 1958), p. 109.
42. *Works,* XI, pp.32-33.
43. General Smuts' cabinet did not encourage the anti-semitic sentiments. A Society of Jews and Gentiles, having branches in important centres in the Union, was formed to nip anti-semitism in its bud. Although the Jewish people were outwardly sympathetic

towards the Indian cause, inwardly they remained antipathetic. In business activity their ideal was predominance and as such they intended to stop competition. They were not in a position to act against the English or the Dutch for obvious political reasons; the Jews attempted to oust the Indians out of the commercial arena. Still, some benevolent personalities sided with Indians. P.S. Joshi., op. cit., p. 37.

44. CO, 551110. Telegram from Governor General to Secretary of State, April 14, 1911.
45. *Ibid.*
46. NAI, July 1911, proceedings 1, July 1, 1911.
47. *Ibid.*
48. Gokhale had presented the motion in the Indian legislative council to end the Indian indentured immigration to Natal. His confidence in the South African Government was to some degree justified. P. Moon, *Gandhi and India,* op. cit., pp. 49-71.
49. SANA, prime minister's office, 12/4/1912. Extract from the *Times of India,* December 21, 1912.
50. *Ibid.*
51. "Works," XI, pp. 577-586.
52. W.K. Hancock, *Smuts: The Sanguine Years, 1870-1919,* (Cambridge, 1967), p. 342 and also L.M. Thompson, *Indian Immigration into Natal, (1860-1872),* (Cape Town: 1952).
53. *Satyagraha,* op. cit., pp. 269-70.
54. "Works," XII, p. 315. "I am sure," C.F. Andrews said to Gandhiji, "that you are right to stand out. There must be no sacrifice of honour." Gandhiji and C.F. Andrews became friends from that moment on. Furthermore, within two or three days they were known as "Mohan" and "Charlie" to each other.
55. *Satyagraha,* pp. 325-26.
56. *Ibid.*, p. 326.
57. *Ibid.*, p. 327. Gladstone wrote to Smuts that it was not easy to conduct negotiations with Gandhiji who represented an unusual type of humanity. Gandhiji's ethical and intellectual attitude. He said that was the product of a curious compound of mysticism and astuteness baffling the ordinary train of thought. "*Satyagraha.*"
58. *Ibid.*
59. NAI, July 1914, proceedings 10-12. Viceroy to Secretary of State, May 28, 1914.
60. Sections 1, 2 and 3 of the major proposals regarding the Indian marriages.

61. "*The Star,*" July 15.
62. *Ibid.*
63. W.H. Hancock, "Smuts," op. cit., p. 345.
64. *Ibid.*, pp. 345-47.
65. *Ibid.*, pp. 346-47.
66. "*The Times,*" December 6, 1913.
67. M.K. Gandhi, *The Story Of My Experiments With Truth,* (Boston: 1975), p. 265
68. *Transvaal Hansaard,* April 7, 1907.
69. *Satyagraha,* pp. 24-26.
70. NAI. Papers with Acts. India Act XIV of 1914, sec. of state to government, May 9, 1907.
71. *Ibid.*
72. *Ibid.*, carefully screened members of the Indian community were allowed to return to the Transvaal after the British occupation of the Colony in 1900. M. Palmer, "The History of the Indians in Natal," (Natal Regional Survey No. 10) Cape Town: Oxford University Press, 1957) and N. Iqbal, "The Politics of Racism," (Ahmedabad: Navajivan, 1965).
73. T.A. British India Office to Colonial Office, April 7, 1907.
74. The Act 15 of 1907 which repealed the Peace Preservation Ordinance of 1903. In section 2, the formula of excluding the Indians without having to mention them had been established.
75. T.A. British Indian Association to Colonial Office, op. cit.
76. T.A. Pathans and Punjabis to Secretary of State, September 14, 1908.
77. *Ibid.*, Also in G.H. Calpin, *Indians in South Africa,* (Pietermaritzburg: Shuter and Shooter, 1949).
78. "*Works,*" VII, 468. Gandhi to Johannesburg, *Star,* December 10, 1907.
79. *Ibid.*, In India indignation was expressed at public meetings and in the mainstream media. Dailies wrote editorials denouncing South Africa's racial polity. Please see, *Kesari,* February 4, 1908.
80. T.A. Tel., government to secretary of state, January 28, 1908
81. Draft of Tel. to undersecretary, colonial office to high commission, January 25, 1908.
82. *The Times,* January 7, 1908.
83. The issue of legal representation for Indians drew much attention. On April 25, 1907, Gandhiji delineated his news that if anyone was prosecuted under the new Act and if he had a permit to reside in the Transvaal, he would "defend him in the court free if charge. If

the case is to be heard outside Johannesburg, the Association will pay Mr. Gandhi's railway fare. *Indian Opinion,* April 25, 1907.

84. W.K. Hancock, *The Sanguine Years, (1807-1919),* (Cambridge, 1962), pp. 332-33. The author explains the difficult nature of the relationship between the Indians and the government. The nature of the problem is discussed in C.J. Fergusson-Davie, *The Early History of Indians in Natal,* (Johannesburg: South African Institute of Race Relations, 1952). Especially chapters 4 and 5.
85. *The Times,* January 7, 1908.
86. *Ibid.*
87. P. Moon, *Gandhi and Modern India,* op.cit., p. 49.
88. *Ibid.*, p. 50. The author states that "in face of this criticism and with other grave internal problems looming ahead, the Union Government shrank from keeping the hundreds of non-resisting Indians in jail and decided to give in. To cover their retreat, they appointed a commission of three members to inquire into Indian grievances and immediately afterwards released Gandhi unconditionally, along with his coadjutors, Kallenbach, Polak, and West, who had also been imprisoned." *Ibid.*, p. 71.
89. Indian in South Africa were placed between the African people and the settlers from Europe constituting 2.8 per cent of the country's total population. The Institute of Social and Economic Research found that at least 50 per cent of Indians in Metropolitan Durban lived in "the grip of poverty". According to the Durban City Council, 80 per cent of the Indian families had income of less than £250 a month when the Household Subsistence Level (HSL) was £310 a month. (The HSL is the index of the amount for subsistence). The Minority Rights Group—Report No. 34. op. cit.
90. W.K. Hancock and Jan der Poel, *Selections from the Smuts Papers,* (Cambridge: 1966), pp. 36.
91. "*Satyagraha,*" p. 161.
92. A Pathan in the crowd was particularly furious accusing Gandhiji of having sold out the Indian settlers to Smuts for £15,000. He shouted: "I swear with Allah as my witness that I will kill any man who takes the lead in applying for registration." *Ibid.*, p. 162.
93. *Ibid.*, p. 168. Also in Pyarelal, *Mahatma Gandhi: The Early Phase,* (Ahmedabad: Navajivan, 1965) and B.R. Nanda, *Mahatma Gandhi,* (London: George Allen and Unwin, 1958).
94. NAI, March 1908, proceedings 5-6, India Office to Colonial Office., October 31, 1907.
95. *Ibid.*, November 11, 1907.

96. Secretary of State to Government, November 27, 1907.
97. *Ibid.*, December 3, 1907.
98. On July 27, 1908, the Africa British Indian Committee forwarded a letter to the Colonial Office complaining against the classification as prohibited immigrants.
99. The goal of such restrictions was to guard against the risks of others, in this case settlers from Europe, women and children being jostled off the sidewalks "by unsavory and ill-mannered coloured people." TA, minute no. 463, July 29, 1908. If such a criterion had been accepted and fairly applied, heavy penalties should have been imposed on those who had mistreated the Indians.
100. TA, minute no. 463, July 29, 1908. Governor General to Secretary of State, August 3, 1908.
101. *Ibid.*
102. NAI, July 1908, proceedings 1 of July 6, 1908.
103. TA Colonial Office to India Office, April 1,1908.
104. "*Works,*" VIII, 230; Gandhi to Smuts, May 13,1908.
105. *Ibid.*, p. 248.
106. *Transvaal Leader,* August 22, 1908.
107. *Ibid.*, Gandhiji and Smuts held diametrically opposed interpretations on the development.
108. "*Satyagraha,*" p. 156.
109. Gandhiji held the view that the rest of the Indians would have voluntarily registered provided the Government had not stopped the procedure on May 9. Further details are provided in C. Kondapi, *Indians Overseas, 1838-1949,* (Bombay: Oxford University Press, 1960). Especially chapter 3.
110. *Transvaal Leader,* August 25, 1908.
111. *Ibid.*, The Chinese also mounted the podium dropping their certificates in the pot to demonstrate solidarity with the Indian residents and the goals of the peaceful campaign.
112. TA, India Office to Colonial Office, September 3,1908.
113. *Ibid.*
114. *Ibid.*
115. *Ibid.*
116. *Ibid.*
117. *Ibid.*
118. TA, September 7, 1908.
119. *Ibid.*, October 23, 1908. The news widely circulated in India and meetings were held in many parts of the country to show their

support for and solidarity with their fellow countrymen in South Africa.

120. TA, December 15, 1908.
121. *Ibid.*
122. October 15, 1908.
123. TA, October 15, 1908.
124. South Africa British Indian Committee said, Gandhiji was put to hard labour on the road. The Government denied the accusation that Gandhiji tended a garden. *Honsaard*, March 24,1909.
125. P.C. Joshy, *Tyranny of Colour—A Study of the Indian Problem in South Africa,* (New York: Kennikat Press, 1942), p. 69. The author praises Gandhiji's non-violent campaigns in South Africa.
126. *Ibid.*, p. 75.
127. *Ibid.*, Related data provided in S.B. Mukherji, *Indian Minority in South Amca,* op. cit. According to the author, the "new struggle was directed against the Asiatic Registration Amendment (Act XXXVI, 1908)". It is treated as 'prohibited immigrants' who could pass the education tests under the Immigration Restriction Act (Act XV, 1907), but were ineligible under the Black Act (Act II, 1907).
128. P.C. Joshi, op. cit., p. 70. The author pointed out that "the struggle displayed before the world the heroism of South African Indians. It brought to light the long lost truth that Indians can sacrifice their all for the sake of their self-respect." p. 73.
129. *Ibid.*, p. 75.
130. *The Times,* March 8, 1920. "Many a striking memorial to his [Gandhiji's] services and inspiration exists today. The impression he made on South Africa by his purity, learning and self-sacrifice has not yet been effaced. Thousands of white men and women experience an ecstatic pleasure when they hear the word 'Gandhi.'.... Some enthusiastically recollect the occasion on which they shook the thin, soft hand of this brown emaciated figure. There are clergymen who refer to his gospel in their churches. "India is Mahatma Gandhi, and Mahatma Gandhi is India"—this is the belief that South Africa cherishes. His method was deliberately to break the law, and to organize his followers into a mass movement of passive resistance in disobedience to the law objected to. South Africa again has a perennial interest in the personality and actions of this great man." *Ibid.*, pp. 75-77. In P.C. Joshi, op. cit.
131. *Ibid.*, p. 124.

SEGMENT-C

# CHAPTER-VII

# AHIMSA IN ALABAMA (Background and Boycotting the Bus)

## ARTICLE -1

### (A) The Foundation

Notwithstanding the fact that Rev. Dr. King has visited several parts of the world, his stay in India, and the wealth of experience he gained, had been a definite spiritual experience. In India he reached the firm conclusion that non-violent approach was morally superior and a system based on humanitarian principles.

His campaigns in the United States in typical Gandhian mould consisted of boycotts, non-violent protests, and petitions to Government officials to bring serious problems of injustice and racial bias into sharp focus. Before we analyse the circumstances, which had led to the famous bus boycott in Montgomery launched by a young Rev. Dr. Martin Luther King Jr., and how it had changed the course of his struggle, it is important to delve into his philosophy of non-violence. We will try to find out to what degree Gandhian ideology provided the foundation for the historic bus boycott in Montgomery.

The American civil rights leader, like Gandhiji, had defined non-violent opposition as readiness to accept suffering without any retaliation and concerning this basic aspect of non-violent resistance, Rev. Dr. King fully adhered to the Gandhian ideals. His interpretation of one point deserves special attention:[1]

> A fourth point that characterizes non-violent resistance is a willingness to accept suffering without retaliation, to accept the blows from the opponent without striking back. "Rivers of blood may have to flow before we gain our freedom, but it must be our blood," Gandhi said to his countrymen. The non-violent resisters are willing to accept violence if necessary, but never

> to inflict it. He does not seek to dodge jail. If going to jail is necessary, he enters it as a bridegroom enters the bride's chamber.

Armed with strong convictions in the moral force of non-violence, Rev. Dr. King organized a number of peaceful campaigns, despite facing opposition from both friends and foes, in Montgomery, Selma (Alabama). Albany, Atlanta (Georgia), to name but a few cities. The Montgomery pastor had came to oppose violence and acrimony on humanitarian grounds long before he started his campaign in Montgomery:[2]

> **It [violence] thrives on hatred rather than love...destroys community and makes brotherhood impossible on grounds of pragmatic reasons.**
>
> **It solves no social issue, but it only adds new and more complicated problems to one's existence.**

Montgomery became Rev. Dr. King's testing ground for the successful experiment of his non-violent philosophy. The Gandhian ideals showed him the way to tackle a problem, however, formidable it might be. A compendium of his visit to what he termed "the land of Gandhi" is within the phew of our study as it had strong influence on Rev. Dr. King's life and activities.

The champion of the greatest civil rights movement in the United States, Rev. Dr. King, considered peaceful resistance as a personification of the best in human beings placing it at a point equidistant between what he had considered the two extreme responses. "To accept passively an unjust system," he argued, "is to cooperate with that system; thereby the oppressed become as evil as the oppressor."[3] He acted on the principle of non-co-operation with evil. Rev. Dr. King stressed: "Non-co-operation with evil is as much a moral obligation as is co-operation with good."[4]

While in India, Rev. Dr. King could gain greater insight into the practical application of *ahimsa* as an instrument of resistance in Montgomery. A letter from Chester Bowles, then ambassador to India, reinforced his conviction that no other method of combat could produce the desired results in the conditions in America. The U.S. ambassador made it clear that the only practical way out of "our present dilemma"[5] was the strict adherence to "the Gandhian techniques..."[6] Several previous engagements had prevented Rev. Dr. King, Mrs. Coretta King, and Professor Lawrence Roddick, a close associate, from visiting India. In the days following a near-fatal assault on him at Blumstein's department store in Harlem, New York City, Rev. Dr. King had an enforced rest. He was thinking seriously about visiting India. While he was signing copies of his monumental book, *Stride Toward Freedom,* Mrs. Izola Curry, carried away by extreme psychotic impulses, plunged an eight-inch letter-opener into Rev. Dr. King's chest. It was during the period of convalescence that he began to think seriously about his long cherished wish to visit India, Dr. King had pondered over the relevance of Gandhian ideals to the American dilemma in Montgomery and elsewhere in the nation. While the struggle for racial justice was raging the advocate of American's civil rights movement convincingly stated, **"India's Gandhi was guiding the light of our technique of the non-violent social change."**[7]

He recalls:[8]

> We spoke of hun [Gandhji] often...So some of my fiiends asked: "Why don't you go to India and see for yourself **what the Mahatma, whom you so admire, has wrought?"**

## (B) India: Enduring Impressions

After months of negotiation, a grant from the American Friends' Society financed a major part of Rev. Dr. King's tour of India and the visit to the country was considered so paramount to the full flowering of Gandhism in his life that the American leader openly declared on arrival in New Delhi:[9]

> **To other countries I may go as a tourist, but to India I come as a pilgrim. This is because India means to me Mahatma Gandhi, a truly great man of our age.**

The pilgrim made much progress in the land of his idol. An honoured guest of Gandhi National Memorial Fund, Rev. Dr. King, in a maelstrom of activity in India held talks with several Gandhians including Jawaharlal Nehru and Dr. S. Radhakrishnan. Nehru explained to Rev. Dr. King that caste. discrimination was a serious crime punishable with imprisonment under the terms of the Constitution of India. Referring to the policy of reservations to backward communities, Professor Roddick put the question if that was not discrimination. "Well, it may be," Nehru replied, "but this is our own way of atoning for the centuries of injustice we have inflicted upon these people."[10] (In the United States the quota system for the Afro-Americans-Americans is considered a discriminatory practice euphemistically called reverse discrimination as part of systematic attempt to keep the blacks away from attending colleges and in obtaining lucrative jobs). Nehru's words and the Indian Government's policy of allotting quota to untouchables or Harijans as

Gandhiji preferred to call them were the outcome of the influence of the Gandhian ideals. India's egalitarian attitude exerted a profound impression on Rev. Dr. King unquestionably helping in chalking out a detailed government programme of fostering compensatory preferential treatment of Afro-Americans.[11] Rev. Dr. King points out:[12]

> We were surprised and delighted to see that India has made greater progress in the fight against caste untouchability than we have made in our country against race segregation. Both nations have federal laws against discrimination acknowledging, of course, that the decision of our Supreme Court is the law of the land.

Despite the large catalogue of federal laws and regulations meant to wipe out racism, the United States still is one of the worst racist countries in the world and alluding to the gulf in racial harmony between India and the United States, Rev. Dr. King remarks:[13]

> ...We must recognize that there are great differences between what India has done and what we have done on a problem that is very similar. The leaders of India have placed their moral powers behind their law.

The American civil rights leader, highly impressed by India's policy under Gandhiji's guiding principles, stressed during his Indian tour that "from the Prime Minister down to the village councilmen, everybody declares publicly that untouchability is wrong,"[14] adding that:[15]

> But in the United States some of our highest officials decline to render a moral judgment like the Supreme Court decision, a pronouncement of justice itself does not mean that the millions of Negro children will be treated in conditions of equality.

Rev. Dr. King's stay in India, from February 10 to March 12, 1959, with a sojourn in Kerala, included memorable visit to Raj Ghat, lectures at Indian universities, interviews with a large number of journalists who gave him lead press coverage, visits to Gandhiji Village, i.e. two villages established by Vinoba Bhave as part of his Bhoodan Movement. "Bhave" according to Rev. Dr. King, "was a great spiritual man, moving in a humble way to keep the spirit of Gandhiji's philosophy alive."[16]

While in the subcontinent, he acquired a reservoir of knowledge on Gandhiji's Salt Satyagraha, a memorable part of the history of the non-violent struggle—an event that had a strong influence on Rev. Dr. King himself. He learned from his many talks with Gandhiji's disciples that in March 1930, near the city of Ahmedabad, Gandhiji had left the banks of the Sabarmati river to walk with a group of seventy-nine volunteers for the shores of the Arabian Sea, solemnly vowing never to return to Sabarmati Ashram until the British government had abolished the infamous salt tax once and for all Rev. Dr. King stated that "this highly publicized 'Salt Satyagraha' was the signal for a national eruption of civil disobedience."[17] The spirit of Salt Satyagraha, a nail in the coffin of British aggrandizement in India and the massive civil disobedience, spreading like wild fire in the country had been a well-spring of inspiration to Rev. Dr. King's home-grown Satyagraha in America.

### (C) The Pilgrim from America

The pilgrim from America pointed out that as he worked for justice and freedom in Alabama, he perceived the near identity of *Agape* and *Satyagraha.* Rev. Dr. King's thought was equally self-assured in the moral sense notably when one speaks of love which finds its expression in the word *agape* as the term *agape* implies nothing sentimental or basically affectionate. It means understanding, demonstrating goodwill towards all individuals, an overflowing love seeking nothing it return from anyone. It is the love of God working in the lives of human beings. When we express love at the *agape* level, as Gandhiji did, we love other human beings not because we like them or because their attitudes and ways appeal to us, but because God loves them.[18]

How did the Indian people react to the visit by Gandhiji greatest disciple in America? Rev. Dr. King says that he had "a great reception,"[19] besides **being overwhelmed by the extreme hospitality of the Indian people ewerywhere:[20]**

> The people showered upon us the most generous hospitality imaginable. We were graciously received by the prime minister, the president and the vice-president of the nation; the members of Parliament, governors and Chief ministers of various Indian states: writers, professors social reformers and at least one saint.... **Virtually every door was open to us.** We were **looked upon as brothers** with the colour of our skin as something of an asset. But the strongest bond of fraternity was the common cause of minority and colonial peoples in America, Africa and Asia **struggling to throw off racialism and colonialism.**

Montogmery as a result of the coverage in the vibrant Indian press, the 381-day bus boycott was well known in the nation, prompting Rev. Dr. King to praise the Indian journalists about whom he said "they were scrupulously fair with us and in their editorials they showed an amazing grasp of what was going on in America and other parts of the world."[21]

Rev. Dr. King, had been Gandhiji's greatest disciple who had espoused the Gandhian ideals as the bedrock of his civil rights movement in the United States and in that sense little wonder, the Indian people showered upon him "the most generous hospitability imaginable" (Rev. Dr. King remained critical of the philosophical bent of several writers and social thinkers, for instance, Reinhold Niebuhr, but he had accepted the Gandhian ideals).

Equally, the Afro-Americans-American leader was impressed by the reactions of the people to his visit. Referring to the economic condition of the Indian masses he says:[22]

> Great ills flow from the poverty of India, but strangely there is relatively little crime in **India. Here is another concrete manifestation of the wonderful spiritual quality of the Indian people.** They are poor, jammed together and half starved but they do not take it on each other. **They are a kindly people.** They do not abuse one another, verbally or physically as readily as we do. We saw but one fist fight in India during our stay.

Mrs. Coretta King felt that India's poverty and the related economic backwardness were the results of the colonial misrule of India when Rev. Dr. King opined "Indians who at rich, have luxurious houses, landed estates, line clothes and show evidences of overeating."[23]

Rev. Dr. King's memorable visit to India deeply touched him;[24] his observations on and impressions about the land of Gandhiji need to be quoted in their entirety in order to grasp the full meaning and impact the visit had on his struggle in Alabama and elsewhere in the United States:[25]

> The trip had a great impact upon me personally. It was wonderful to be in the land of Gandhi, to talk with his son, his grandsons, his cousins and other relatives and to share the reminiscences of his close comrades, to visit his ashram, to see the countless memorials for him, and finally to lay a wreath on his entombed ashes at Rajghat. I left India more convinced than ever before that non-violent resistance is the most potent weapon available to oppressed peoples in their struggle for freedom. It was a marvelous thing to see the amazing results of a non-violent campaign. **The aftermath of hatred and bitterness that usually follows a violent campaign was found nowhere in India. The way of acquiescence leads to moral and spiritual suicide.**
>
> The spirit of Gandhi is very much alive in India today. But any objective observer must report that Gandhi is not only the greatest figure in India's history, but that his influence is felt in almost every aspect of life and public policy today.

## (D) Manifest Influence

Gandhiji's strong influence was manifest in Rev. Dr. King's persistent resistance to the collective denial of justice to Afro-Americans. As a fervid advocate of racial justice and equality, he was highly gratified that India and its leaders were integrating, 'the Harijans', at a much faster pace than the United States. In contrast to the violent confrontation between the Government and the Afro-American people in the United States, Gandhiji's compassion for and love of Harijans helped speed up the process of integration in India without violent upheavals besides opening up new doors of opportunity for them. Rev. Dr. King summons up his experience in India in the following words:[26]

> I left India more convinced than ever before but non-violent resistance is the most potent weapon available to the oppressed people in their struggle for freedom and justice. It was a marvelous thing to see the results of a non-violent campaign.

Rev. Dr. King's visit to India was an important milestone in his long journey to find an equitable solution to the injustice rampant in the multi-racial American society.[27] After returning to United States on March 17, 1959, Rev. Dr. King was ever vociferous in relating his experience in India whenever an opportunity presented itself. L. Davis observes that "this was a 'new' Martin Luther who was speaking,"[28] and adds:[29]

> The Negro must have Christian faith to met hate with love... You must say: [to your tormentor]: you will match his capacity to inflict suffering with your capacity to suffer. You will not abide by his unjust laws, but you will not hate him for making them. Non-violence is the most potent weapon available to the people in the struggle for human dignity. The eye for eye philosophy leaves everyone blind.

Mrs. Coretta King makes the following observation about the results of the Indian trip:[30]

> When we left, Martin had said that our first twenty-four hours in India has heen like meeting George Washington, Thomas Jefferson and James Madison in a single day.

After he had returned from India, he revitalized his non-violent struggle in the South, which, historically, had been a synonym of obtuse racist feelings with the reaffirmed faith that, the problem could be remedied by non-violent means, as did Gandhiji prior to him. The success of the famous bus boycott in Montgomery catapulted Rev. Dr.

King into a national hero. He opened up a new frontier of Gandhian non-violence in the United States, where the great experiment in non-violent resistance to institutionalized discriminatory practices was facing serious challenges. They chiefly rose from the misconception that non-violence would be impractical and unproductive in a country where non-violence had never been practiced on a large scale. The Afro-Americans applied it. It further helped remove the false impression created by the misguided media that the Afro-Americans were, by their very nature, violent and so incapable of practicing Satyagraha. The new method adopted by Rev. Dr. King started gaining credibility, giving him wide recognition. He stuck to Gandhian ideology with Biblical fervor. His prestige and power in American politics grew by leaps and bounds, giving a rude shock to bigots and charlatans who had proclaimed themselves as the guardians of a defunct moral code.

## ARTICLE -2

### (A) The Gust of Wind

In Montgomery, a city with radio-active racist views, Mrs. Rosa Parks' tart experience proved to be the catalyst for Rev. Dr. King's successful boycott of the city buses. On December 1955, a fateful day, a tired Mrs. Rosa Parks had boarded the Cleveland Avenue bus in downtown Montgomery. After standing on her feet for hours, the physically exhausted Afro-American lady sat down in the first seat behind the section which had been generally reserved for white skinned passengers, but only to be ordered by the driver to move further back to accommodate white-skinned people. By that time, every seat on the bus had been occupied and Mrs. Parks saw no good reason to stand to suit a white-skinned person. While three other Afro-American passengers immediately complied with the driver's order, an intrepid Mrs. Parks defied it and asserted her right to sit in any seat in a free country. She was arrested.[31]

Questions were raised about her insolence while her bitter experience resulted in widespread condemnation of the racial attitude rife in Alabama:[32]

> The reactions of the Negro community in Montgomery were mixed. At first there was some speculation about why Mrs. Parks did not move. Some individuals in the white community alleged that she had been 'planted' by the NAACP as a test case.

"National Association for the Advancement of Coloured People is an Afro-American organization of which Rev. Dr. King had been the vice-president."[33] It was an obvious fact that "the NAACP did not plant her there. In fact, it did not aid or abet the boycotters in the early stages of the movement."[34] Mrs. Parks was a popular woman and naturally her impetuous arrest sparked off a controversy, but no one thought that her defiance of the racist regulation would end up in a challenge, a mass protest led by none other than Rev. Dr. King. It culminated in America's first domestically grown Satyagraha—a spark that ignited a non-violent campaign for freedom. In order to gain a proper understanding of the monumental Montgomery bus boycott, we have to grasp the ramifications of a system, which had been in operation for decades for the sole interests of the white-skinned people. We shall analyze the situation here.

Under that antiquated system, if white-skinned passengers had already occupied their reserved seats and other white individuals got on the bus, the Afro-Americans, who were seated in the unreserved section immediately behind them, were expected to stand up like nice little children and vacate seats for the 'bus guests'. Any non-compliance by Afro-American-American passengers was sufficient ground for their arrest and conviction without question.[35]

Furthermore, the impertinent behaviour of the bus drivers had caused intense resentment among Afro-Americans as the drivers often called them such pejorative names as "niggers," "black apes" and "black cows." Rev. Dr. King movingly wrote that often Afro-Americans would pay the bus fare at the front door, but were forced to get off and reboard the vehicle by the rear door. Often the bus left as Rev. Dr. King said "that with the Negro's dime (a ten-cent coin) in the box before he had time to reach the rear door."[36] The passengers dropped the coin the sealed metal boxes to travel to any destination in the city regardless of the distance. Buses do not have anyone to issue tickets or check them to spare expenses on additional employees.

### (B) Testimony Under Oath

In court Afro-Americans and others testified under oath that when they did not have the correct change, they were threatened and Mrs. Martha Walker gave a sworn testimony to the effect that she was leading her blind husband from the bus and that "the driver whipped out a pistol, and drove the man off the bus."[37] The driver refused to stop the vehicle even though Mrs. Walker called out that her husband's leg was caught in the door and the blind man was dragged some distance before he could free himself. Mrs. Brooks reported the tragic incident to the bus company, which took no action against the offenders.[38]

Lerone Bennett, Jr., of the well-known Afro-American magazine, Ebony, wrote, "It is a point of immense interest that the Montgomery movement began in irony and ended in irony."[39] The irony was that Rev. Dr. Martin Luther King did not start the campaign; but he was pulled into it and put the Gandhian ideals into practice to help the black community.

The arrest and the eventual trial of Mrs. Rosa Parks had galvanized the black community into unprecedented and concerted action, signalling the civil rights campaign. When Mrs. Parks appeared in court on December 5; a committee of Afro-American leaders had called for a one-day boycott of the buses in Montgomery without as much of a thought of the public response. The boycott was non-violent. But for the able leadership of Rev. Dr. King and the most disciplined conduct of the agitation, the boycott might have slipped into violence inviting more violent retaliation. He did not want the boycott to play into the open arms of the enemies.

One of the great imponderables of any boycott is its immediate public response. The organizers took pains to see that the boycott did not whittle away making it a sheer mockery. The Afro-Americans distributed some 37,000 leaflets urging every member of the black community.[40]

> Don't ride the bus to work, to town, to school, or any place on Monday, December 5.
> Another Negro woman has been arrested and put in jail because she refused to give up her bus seat.
> Don't ride the buses to work to town, to school or anywhere on Monday. If you work, take a cab, or share a ride, or walk.
> Come to a mass meeting, Monday at 7:00 p.m. at the Holt Street Baptist Church for further instructions.

It was in a sense what could be regarded as massive civil disobedience campaign among Afro-Americans not only in Montgomery but also in different regions of the country generating faith in the victory of concerted action without resorting to violence.[41] The boycott was the Gandhian non-co-operation directed against an archaic system that struck at the very root of Afro-Americans' self-respect.[42] Self-respect is the core of one's life. All the while the news media played a significant role in Ule campaign by awakening the dormant spirit and by making people keenly aware of the gloomy side of the hitherto unquestioned social practices and conventions. The denial of seat on a bus, in the front, middle or back, is a denial of human dignity. *The Montgomery Advertiser* carried a front-page story of the entire saga, dramatizing the historic boycott. Rev. Dr. King observers:[43]

> ....that newspaper story turned out to the Negroes' advantage, since it served to bring the information to hundreds who had not previously heard of the plan. By Sunday afternoon, word had spread to practically every Negro citizen of Montgomery.

The publicity was so widespread that only "a few people"[44] residing in "the remote of areas"[45] of Alabama had not heard of it. *The New York Times* reported: [46]

> ....the full text of these appeals appeared in the Montgomery newspapers and their substance was broadcast over the Montgomay radio stations. As a result, the one-day protest was almost 90 per cent effective.

Rev. Dr. King, who gave credit to Henry David Thoreau's *"Essay on Civil Disobedience"*, largely due to its non-violent nature zealously guarding the effectiveness of the Montgomery boycott. AU the same, one could not lose sight of Gandhiji's strong influence on the civil right movement inaugurated in the North American continent.[47] While Thoreau had prepared the theoretical framework of Rev. Dr. King's civil rights campaign in the United States, Gandhiji had demonstrated its feasibility, besides elevating the theory into the immutability of science. Whatever be the driving force behind the boycott, it was undoubtedly true that the novelty of the experiment nearly stunned the arrogant perpetrators of atrocious proscriptions and prohibitions they were oblivious of the numerous inhuman restraints on the civil liberties to which their forefathers had been subjected in the New World during the pre-independence era.

At the meeting held in the Baptist Church, there was no hint of civil disobedience. The resolution was read to Afro-Americans by Ralph Abernathy, himself a minister and Rev. Dr. King's close associate. The resolution spelled out:[48]

(i) Passengers receive treatment on a first come, first-served basis—Negroes sitting from the hack of the bus towards the front while the whites sat from the front towards the back.

(ii) Courteous treatment by the bus drivers is guaranteed.

(iii) Negro bus drivers were employed on predominantly Negro routes.

### (C) Spirit of Comradeship

The resolution had been carried unanimously.[49] As far as Afro-Americans in the South were concerned, developments in Montgomery had carried a symbolic significance not only in what was occurring in the shadow of Mrs. Parks bitter experience, but it was "The Cradle of Confederacy" when Jefferson Davis took command of the secessionist elements in the South.[59]

The segregationists in the South as well as the integrationists regarded the boycott a complete success. It had no parallel in the prolonged struggle of Afro-Americans for justice. Afro-Americans woke up as early as three in the morning in a veritable spirit of solidarity, with their brethren walked to work, some as many as twelve miles a day.[52] Others relied on car pools which had turned out to be unexpected a victory for the cause of equality.[53] The car pool had been so remarkable that Rev. Dr. King alluded to it in *Stride Toward Freedom* that "they had to admit it in white citizenship council meetings that the pool moved in military precision."[54] Referring to the effectiveness of the Montgomery bus boycott, a northern reporter writes:[55]

> For most of this past year, Montgomery Negroes operated their own transit service with 'pool' cars and station wagons, while maintaining better schedules than the city system had established.

The highly popular and effective boycott which began in Montgomery, against the racist system served as a model for the whole country. It remained extremely non-violent ever since it began. What effect did it have on Rev. Dr. King? How did the rest of the nation view the struggle by Afro-Americans in Montgomery? The peaceful boycott catapulted Rev. Dr. King into a national figure at the age of 27. The true Gandhian ideals had inspired him and eventually his popularity spread to different corners of the world. Afro-Americans, who had been portrayed as incapable of putting up the most powerful non-violent resistance under the aegis of Gandhism in the United States, acquitted themselves enhancing their credibility to stand up to the demands of America's greatest mass movement. On March 4, 1956, hardly three months after the bus boycott with its unquestionable national impact, *The New York Times* had referred to its leader as "Martin King, Jr., a 27-year old Baptist minister." After a month the same daily wrote about "Rev. Dr. King, Jr.,"[57] in the aftermath of the escalation of the peaceful protest into a full-grown non-violent campaign with no comparison in the recent history of the

United States, thanks to its peaceful and well-disciplined conduct. More encomiums were to follow for Rev. Dr. King's burgeoning popularity and on December 12, 1956, *The New York Times* lauded him as "the Rev. Dr. King, Jr., whose name should be remembered."[58] None but a few censorious skeptics, the prophets of doom, could miss the rise of a most scintillating star on the American political horizon that lit up the path of a peaceful revolution in a society caught in the sirbonian bog of moral bankruptcy.

### (D) The Campaign Escalates

Rev. Dr. King had a reservoir of experience in organizing and administering community activities as he had been the president of the Montgomery Improvement Association (MIA),[59] the forerunner of his Own Southern Chrisitian Leadership Conference, an influential national Afro-Americans organization. The Montgomery Improvement Association organized the efficient car pool and shouldered the cost of the campaign. The cost of operating the MIA had by now risen to $5,000 a month.[60] Unsolicited donations started pouring in from as far away as Japan thanks to the wide and favourable press coverage.[61] The amount reached a fabulous total of $250000 the largest response being from the various church groups.[62] As the boycott had picked up momentum, Rev. Dr. King had sought permission to establish an Afro-American bus company owned and operated by Montgomery's black people to provide "adequate transportation for our people."[63] Expectedly, the city authorities denied him permission.

Clearly, the city administrators, aware of the rousing response to the call for the non-violent protest, took great care to avoid violent confrontation with Afro-Americans. As the boycott went on, the city began to slide towards a financial crisis, the inevitable result of its perverted policies. *The New York Times* points out:[64]

> There is a tacit agreement by the bulk of both the Negro and the white communities that violence should not erupt, that at all costs the campaign must be confined to the propaganda forums, to the courts, to any peaceful channels.

Before the highly peaceful protest was launched, some 70 per cent of the passengers had been Afro-Americans and eleven months into the popular boycott, the city owned bus company had lost more than $750,000 in addition to the heavy loss to white-operated business enterprises in and around the city while attempts were made to sabotage the campaign from two sources.

(1) Despite the general attitude of the city administrators to refrain from bloody confrontation with Afro-Americans, a handful of trigger-happy clients tried to whip up frenzy and shattered the uneasy peace which had prevailed in Montgomery after the boycott began. (2) Racial bigots let off an explosion that rocked King's house. He was attending a mass meeting at the first Baptist Church when a bomb went off on his porch.[65] Two days later a stick of dynamite was tossed by someone at a car on the front lawn of the house of a member of the Negotiating committee of the MLA.[66] The Afro-Americans, who had assembled to listen to Rev. Dr. King. refused to be provoked and as a police officer said they also averted a disastrous communal riot. That was indeed a great victory for the civil rights crusader and the full value of his commitment to the Gandhian ideology of non-violence started yielding tangible results.[67] Lewis states:[68]

> Back in Montgomery, Martin pondered full dimensions of non-violent involvement. The compelling power of the example of personal physical sufferings increasingly intrigued him.

The social evils, the author goes on, that "once stuck Thoreau were so overwhelming as to compel an honest man to seek imprisonment."[69] Mrs. Coretta Scot King writes:[70]

> We began to think more deeply about the whole philosophy of non-violence. We talked about how superficial and shallow our knowledge of the whole thing was.

L. Lewis further adds:[71]

> **The Mahatma's fasts and lengthy incarcerations offered even nobler guidelines to [Rev. Dr. King's] non-violent resistance to evil...** It was the mid-August three-day visit to Montgomery of the Gandhian disciple and scholar Ranganath Divakar that had convinced Martin that he, too, **must set an example of physical suffering.**

As the initial shock and confusion withered away, the ill-motivated white-skinned people began countering the American civil rights leader with violence and threats in the form of bomb explosions, midnight telephone calls and judicial indictments in the vain hope that the new challenge, quite novel in its form, could be nipped in the bud.

Although Rev. Dr. King and many Afro-Americans had to go through unsavoury experience, facing challenges, a few words must be mentioned about the bright side of the boycott trapped in the iron mesh of racial rivalry.

## ARTICLE-3

### (A) The Hands of Co-operation

Every cloud has its silver lining. It should not be mistaken that the sporadic outbursts of violence and intimidation constituted a true reflection of the general sentiments entertained by the white community. A remarkable number of white-skinned people openly expressed their sympathy for the constant demands of the blacks for fairness. The exhortation of the Mayor of Montgomery, an unrepented segregationist to refrain from transporting Afro-Americans to and from the places of work, went unheeded as several white people lent a helping hand to the forsaken section of the city's population. A white-skinned a resident of Montgomery, drove up to a group of Afro-Americans awaiting an MIA station wagon to go to their places of work. "You people waiting for ride or pick-up?" he enquired. "Yes," one man replied after a moment of hesitation. "You stay off those city buses, mind the well-wisher encouraged them, "You'll never win, once you get back on those damn buses. Stay away." He drove off. A genuine expression of sympathy by a city resident for a noble cause!

Even though the city fathers had initiated a few abortive efforts at negotiation, there was no agreement on the horizon.[73] But they forged a clandestine deal with the White Citizen's Council, a coterie of incorrigible segregationists[74] with a firm resolve to defeat the boycott which had caused considerable loss of revenue to the city and loss of business to the local merchants. The dialogue had reached an impasse. Under the guise of a quick solution to the problem, traffic tickets were liberally issued by the police to Afro-Americans who were then depending on the car pool. Besides, several others were booked at the police station, later imprisoning them.[75]

**Montgomery soon had the notoriety of being the Zirrt Southern city to imprison IUng for the Zirrt time in his public life for advocating justice and for practicing Gandhian *ahimsa* in the United States.**

The charges levelled against him for practicing peaceful means were flimsy. America's foremost advocate of *ahimsa* was arrested on the ground of driving over the speed limit, at thirty miles an hour in a twenty-five mile zone and for having picked up three passengers from the city's bustling commercial area.[76] So in the eyes of the law, picking up three passengers was illegal. The denial of justice to three million black people was not.

Rev. Dr. King was imprisoned for the first time in his life in the city of Montgomery for **leading the Gandhian non-violent struggle for social justice in the United States.** The news of his imprisonment dominated headlines in the media projecting him as an advocate of non-violence engaged in a great mission to eradicate discrimination against Afro-Americans. Lionell Lokos wrote that "King languished in the prison"[77] only to enable the officials "to go through the finger-printing piocess."[78] No sooner had the news of the civil rights leader's imprisonment spread than a large number of Afro-Americans assembled outside the jail. Lokos goes on:[79]

> The jailer became a little panicky, and his panic increased along with the size of the crowd. Evidently, he had feared that the situation would soon get out of hand.

In the spirit of exchanging love for hate Rev. Dr. King did not resist arrest, nor did he show any reluctance, entirely co-operating with the prison officials. He expressed satisfaction that the people who had assembled outside the jail showed great discipline and self-control, two hallmarks of non-violent resistance. Rev. Dr. King himself says:[80]

> ... non-violent resistance would be a willingness to accept blows from the opponent, without striking back, a willingness to accept suffering without retaliation.

And during the course of his non-violent struggle in Montgomery, Selma, Albany and in other urban centres in the United States, Rev. Dr. King made steady progress in *ahimsa* transforming it into a way of life rather than hollow dogma. He was stabbed, jailed. His residence was bombed three times. His daily mail brought an avalanche of death threats. Vituperative epithets against him were common. Undaunted, he pursued his goal with indefatigable courage, travelling wide and delivering numerous speeches **vehemently pleading for non-violence, justice and freedom.** Alluding to his faith in non-violence. Lokos makes the following comment:[81]

> The doctrine of non-violence had always been the fixed star in Martin Luther King's civil rights movement. And yet he had been muddied in the ideological waters with a none to threat of violence if his methods should fail.

This statement suggests that although Rev. Dr. King had been fully committed to non-violence he had, nevertheless, reservations that "if Negros do not achieve their objective through non-violence, they will then feel free in restoring to force and violence."[82] No one is born with ideals, one develops them. The apparent ambivalence in Rev. Dr. King's position should not be construed as leaving an option for violence as a last resort, rather as a calculated attempt to leave for possible error in the hypothesis of a researcher until his assertions are irrefutably proved by convincing results. Yet, his life-long adherence to Gandhian ideals showed black and white America the efficacy of non-violence and for their just cause Afro-Americans filled the jails in Alabama. According to Rev. Dr. King:[83]

> ... at the jail an almost holiday atmosphere prevailed ... Many Negroes had gone voluntarily to the Sherif's office to see if their names were on the list and were even disappointed when they were not.

Faith comes from convictions and convictions in turn, come from experience acquired over a period of time. Naturally, Rev. Dr. King became, in later years, unequivocal in stressing non-violence as a method of resisting evil. He learned from experience and the dramatic changes in the attitude of his fellow Afro-Americans and the readiness with which they atoned for the sins of their oppressors dispelling the last lingering doubts in his mind about the feasibility of the Gandhian technique. Afro-Americans, who dared defy laws in Montgomery and elsewhere, had a different view of the laws. Rev. Dr. King pointed out that "those who had previously trembled before the laws were now proud to be arrested for the cause of freedom."[84] In court the defence attorneys were in no mood to concede that Afro-Americans had violated the law and that the prosecution's evidence was insufficient to prove beyond any reasonable doubt that their action was in violation of Alabama's anti-boycott statute.[85] The defence attorneys had argued that no evidence had been presented to prove that Afro-Americans did not have "just cause or legal excuse"[86] as stipulated by the anti-boycott law.

## (B) The Parade of Witnesses

Altogether the attorneys had called 28 Witnesses who had bitter experience of rude, and unjustifiable treatment of the bus drivers,[87] who themselves probably came from uneducated and economically backward families in and around Montgomery. Countless reporters from all over the United States, India, France and England had covered the trial. (When Rev. Dr. King visited India, he was surprised that the people of India had been well informed of the problems faced by Afro-Americans in the United States, notably in Montgomery).

Judge Carter tried Rev. Dr. King and found the foremost civil rights leader in the United States guilty of violating Montgomery's anti-boycott laws. But it was really strange that the same custodians of the law did not find the unscrupulous drivers and ill-motivated segregationists, guilty of trampling on human dignity highlighting the inherent contradictions in the judicial structure.

Punishment for Rev. Dr. King's crime was $500 in addition to court costs, or 386 days at hard labour.[88] In *Stride Toward Freedom* he exulted:[89]

> I knew I was a convicted criminal, but I was proud of my crime. **It was the crime of joining my people in a non-violent protest against injustice.**

His faith in *ahimsa* was unwavering:[90]

> It is my firm hope that as the Negroes plunge deeper into the quest for freedom and justice, they will plunge even **deeper into the philosophy of non-violence.**

Rev. Dr. King's non-violent appeal to his followers "to endure suffering"[91] at the hands of the opponents was a spirited application Gandhian ideals to bring about a revolution in the American society, of intoxicated by thinking. He called Satyagraha soulforce:[92]

> The Negro all over the south must come to be point that he can say to the white brothers: We do watch your capacity to suffering. We will meet your physical force **with soul force [*Satyagraha*]. We will not hate you, but we will not obey your evil laws. We will soon wear you down by pun capacity to suffer.**

The Supreme Court set aside Rev. Dr. King's conviction and declared that Alabama's laws were unconstitutional, another feather on the cap of Rev. Dr. King. The charge of inciting violence against him was dropped and he came out untarnished with a radiant image gaining remarkable moral power. History repeats itself before our eyes.[93] What occurred in America was a replay of what had come to pass in South Africa where Gandhiji pitted against Gen. Smuts won a parallel victory on the solid foundation of *ahimsa*, a reenactment of the same drama in history, but with different characters. Eleven months into the trial, *The New York Times* noted: "Dr. King has been free on bond since [the trial] serving actively as the boycott leader."[94]

### (C) Bitter Pills

The verdict rendered by the Supreme Court was a bolt from the blue sky. Many individuals, especially the bus drivers, whose impropriety had been instrumental in starting the upheaval, were completely discomfited, finding the court's verdict a bitter pill to swallow. The bus company called 100 drivers, all of them white, and were told unambiguously that they had to abide by the judgment and those among them who could not do so, would have to quit and some in a fury quit without a moment of hesitation.[95]

Fury or not, the transition into the new era was relatively smooth as the whites, did not turn to violent resistance. On the first day of the newly gained prize of equality, the Afro-American passengers entered the bus by the front door which had been slammed on them on previous occasions. They sat in the first vacant seats. They sat in the middle of the bus or in the rear section as they pleased. They did not have to vacate their seats for anyone including the emperors of Montgomery. Lokos observes:[96]

> The first day of bus integration was deceptively quiet—perhaps, at least in part, because much of the world had been looking on. ... They [the Americans] did not get up to give white passenger a seat. **And whites sat with Negroes.**

### (D) A Startling Reaction

The most conspicuous aspect of the 11-month incessant and non-violent struggle was that it brought into sharp focus the social disabilities of the Afro-American society at large. Thousands of people in and outside the United States were pleasantly surprised when Rev. Dr. King rode the bus along the Montgomery streets along with Rev. Dr. King Glen Smiley of New York, a white-skinned cleric by his side. The final chapter in cataclysmic drama of racial confrontation in such a conciliatory manner aroused considerable public interest so much so that it enhanced Rev. Dr. King's public stature. The event fortified the Afro-American cause with non-violence as its guiding light.

Everything looked well and good. It was but the sinister calm before the storm. Montgomery's well-trained fundamentalists were disinclined to relinquish their racist position and indulged in terror unprecedented in its history. Shotgun pellets shattered the windowpanes of Rev. Dr. King's home.[97] A sniper's bullet hit an Afro-American lady in the neck riding the bus forcing the Police Commissioner to suspend the bus service for the rest of the night.[98] During a 10-day hiatus, between the first day of the bus integration and the New Year's Day, four shooting incidents were reported forcing the imposition of curfew on the city. Night bus service was suspended.[99] On the night of January 9, the sworn enemies of racial harmony bombed Afro-American churches and the homes of two black clerics.

In order to allay the fears of the citizenry, James E. Folsom, then Governor of Alabama, offered cash reward of $2,000 for the conviction of individual(s) for indulgmg in criminal actions:[100]

He openly declared:[101]

> Any person who would bomb the House of the Lord endangers the life every man, woman and child in Montgomery. I call on all people of Alabama to help stamp out such lawlessness wherever it may occur.

After a six-day respite, the bus operation resumed on a limited daylight schedule with police assigned to buses and in the vehicles Afro-Americans and others rode together. The segregationists asked the city commissioner for licence to operate a "private" bus service but the request was rejected on the ground that the move would be counterproductive. *New York Times* noted the new configuration by pointing out that Afro-Americans were riding the buses "in amiable, voluntary segregation,"[101] and towards the year's end the buses carried the sign board "sit where you please."[102]

In our study we should not lose sight of a remarkable phenomenon that mitigated the brutality committed against the blacks in Montgomery. A number of white-skinned people assisted Afro-American in their hour of need giving them moral and material support. And the judgment by the Supreme Court, a white dominated body, was decisive in the Afro-American victory over the forces of racism.

The illustration below shows the causes and results of the non-violent bus boycott.

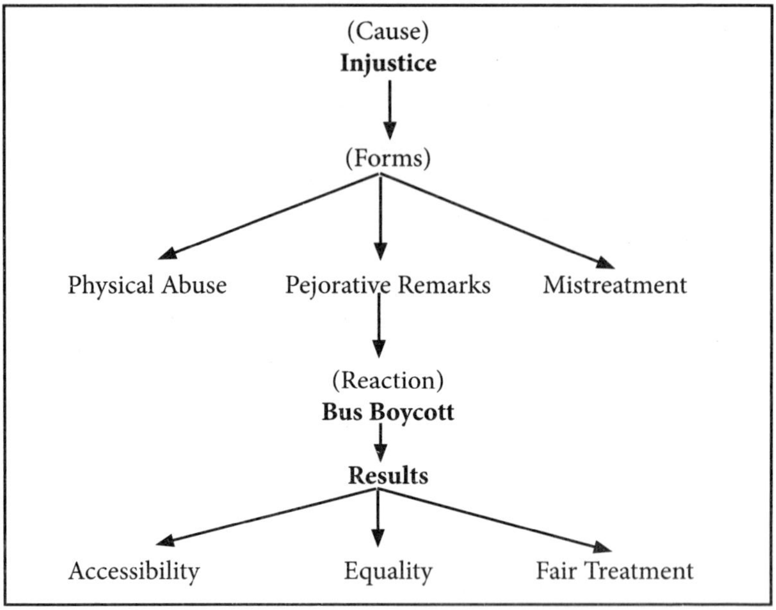


Besides the realization of avowed objectives in the struggle against racism of other social evils mass campaigns produce by-products, which may be of great social value. L. Davis made the following observation on the impact of the Montgomery bus boycott on the future course of Rev. Dr. King's non-violent activities. He pointed out that the "white community learned that there was amazing power of unity [among the Negroes] and that they were no longer dealing with the 'old' Negm, but with a hew one."[103] The author stresses Gandhiji's influence on Rev. Dr. King's non-violent movement in Montgomery and other cities in the United States:[104]

> Another important by-product of the Montgomery Movement was the new philosophy of non-violence and passive resistance, with Martin Luther King, Jr., as the chief architect. He received **worldwide recognition for the way he had translated Gandhi's philosophy of passive resistance.** Dr. King more than anyone else, was the 'backbone' of the Movement, even though he was captivated into its leadership.

In some definite way Rev. Dr. King was a product of the sufferings of Montgomery where **he had applied the tools, which Gandhiji had used**

**on a number of occasions proving that the humanity of non-violence can overcome the brute force of violence.** Non-violence is spiritual and eternal. Violence is ephemeral and brutal. The Montgomery bus boycott went down in history as a reinforcement of Gandhian Satyagraha that proclaims: **Truth dispels fear and generates courage.** After the struggle in Montgomery was over, Rev. Dr. King said, "We no longer have any fear of going to jail."[105] He had both his eyes firmly fixed on problems being faced by Afro-Americans in Birmingham and Selma, to mention two cities. Further attempts will be made in the following chapter to evaluate the American civil rights leader's activities in Birmingham with regard to their relevance to his spiritual progress that was to continue until he turned like Gandhiji, his great Indian predecessor into a synonym of love in the truly spiritual sense. After the bus boycott in Montgomery, became history Afro-Americans began to taste the fruits of their non-violent struggle.

## SUMMARY

1. In the entire history of the civil rights campaign in the United States of America, there was hardly anything to eclipse the historic Montgomery bus boycott. After the successful non-violent boycott, Afro-Americans were able to sit anywhere on city buses, something they were not allowed to do for years. The success of the campaign was entirely the outcome of the non-violent methods adopted by Rev. Dr. King.
2. The boycott became synonymous with non-violent struggle. So great was its impact on Rev. Dr. King's mission to redeem the down-trodden. His campaign received inspiration from Gandhiji, India's emancipator.
3. The bus boycott in Montgomery was triggered of by Mrs. Rosa Parks who had a most humiliating experience on the bus. She was arrested and harassed. Her fellow Afro-Americans took up her cause. Rev. Dr. King called for a bus boycott.
4. Afro-Americans were subjected to rude treatment by bus drivers, shopkeepers and police-men who called them derogatory names such as "niggers", "black cows".
5. Mrs. Parks' arrest impelled the black community in Montgomery into concerted action. Yet, no civil rights struggle in any American city had a more uncertain start. As

days passed by, the movement gathered momention until it became popular, heralding a new era in American history.

6. To virtually everyone in Montgomery it was a bus boycott—pure and simple. But to Rev. Dr. King it was the beginning of a great non-violent war for justice and equality. Thousands of people in the United States and mother parts of the world watched the civil rights campaign in Montgomery.
7. Reporters from India, France and Japan covered the trial, involving those charged with the violation of the law. Rev. Dr. King was amazed to know later that the people of India were well-informed of the racial situation and of his campaigns in the United States.
8. The Montgomery boycott transformed Rev. Dr. King into a national figure because of his emphasis on non-violent methods to achieve racial equality and justice. No one in the United States had applied non-violence on such a large scale as Rev. Dr. King. His received international recognition as a champion of the oppressed and a protagonist of the Gandhian philosophy.
9. During the highly successful boycott, the bus company landed in a great financial crisis since the overwhelming majority of its clients, Montgomery's Afro-Americans, had refused to ride the bus, but relied on car pools, which were organized by Montgomery Improvement Association and its supporters.
10. Despite the opposition by the city administrators against the Montgomery bus boycott, numerous white people had supported Afro-Americans and urged them to stay off the bus until their just demands were met. The encouragement and support were invaluable.
11. Rev. Dr. King was arrested for masterminding the boycott. He sought the legal assistance of Afro-Americans lawyers, particularly Fred Grey who defended the Afro-Americans in several court cases.
12. America's renowned civil rights leader refused to pay a fine and went to jail, for a just cause. He said that he would never pay a fine for his cause was just and the penalty was unjust.
13. The court proceedings against Afro-Americans were widely reported in the world press. The reports created world opinion in favour of the agitation for justice and equality.

Several witnesses testified to the bitter experiences on bases and in shops. At the end of the successful bus boycott several drivers quit jobs.

14. The Supreme Court of the United States of America declared Alabama's segregation laws on bus unconstitutional, signalling the end to the 11 month boycott. Rev. Dr. King rode the bus sitting side by side with a white philanthropist. Today, the boycott is history. We are indebted to Martin Luther King and his 'teacher' Mohandas Karamchand Gandhi for this 'glorious revolution.'

**Notes and References**

1. Martin Luther King, Jr., *"Stride Toward Freedom,"* op. cit., p. 103. Rev. Dr. King expressed the belief in non-violence in another article, *Christian Century,* a conservative publication that "the method of non-violence is based on the conviction that the universe is on the side of justice. It is this conviction that prompts the non-violent resister to accept suffering without retaliation." February 6, 1957, pp. 165-66.
2. *Ibid.*
3. *"Stride Toward Freedom,"* op. cit., p. 212.
4. *Ibid.*
5. In David L. Lews, *"King: A Critical Biography"*, (New York: Praeger Publishers, 1970), p. 98. Chester Bowles had told Rev. Dr. King that he should certainly visit India and in his reply to the U.S. Ambassador the civil rights leader indicated that he had travelled much along the road to philosophical non-violence.
6. *Ibid.*
7. *Ebony,* (July 1959).
8. *Ibid.*
9. *"King: A Critical Biography,"* op. cit., p. 99.
10. *Ibid.*, p. 100.
11. During his stray in India, Rev. Dr. King had received valuable information about Vinoba Bhave's Bhoodan. He said that the movement was led by "the saints Vinoba Bhave and Jayaprakash Narayan" and that their "ideal is self-sufficiency". Rev. Dr. King also stated: "Such ideas may sound strange and archaic to Western ears. However, the Indians have already achieved greater results than we Americans would ever expect." *Ibid.*, p. 103.

12. *Ebony,* op. cit., Mrs. Coretta King said "Nehru talked with Martin, comparing the Indian struggle for freedom with that of the American Negro for civil rights." Coretta Scott King, *My Life with Martin Luther King,* p. 172, (New York: Holt Rinehart and Winston, 1969).
13. *Ibid.*
14. *Ibid.*
15. *Ibid.*
16. *"King: A Critical Biography,"* Lewis., op. cit., p. 104.
17. *Ibid.*, p. 102.
18. Rev. Dr. King says: When we speak of loving those who oppose us we refer to neither "eros" nor "philia", we speak of a love which is expressed in the Greek word "agape", which means "understanding." *Christian Century,* (February 6, 1957); p. 165.
19. *Ebony,* op. cit.
20. *Ibid.*, He noticed that there was little rime in India notably compared with the United States.
21. *Ibid.*
22. *Ibid.*
23. *Ibid.*, Dr. King said "India had a problem of segregation, but it is solved more peacefully than the United States."
24. *Ibid.*
25. *Ibid.*
26. L.G. Davis, op cit., p. 105.
27. *Ibid.*, p. 89.
28. *Ibid.*
29. *Ibid.*
30. Coretta King, *"My Life with Martin Luther King,"* op. cit., p. 183.
31. *"Stride Toward Freedom,"* op. cit., p. 213. In the same work, the champion of the American civil rights movement argued with a high degree of compassion that "non-violence does not seek to defeat or humiliate the opponent, but to win his friendship and understanding." p. 102.
32. Quoted in L.G. Davis, *"I Have A Dream,"* op. cit., p. 38.
33. *The New York Times,* March 4, 1956. All through Rev. Dr. King's campaigns for justice, this daily had adopted a favourable attitude towards him while many newspapers and individuals, especially in the South, had denounced him.
34. L.G. Davis, *"I Have A Dream," supra,* p. 38.

35. *The New York Times, Ibid.*, p. 41. Also many of its special Sunday editions carried full reports and interesting reviews on the activities of Rev. Dr. King and those of other black leaders.
36. *Ibid.*, pp. 40-42. The frustrated Afro-American passengers had no other alternative prevailing conditions no matter how harsh the situation had been. Related accounts are given in Louis Lomax, "*The Negro Revolt,*" (New York: Harper and Row, 1962). Especially chapters 3 and 5. Also in Edward Preston, "*Martin Luther King, Jr., Fighter For Freedom,*" (New York: Double Day, 1969).
37. *The New York Times,* March 4, 1956, p. 40.
38. *Ibid.*, p. 52. Other related information in L.D. Reddick, "Crusader Without Violence," (Harper and Brothers, 1959).
39. Lerone Bennett, Jr., "*What Manner Of Man,*" (Chicago: Johnson Publishing Co., 1964), p. 77.
40. *The New York Times,* March 4, 1956.
41. Montgomery Advertiser, December 3, 1956, pp. 21-22.
42. *The New York Times,* March 4, 1956, p. 48. Mrs. Parks appeared in court and was fined for violating the bus segregation laws in Montgomery. Today, thousands of people, crossing colour barrier, remember her as a key figure in starting the bus boycott. She had been a great source of inspiration to the Afro-Americans in their strenuous efforts for justice. Her bold refusal to give up her seat received wide publicity and was followed the year-long non-violent boycott under the leadership of Rev. Dr. King who championed the cause of the black people.
43. *Ibid.*, p. 18.
44. The fundamental reasons for the marches and demonstrations are narrated in Doris Saunders, "*The Day They Marched.*" (Chicago: Johnson and Co., 1963). "*In Stride Toward Freedom*". Rev. Dr. King also described the ordeal faced by the Afro-Americans in Selma and Albany (State of Georgia).
45. *The New York Times,* March 4, 1956, p. 11.
46. *Ibid.*, p. 14.
47. For a brief historical study of colonial America and race relations, please see Thomas Pearce Bailey, "*Orthodoxy in the South,*" (New York: The Star Publishing Company, 1914).
48. *The New York Times,* News of the Week in Review, p. 6E.
49. "*Stride Toward Freedom,*" op. cit., p. 52.
50. Jefferson Davis (1908-1889) had served as president of the Confederate States of America during the Civil War. He was also

known as the man who "symbolized the solemn convictions and .tragic fortunes of millions of men." Davis became interested in politics in 1843, winning a seat as a Democrat in the U.S. House of Representatives in 1845. *The World Book-American Encyclopedia,* Vol. 4, pp. 42-43.

51. *The New York Times,* December 16, 1956, p. 32.
52. *Ibid.*
53. *Ibid.*, March 4, 1956. The anti-integrationist sentiments had become the cherished tradition of thousands of white-skinned people. About ten thousand men and women jammed the City Coliseum in Montgomery to hear Senator James O. Eastman of Mississippi deliver an emotional and feverish oration in support of such aspirations. Actions of such individuals could be described as pouring oil on fire and in the absence of such support the segregationists might not have put up such fierce resistance.
54. *"Stride Toward Freedom,"* op. cit., p. 77.
55. *The Naw York Times,* December 16, 1956.
56. *Ibid.*, March 4, 1956, p. 22. The favourable attitude in the media, mainly the result of Rev. Dr. King's emphasis on the Gandhian philosophy of *ahimsa,* was highly instrumental in the recognition of his methods for justice. In America it was a novel concept in the sense that no one before him and applied it on a mass scale.
57. *Ibid.*, April 3, 1956.
58. *Ibid.*, December 2, 1956, p. 18. By this time, Rev. Dr. King's burgeoning renown had become well known in the United States and in many parts of the world. For a descriptive account of his non-violent activities, please see William Robert Miller, *"Martin Luther King, Jr., His Life, Martyrdom and Meaning for the world,"* (New York: Weybright & Talley, 1968).
59. *Ibid.*, March 21, 1956. p. 1.
60. *"Stride Toward Freedom,"* op. cit., Rev. Dr. King's philosophy of non-violence is also vividly described in William Robert Miller, "*Won-violence: A Christian Interpretation,*" (New York: Schocken, 1966).
61. *"Stride Toward Freedom."* op. cit., p. 80.
62. *Ibid.*, The total number of vehicles was impressive. When the boycott ended, there were 300 private cars and twenty station wagons. The vehicles were lent to the MIA by churches and Afro-American groups from different parts of the country to express solidarity with their brethren struggling for justice. The donations helped the MIA run the successful car pools in Montgomery.

63. *The New York Times,* December 16, 1956, p. 14.
64. *Ibid.*, p. 48.
65. *"Stride Toward Freedom"*, p. 135. Rev. Dr. King had entertained serious concern about the safety of his family while he was imprisoned for one reason or another. He had made provisions for the welfare of family and explained to his daughter's frequent enquiries that someone had to work better to the condition of the Afro-Americans. Further details are provided in J.M. Washington, *"A Testament of Hope: The Essential Writings of Martin Luther King,"* op. cit., p. 140.
66. The dynamite was thrown into the front lawn of the harvester E.D. Nixon, who was a member of the Montgomery Improvement Association. Such violent acts had created fear in the minds of people.
67. *"Stride Toward Freedom,"* p. 140.
68. David L. Lewis, *"King: A Critical Biography,"* op. cit, p. 96.
69. *Ibid.*
70. Rev. Dr. King believed that non-violence is a method that impresses and inspires all people struggling for justice and freedom. Gad grant that says we wage the struggle with dignity and discipline. May all who suffer oppression in this world reject the self-defeating method of retaliatory violence and choose the method that we seek to redeem." *Christian Century,* op. cit.
71. David L. Lewis, *"King A Critical Biography,"* p. 96.
72. *The New York Times,* December 16, 1956, Magazine Section, p. 50.
73. *Ibid.*
74. *"Stride Toward Freedom,"* p. 126.
75. Rev. Dr. King found that a jovial atmosphere prevailed in the jail. In his numerous encounters with the city authorities, he could easily rely on Fred Grey's 'expert legal counsel,' as he was effusive in his praise for Grey in *"Stride Toward Freedom."* Grey, an Afro-American, was a protestant minister and as such he was not drafted into the national army. As soon as his involvement with the civil rights movement was known, the Government changed its policy toward him on the spurious ground that the church had acquired a new pastor. (*New York Times,* August 7, 1956, p. 18). It may also been noted here that the Rev. Dr. King was highly skeptical of the motives of the sudden change in Government policy, which had clear racial overtones.

76. About his experience in prison, Rev. Dr. King recalled with obvious relish: "Rushing into the fingerprinting room, he (the prison official) said: 'King, you can go now', and before I could get half my coat on, he was ushering me out, released on my own bond."
77. *"Stride Toward Freedom,"* pp. 127-28.
78. *"House Divided,"* L. Lokos, p. 99.
79. *Ibid.*
80. *"Stride Toward Freedom,"* p. 217.
81. *Ibid.*
82. *"House Divided,"* As the indispensable solution, Rev. Dr. King endorsed non-violent resistance. His movement was to be non-violent, there would be no reliance on the use of physical force against the oppressors and there would be a willingness "to accept blows from the opponent, without striking back."
83. *"Stride Toward Freedom,"* p. 146.
84. *"House Divided,"* p. 83.
85. *Ibid.*
86. *"With this feeling of solidarity,"* Rev. Dr. King added, "I walked with the firm steps toward the rear of the jail. After I had received a number and had been finger printed, one of my church members paid my bond and I left for home .... In all, twenty-eight witnesses were brought to the stand by the defense." *"Stride Toward Freedom,"* pp. 146-47.
87. Mrs. Stella Brooks provided the most moving testimony. Her husband paid the fare, but the driver asked him to reboard the bus by the back door. There was no room in the rear section and Mr. Brooks said that he would rather walk if the driver would return the fare. The driver called the police. The police officer abused Mr. Brooks. Rev. Dr. King said: The policeman shot him. It happened so suddenly that everybody was dazed. Brooks died of his wounds." *"Stride Toward Freedom,"* pp. 147-48.
88. *Ibid.*, p. 147.
89. *Ibid.*, p. 148.
90. Rev. Dr. King had always urged his followers to refrain hm violence. When the porch of his house had been burned down, he asked the large group of followers to remain peaceful. "Now let's not become panicky. If you have weapons, take them home; if you do not have them, please do not seek to get them. We cannot solve this problem through retaliatory violence. We must meet violence with non-violence. **Remember the words of Jesus: "He who lives by the**

**sword will perish by the sword."** Similar views on non-violence can be found in the articles published in *Christian Century.*

91. In *"King: A Critical Biography,"* op. cit., p. 98.
92. *Ibid.*, In these views held by Rev. Dr. King, one finds a clear strain of the Gandhian thought and philosophy; non-compliance with the enemy's oppressive an evil laws calls for courage and a strong will.
93. *Ibid.*, p. 98.
94. *The New York Times,* October 14, 1956, Main Section, p. 48.
95. *Ibid.*, December 16, 1956. Magazine Section, p. 48.
96. *"House Divided,"* op. cit., p. 189.
97. *The New York Times,* December 24, 1956, p. 6.
98. *Ibid.*, Similar racial incidents are also described in Nathan Wright, Jr., *"Black Power and Urban Unrest,"* (New York: Hawthorne and Company, 1967). Police dealt with the demonstrators using clubs and water hoses.
99. *Ibid.*, December 30, 1956. The nation's attention was riveted to the violence which had erupted in Montgomery following the victory of the bus boycott by the Afro-Americans. The police imposed curfew.
100. *Ibid.*, January 10, 1957. The members of the racist organization. Ku Klux Klan (KKK) with their hooded faces staged counter-demonstrations against the Afro-Americans by burning wooden crosses, representing a normal practice during such protests by KKK. Its members lynched the Afro-Americans, besides setting fire to churches, schools and houses belonging to black people. It also opposed immigration from Asian and African countries. Today its power is on the wane.
101. *Time,* January 21, 1957.
102. *The New York Times,* February 2, 1956, p. 65.
103. *Ibid.*, December 7, 1956, p. 59.
104. *"I Have A Dream,"* L.G. Davis, p. 58. The need for equality and individual freedom during the bus boycott was perhaps best summed up by an elderly Afro-American lady: "I'm not walking for myself," she said, " I'm walking for my children and grandchildren." Another Afro-American said: "My feet are tired, but my mind is rested." Similar accounts are given in *"Black Rage,"* William L. Grier and M. Cobbs (New York: Basic Books, 1958) and also in *"Freedom Summer,"* Sally Belfrage (New York: Viking Press, 1965).
105. *"I Have A Dream."* p. 58. Although Rev. Dr. King did receive public recognition for his non-violent campaigns in the United States and

in several parts of the world much more than all Afro-American leaders combined, there was, nevertheless, opposition to him, including a few publications, which included *The States 'Rights Advocate* and *The Alabama Journal.* The criticism by individuals or publications did not deter him from continuing his campaigns for civil rights in Montgomery. The immediate cause of the boycott in Montgomery had been the humiliation of Mrs. Rosa Parks, her tired feet and her dauntless spirit. Rev. Dr. King and his followers seized that entirely unexpected opportunity to plunge into a year-long boycott with remarkable results. The anticlimax came when Rev. Dr. King rode the bus with a white-skinned by his side. In Montgomery, the chief architect of the peaceful campaign was minister seated an eminent Afro-American leader advocating Gandhian ideals providing leadership to a campaign composed of local residents determined to implement reforms for equality. The chief goal was to bring about a local solution to a local problem, but with global implications. The problem had been simmering for years. Rev. Dr. King related the steps he had adopted in Montgomery (and that was true of his other campaigns) which Thoreau describes in his *Essays On Civil Disobedience.* "From that moment on," Rev. Dr. King stated, "I conceived of our movement as an act of massive non-co-operation. From then on, I rarely used the word boycott." The boycott in Montgomery was not the first of its kind in the United States in the struggle of the Afro-Americans. Rev. Dr. King Theodore Jamison, a friend of Rev. Dr. King, had organized bus boycott in Baton Rouge, Louisiana, with a successful car pool, a precursor to the Montgomery boycott. Further details are given, *"The Non-violent Cross: A Theology of Revolution and Peace,"* James W. Douglas, (New York: Macmillan and Company, 1968) and James McBride Cobbs, *"Who Speaks for the South?"* (New York: Funk and Wagnalls, 1964). But for Rev. Dr. King's peaceful approach there would have been violent confrontations and the buses might have been burned down with dire consequences. "It is becoming clear," the civil rights leader prophesied even after the boycott, "That the Negro is in for a season of suffering." *"King: A Critical Biography,"* L. Lewis, op. cit, p. 85.

# CHAPTER-VIII

# NON-VIOLENCE IN BIRMINGHAM (The Tide of Change)

## ARTICLE -1

### (A) The Paramount Aspect

In the preceding chapter we noticed the peaceful results of the bus boycott in Montgomery and how it transformed Rev. Dr. King into America's paramount advocate of non-violence, proving as Gandhiji did that non-violence was a much better means than mass violence to achieve the desired end. This chapter would assess his campaign in Birmingham where the Afro-Americans had been subjected to the convulstive twists and turns of racial discrimination.

The non-violent struggle for racial equality in Birmingham, Alabama, was crucial in King's life as the stake was so high that its collapse would have proved disastrous. A debacle might have seriously abraded his non-violent crusade with its negative effects on its recognition by the Afro-American community as a weapon, especially at a time when served other black leaders preferred violent confrontation to end racism. Lerone Bennett, Jr., Rev. Dr. King's personal biographer, says:[1]

> ....a defeat in Birmingham would probably weaken his career and the non-violent crusade. King sent Walker and other SCLC aides to Birmingham secretly to recruit workers and to lay the groundwork for a crisis.

In order to gain a better insight into the implications of Rev. Dr. King's non-violent approach with its significance for Afro-Americans residing in Birmingham in particular and in the country in general, we ought to analyze the racist situation that had been in existence in

Birmingham. In the analysis we have to consider three main aspects as they are related to the historical process of this Southern city and its administrators operating behind the confined racist walls.

(A) From time immemorial Birmingham had earned notoriety for its virulent racist attitude with few parallels in other parts of the United States of America. "Bull" Conor, and others of the same venomous breed, had headed the city's police force. They had been highly prejudicial towards the black people resorting to the most malevolent methods to keep them under the roof of subservience with virtual impunity. In general the judiciary did nothing to ameliorate the situation, all the while remaining a patient witness to its own disgrace.

(B) The official impudence was but a reflection of the general attitude of the rest of the society towards Afro-Americans, who were despised, ill-treated, looked down and were subjugated to dire humiliation.

(C) Being a railroad terminus and an industrial hub of mining and mill town, Birmingham was known for dissension and violence with trigger happy individuals reigning supreme with a blatant disregard for law and order, justice and equality. Indiscriminate use of dynamite was comrnon.[2] Afro-Americans had been the hapless victims and since the thirties at least 50 bombings of their houses and buildings had occurred while none had been booked. The legal machinery stood by as a silent witness of its own dishonour resulting in deep undercurrents of discontent in the black population. The odious atmosphere had compelled a law enforcement agent to make the following stark observation:[3]

> Kids in the black county around Birmingham grow up knowing how to handle dynamite. And dynamite is readily available. So they know how to obtain if what to do with it. As a result, they're experts in hit-and-run dynamite raids.

In Birmingham, Afro-Americans were butchered *en masse* (The fate of the American Red Indians had been no better either). The appalling racial situation that prevailed in Birmingham had drawn the attention of many black leaders.[4] For instance, Roy Wilkins, a prominent Afro-American leader had clearly stated that Afro-Americans in Birmingham were extremely rough, arguing further that:[5]

> Negroes [in Alabama] are some of the roughest in the United States. If there is an incident there, I shudder to think what will happen, because they will no...the great rank and file of the 140,000 Negroes will not easily accede to the fine discipline of Dr. King.

It was true that Negroes in Alabama and elsewhere had resorted to violence out of sheer frustration as a result of years of fruitless struggle for justice. Nonetheless, violence is violence and it can in no way be justified. Violence is the spontaneous reaction when human dignity is trampled upon, but non-violent resistance calls for rigorous mental training and discipline. The sporadic violent reprisal carried out by the black community should not be equated with the persistent and calculated atrocities perpetuated by the white ruling class with no pretext to offer but the colour of the skin and a brutish attitude. Beyond the colour an aggressive attitude played a major role in the drama of racism as white-skinned people living in different parts of the globe did not start racist conflicts as in the United States. Hostile elements... factors... had conspired against the interests of Afro-Americans for upward social and economic mobility indicating one of the worst forms of injustice directed against a viable social group by another that extolled the virtues of human dignity to the extent of the Sermon on The Mount.

Thus, it is easy to understand that the task that awaited Rev. Dr. King in Birmingham was by no means an easy one; it was indeed a Herculean labour which called for a true Gandhian endurance and a spirit of sacrifice.

Encircled by the clouds of opposition from within and outside his circle of friends and colleagues, Rev. Dr. King stopped short of recruiting volunteers even from the cradle as one of his demonstrators in Birmingham was "no more than eight"[6] tagging along with her mother in a Birmingham protest rally. A large number of his demonstrators had been black teenagers who were encouraged to stay out of schools to demonstrate in full view of the public and television camera. A few years before, *The New York Times*, referring to a group of Freedom Riders remarked that "non-violence that deliberately provokes violence is a logical contradiction."[7] In his well-known work, *Why We Can't Wait*, Rev. Dr. King recalls with great exhilaration that the youngsters climbed over the gates of a school "'and ran toward freedom,' even though the headmaster had given firm order to lock up the gate to prevent the pupils from joining the march. "Looking back, it is clear that the introduction of Birmingham's children into the campaign was one of the wisest move we made."[8] *The New York Times* had a different perspective: "The presence of hundreds of children among the marchers made all these marches especially perilous adventures in actual brinkmanship."[9]

Although the marches and demonstration had remained peaceful, the obvious hazard was in the city's ferocious past with the ever-looming possibility that Birmingham's bloody racial history might repeat itself during the demonstrations. Yet, it was a foregone conclusion that Afro-Americans were in the throes of a struggle for equal rights and dignity as stated by Roy Wilkins, a close associate of Rev. Dr. King and one of the most moderates of all the civil rights leaders.

> The Negro in this country is engaged in a war for his rights, and for his status as a citizen of the country. It is, in this sense, literally a war.

### (B) The End of Novices

Assessing the difficult social situation in Birmingham, Lerone Bennet, observed that the Southern Christian Leadership Conference had recruited a large cadre of black students demanding assignment to the front lines of the non-violent movement. As a result of the American civil rights leader's previous non-violent attempts in the South, specifically in Montgomery, Afro-Americans in Birmingham were not novices in the non-violent ideology. Rev. Dr. King stated his goals stressing:[11]

> We require an army of captains and sergeants to fight the white man this summer. I want captains to march whole schools to jail after their graduation.

America's acclaimed civil rights leader left no doubt in comparing the serious developments in Birmingham to war when he stated that the road to the conquest of racism in Birmingham would be **the refusal by Afro-Americans "to be intimidated"**[12] by the white-skinned people further emphasizing that the victory depended on what he had strongly felt:[13]

> ...the indomitable spirit of Negroes to endure; their willingness to fill the jails; their ability to love their children and take them by the hand into the battle; to leave on that battlefield of **six murdered Negro children, I too suffer the grief and resist demoralization and provocation to violence.**

The view held by many people in Birmingham, including C.B. Hanson, the publisher of the Birmingham *Post Herald,* was in support of a rehabilitation of the city administration which had denied jobs, voting rights and access to proper housing to Afro-Americans. In the Birmingham campaign, Rev. Dr. King wanted to efface social injustice at its worst. How did the racist system operate? And who was responsible for the perpetuation of that system? We shall try to examine these questions now for a clear understanding of the problem as discriminatory laws had been at the root of the civil rights movement.

The problem was serious. Until April 1963, a three-man commission "shadow form" of Government existed in the city. The city's prominent leaders believed that it could not bring about a peaceful accord between the Afro-American community and others. The brazen refusal by the city government to meet the fair, and unquestionably democratic demands, of the Afro-American community had constituted the nucleus of the problem. T. Eugene "Bull" Connor, a segregationist par excellence and a "power, on the city commission for quarter of a century, was quite adamant in his antipathy to any compromise being forged with the Afro-American community. Rev. Dr. King was fully aware that as long as "Bull" Connor had remained in the halls of power, the chances of any improvement in the racial situation would be quite remote. Albert Boutwell, who held moderate views, had won mayoral election by a margin of 8,000 votes out of a total of 50,000 votes."[14] According to *The New York Times* the Afro-American vote was "decisive not only in the referendum... but also in the election of Mr. Boutwell."[15] Even so, Rev. Dr. King had never wavered in his decision against providing the mayor-elect with an opportunity to handle the city's taut racial atmosphere. Concerning that important problem, *The Birmingham News* stated the obvious:[16]

> Virtually the day after the election, when at least the road was open for a proper solution of the segregation problem, the Rev. Martin Luther King and several other outsiders, some of whom were frankly publicity seekers, came into Birmingham and started raising Hell.

Paradoxically, Albert Boutwell had garnered enough votes to take over the regions of the city administration, but he remained a nominal mayor while Connor, a born segregationist, had severely challenged Boutwell's legal claims to office leading to an unpredicatable situation in race relations, not to mention in the city administration. Birmingham had two mayors in April and early May 1963. It was like a man with two heads attached to the neck. Moreover, the city government had been led by the three previous city commissioners who were unwilling to give up power or even to effect changes in improving race relations. It was unquestionably a legal justice issue to be decided by the Supreme Court as a hearing had been set for May 16[17]. Until that time, Albert Boutwell remained a mayor devoid of any vestige of power. Until he was officially declared as the mayor, it was debatable that Boutwell, with his moderate learnings, could have introduced legally binding regulations in Birmingham.[18]

Rev. Dr. King, his aides and the residents of Birmingham were aware of all this. Although the American civil rights leader had scant regard for Mr. Boutwell for his public pronouncements, he did consider him a moderate as compared with Connor's hard line policies. Comparisons can be misleading, but we all get caught up in them. Rev. Dr. King emphasized that Afro-Americans were hopeful that "Connor would be thoroughly defeated"[19] and in such an eventuality "we would not have to deal with him"[20] [Connor]. In addition, he even held off the peaceful demonstrations based on the rationale that the move "might eventually have had the effect of helping Connor win"[21] the crucial election. It was common knowledge that the city's Afro-American community had treated Rev. Dr. King's decision to go into Birmingham with mixed emotions as he had made the decision against the advice of some of the black community leaders. But is there anything novel about opposition from within an organization? Didn't Gandhiji himself have to content with the voices of dissent? Even with such internal opposition wasn't Gandhiji highly efficacious in his campaigns? Some leaders have an unerring understanding of human nature, woefully lacking in their followers. Referring to the issue of Dr. King's decision to go into Birmingham without informing the city's Afro-American leaders. *The New York Times* editorialized:[22]

> Many prominent members of the Birmingham Negro community are known to have opposed a direct-action campaign at this time. They believe that the new administration should be given the opportunity to disclose its intentions.

### (C) A Racially Tormented City

Rev. Dr. King, by no means, was an uninvited guest in Birmingham since the invitation to visit the racially tormented city had come from none rather than Rev. Fred Shuttleworth, president of the Alabama Christian Movement for Human Rights, an affiliate of Rev. Dr. King's highly influential SCLC.[23] The followers of the American civil rights leader had decided to hold its annual convention in Birmingham and they had given considerable importance to joining hands with Rev. Dr. King Shuttleworth in the massive non-violent campaign in order to demonstrate their solidarity. At the same time, a number of Afro-Americans had sought the intervention by the Alabama Christian Movement for Human Rights to invalidate the city ordinance on racial integration at Birmingham's lunch counters as Afro-Americans in Birmingham and in other cities in the United States were not permitted to enter local restaurants.[24] Their children were denied admission into common playgrounds. In his book, *Why We Can't Waif?* Rev. Dr. King explains the main reasons for embarking on the movement without again waiting for the officials to adopt appropriate measures. His campaign in Birmingham, regardless of the voice of dissent, **was aimed at obtaining the basic constitutional right of individual freedom for Afro-Americans society by relying on the Gandhian ideals of non-violence and reconciliation with the opponents, who could only be transformed by the power of love.** Rev. Dr. King replete with humane spirit followed Gandhiji's footprints. You cannot change the colour of a person. But you can change the inequity against that person.

The SCLC had decided to hold its crucial annual convention in Birmingham any way while militant "Bull" Connor allegedly threatened to cancel licences of those merchants who supported the Afro-American agenda. He earned the notorious reputation of being the most implacable adversary of integration. Integration had been the legitimate goal of Rev. Dr. King's non-violent campaign. By then he had reached the inevitable conclusion that "we had no alternative but to go through with our proposed combined-action campaign"[25] as his signatures could be seen in the entire odyssey.

Rev. Dr. King who had thoroughly imbibed the Gandhian ideals, decided to organize peaceful demonstrations reminiscent of Gandhiji's call for similar campaigns in colonial India. In order to receive ample support for the epoch-making non-violent campaign, he sent confidential letters to NAACP, CORE, SNCC and the SRC in addition to maintaining correspondence with some seventy five leaders of the earlier Albany movement. He discussed plans with seventy-five prominent New Yorkers including unofficial representatives from the office of the late Governor Nelson Rockefeller,[26] who had genuine sympathy for the Afro-American cause.

Rev. Dr. King had committed hundreds of Afro-American volunteers to brave the outgoing rabidly anti-integrationist city administrator. His refusal to wait for the decidedly moderate mayor to be confirmed as mayor and his unwillingness to talk with the leaders of the Afro-American community in Birmingham had the ingredients of a recipe for a much larger objective than was the case in the previous campaigns. The peaceful Birmingham struggle was a preface. What was his ultimate aim? Rev. Dr. King's eyes were set on an unprecedented Civil Rights Act meant to improve the status of his people even when he had been told by the President of the United States that Afro-Americans did not require legal assurance to safeguard their rights and prerogatives. In January 1963, Rev. Dr. King blurted out.[27]

> High government officials here in Washington were telling me that we did not need civil rights legislation. Even President John Kennedy was saying that.

The stage was set. The peaceful struggle in Birmingham began in earnest and developments had captured the headlines in the media. President John F. Kennedy wanted the Congress to enact three pieces of legislation: (i) relating to voting rights; (ii) on school desegregation; and (iii) for the Civil Rights Commission. President Kennedy sent a message to the Congress on the civil rights including equal access to jobs for Afro-Americans. The brick walls of opposition in Birmingham slowly began to crumble as though they were hit by cyclone. The President made the following recommendations:[28]

> ...that the Congress stay in session this year until it has enacted—preferably as a single omnibus bill—the most responsible, reasonable and urgently required solutions to this problem for which solutions should be acceptable to all fair-minded men. This would be known as the Civil Rights Act of 1963 and would include in addition to the aforementioned provisions on voting rights and the Civil Rights Commission additional titles on public accommodations, employment, federally assisted programs, a Community Relations Service and education.

## ARTICLE -2

### (A) A Silver Platter

Physically, Rev. Dr. King was in Birmingham, but his non-violent mind and ideas were fixed on the White House, hungry for justice for the Afro-Americans. As a deft civil rights leader, he was armed with sufficient knowledge that "Bull Connor's uncompromising stance would play right into his two hands. He was waiting for a crisis to precipitate. An ideal opportunity presented itself on a silver platter to Rev. Dr. King. The well-known Montgomery pastor and the advocate of *ahimsa* steadfastly adhered to the Gandhian ideal of non-violence in his campaign in Birmingham, which sowed the needs of the historic Civil Rights Act and "Bull" Connor, had been its unwitting father. "The civil rights movement," according to John F. Kennedy, "owes Bull Connor as much as it owes Abraham Lincoln."[29] The apparent contradiction implicit in that assertion was that while Lincoln had vehemently supported the cause of the Afro-Americans, Connor had opposed it tooth and nail, resulting in a final confrontation and victory, auguring a new era in American's socio-political history. On April 3, 1963, Rev. Dr. King inaugurated the Birmingham campaign a veritably non-violent resistance against unjust laws, with his unbending declaration:"[30]

> Pharaoh lets God's people go i.e., until the city established fair practices, formed a biracial committee, and desegregated facilities in downtown stores.

Since he was preoccupied with activities behind the scene to muster wide support, he was unable to throw himself into the struggle for a full week. Although the campaign had had a slow beginning, it soon gathered momentum and 35 demonstrators courted arrest[31] while thousands flooded the streets clamouring for justice. On April 6, 1963, demonstrators or Satyagrahis peacefully marching towards the City Hall, were stopped three blocks from their ultimate destination. Forty-two Afro-Americans were arrested and charged with parading without obtaining a permit.[32]

The Afro-Americans had tasted the bitter fruits of racial discrimination in housing and jobs in Birmingham for years so much so that Rev. Dr. King had been forced to act even in defiance of some of leaders in the Afro-American community and also against the advice of the Federal Department of Justice. In his previous public pronouncements he had made it clear that non-violence does not presuppose the acceptance of unjust laws and that the defiance of such laws does not mean animosity towards the law makers. As the campaign began to accelerate on all cylinders, the general tide of resentment against Rev. Dr. King's alleged obstinacy began to ebb away. *The New York Times* reported:[33]

> Some Negro leaders were sad to feel that the city's entire Negro population of 1,50,000 had now been summoned, whether they liked it or not.

True to the spirit of the philosophy of Gandhian non-violence, Rev. Dr. King added a new chapter to the emerging history of America's civil disobedience campaign. He brought down two birds (maybe three) in one shot. He upheld the basic human right in peacefully challenging unjust laws and awakened the judiciary with a rude shock from the overdose of lethargy that precipitated the crisis. Rev. Dr. King succeeded in bringing into focus the crucial fact that an indolent judiciary is as much culpable as insolvent legislature or an indolent executive. A judicial injunction barring a peaceful protest was tantamount to abetting the perpetration of injustice. The volunteers defied the injunction and picketed the department stores that had refused to hire the services of the Afro-Americans.

Rev. Dr. King, the living symbol of the Gandhian philosophy in the Untied States, was arrested in Birmingham for violating the court injunction and for leading a non-violent march of his Afro-American followers towards the city's business area. That was his thirteenth arrest and he courted it without offering resistance each time and each arrest increased his popularity.[34]

The popularity of America's Gandhian disciple was so great that more than a thousand demonstrators had joined the peaceful rally as it was also the first Birmingham march in which Rev. Dr. King had himself participated.[35] The Federal government refused to interfere harping on the technical ground as if Birmingham was part of a separate political entity. Assistant Attorney General Burk Marshall pointed out that "that federal government has no authority to take legal action and to intervene in the local affairs of Birmingham as the situation now stands."[36] The ambivalence in such a statement was obvious to an impartial observer of the American scene laws, which were interpreted to the advantage of the white-skinned people. Alabama was particularly notorious for its bigotry and partisan attitude and the judicial system had little credibility. To add insult to injury, the Federal Government often shirked its responsibility seeking the cover of legal technicalities. What is more? Even some black leaders were non-cooperative and felt that the campaign was "untimely and unwise."[37] A black clergyman urged:[38]

> ...our own Negro community to withdraw support from the demonstrators and to unite locally in working peacefully for a better Birmingham and a for a better future.

## (B) A Letter from the Jail

The clergyman's letter to the city's restive black community indicated a clear admission that racial harmony in the region was indeed a far cry.[39]

> When the rights are consistently denied, a cause should be pressed in the court and in negotiations among local leaders, and not in the streets. We appeal to both our white and Negro citizens to observe the principles of justice, order and common sense.

From Prison Rev. Dr. King sent a letter to the religious leaders, *Letter From A Birmingham Jail,* portraying the horrid racial situation that existed in Birmingham stating the cardinal truth: "Birmingham is probably the most thoroughly segregated city in the United States."[40] He strongly felt that the city made a mockery of the democratic ideals upheld by the United States. The letter, beyond any doubt, one of the most significant documents in the entire history of the American civil rights movement, a document which had been reprinted, excerpted and studied *ad infinitum* in religious as well as scholarly publications (Appendix-9).

It may be noted as a point of contrast that while Gandhiji's struggle was directed against an alien colonial tyranny, Rev. Dr. King had a more subtle and sensitive role as his opponents were a segment of his own misguided countrymen. They unscrupulously denied an ethnic group even the basic human rights. Gandhiji was trying to attain freedom from colonialism. Rev. Dr. King was trying to freedom from racism. The champion of American civil rights movement had no illusions about the challenges ahead. His letter explains:[41]

> The main purpose of our direct-action program is to create a situation so crisis-packed that it will inevitably open doors to further negotiations in a peaceful and just manner.

He had solid reason not to wait:[42]

> I have hope that Mr. Boutwell will be reasonable enough to see the futility of massive resistance to desegregation. But he will not see this without pressure from hundreds of devotees of civil rights in our country.

As an experienced civil rights leader and as a person who had a deep knowledge of the country's racial climate, Rev. Dr. King knew of the subtle aspects of "the white moderate who is more committed to 'order' than] justice."[43] He stated:[44]

> I have almost reached the regrettable conclusion that the Negro's great stumbling block in his stride toward freedom is not the White Citizen's Council or the Ku Klux Manner, but the white moderate who is more devoted to 'order' than justice; who prefers a negative peace which is the absence of tension to a positive peace, which is the presence of justice.

It was but an exercise in futility.[45]

> I agree with you in the goal you seek, but I cannot agree with your methods of direct action; who peternistically believes that he can set the timetables for another man's freedom.

Rev. Dr. King would not plod the violent route of brute force for freedom and justice, for violence invited devastating retribution and he had no intention of raising the spectre of force. He pointed out that if the non-violent principles "had not emerged, by now many streets in the South would, I am convinced, be flowing with blood";[46] arguing further that a "few members of the oppressor race can understand the deep groans and passionate yearnings of the oppressed race."[47] Gandhian vision was an untested factor in the United States and Dr. King was bent on proving its effectiveness in The New World, for he more than anyone else in the United States was convinced of the overwhelming power of non-violence anywhere and at any time.

He was strongly impelled by the hopeful vision of applying non-violence in Birmingham, even taking into account the chances of scattered outbursts of Afro-American violence. Violence did erupt outside Birmingham prison gates in the course of a protest march against the summary arrest and detention of a demonstrator for hurling stones at a policeman. Such stray instances could not be prevented in any organized resistance, and at times they ran out of gear and mob frenzy was difficult to contain despite the best efforts of the noblest leader.

### (C) The Solemn Pledge

If Rev. Dr. King had not refused the bail, he would have been released from prison on the first day of imprisonment; but his refusal to do so had been the result of the earlier pledge not to pay money to win freedom. On April 26, 1963, the court found him guilty of contempt of the Circuit Court injunction prohibiting him from organizing demonstrations, peaceful or otherwise. The penalty for his recalcitrant action was five days in jail and a fine of $50.[48] He was permitted to remain at liberty, pending appeal to the State Supreme Court (High Court).[49] Meanwhile, the two city administrations in Birmingham, waning against each other, had buried their wide differences of views, joined hands and refused the requests by the Afro-American society to organize non-violent protest marches, but undaunted by the decision of the city fathers, countless Afro-American people, many in their teens, defying the law marched through the Birmingham streets. During the demonstrations, 500 persons were arrested[50] and the entire nation stood witness to a grisly sweep of choler, as the swirling smoke of racial bitterness was visible all over Birmingham plunging the city into darkness. Nobody could easily forget May 3, 1963 when "Bull" Connor who had given assurance of ordered the use of fire hoses, ferocious dogs and clubs to break up a gathering of peaceful demonstrators. The move had inflamed the feelings of many people, especially when the riot squad and police dogs attacked young Afro-American volunteers holding hands together under the pelting spray. Rev. Wyatt Tee Walker, Rev. Dr. King's partner in peace, offers a portrayal of the ghastly episode:[51]

> ... they'd [police] been saying, 'turn the water hose on, turn the water hose on, turn the water hose on.' Then somebody threw a brick, and they started turning them on. So, they just danced and played in the spray. This famous picture of them holding hands, it was just a frolic, they'd get up and run back, and it would slide them along the pavement.

The serious nature of the racial dilemma facing Birmingham at the height of Rev. Dr. King's non-violent struggle drew the attention of Attorney General Robert Kennedy who issued warning from Washington that "a deep turmoil" would be the unavoidable result of the denial of equal rights to the Afro-American, who has become restive. After making the public pronouncement, Robert Kennedy, in a circuitous manner, called on Rev. Dr. King and the black leadership to exercise their influence to end the racial saga by pointing out that "for the sake of everyone,"[52] a remedy could be found in resolving the problem, but not "in the streets."[53]

How did Dr. King react? He strengthened his campaign rather than halt it as Gandhiji had done under analogous circumstances when the British had made overtures under the pretext of resolving an emerging crisis. Firemen were in full force turning water hoses on Afro-American demonstrators some of whom were gristle steelworkers who had stormed the city's main parts. When Dr. King felt: that the movement might slip into violence he decided to call off further protest marches demonstrating his exeeme abhorrence to violence when he saw knives and pistols being openly carried by several people.[54] He wanted to prevent the head on collision of the locomotives in the middle of the night. In three days well over 1,100 arrests of adults and juveniles[55] were made in Birmingham, many not older than 10 and 12 years of age as a tornado of fury had swept the city from one end to the other.[56]

## ARTICLE -3

### (A) Defying the Unjust Law

A determined Rev. Dr. King would not just call off the peaceful demonstration and keep the kettle boiling in Birmingham he reminded his followers: "Today," he declared, "was D-day. Tomorrow will be double D-day."[57] (D-day was a reference to the allied invasion of

Normandy, France, to end the German occupation of France. D-day marked a turning point in the last war and the term has received great currency all over America and Europe). The Afro-American educational institutions, as expected, were in the forefront of the defiance as only 87 students were present as against 1,339 who were absent in one school. A leaflet distributed by the black volunteers urged the students: "Fight for freedom first, then go to school."[58] Black people, who had not even heard of Gandhiji and Thoreau, were now keenly aware of the implications of the term freedom.[59] Freedom is to the mind of man as light is to his eyes. *Hemld Tribune* made the following comment on "a majestic possibility in the Negroes' progress," pointing out:[60]

> Ironically, Birmingham seemed on the verge of new era when Dr. King moved in on it as his proper target...There was an air of optimism that harmonious racial progress was about to be made.

Five weeks into the Birmingham imbroglio, a consensus was evolving with the president, the nation's Attorney General and the Congress engaged in lengthy negotiations to work out an accord ushering in a series of fundamental changes in Birmingham's racial landscape. We shall now make an impassionate analysis of the proposed changes in the order of their importance:[61]

(i) Promotion and hiring of Negroes on a non-discriminatory basis in stores and industries, hiring of Negro clerks and within 60 days by the stores, and appointment of a private fair employment committee.

(ii) Desegregation of lunch counters, rest rooms (toilets), fitting rooms and drinking fountains in large downtown department and variety stores within the next 90 days.

(iii) Establishment of a bilateral committee within two weeks.

(iv) The release of jailed Negro demonstrators on bond or on personal cognizance.

Although the accord had symbolized an optimistic development in healing the wounds of the past, its terms had fallen short of Rev. Dr. King's original objectives as the most serious shortcoming, from the Afro-American vantage point, was that the agreement was far from obligating the Government officials to make any serious commitment to it. The agreement was between Rev. Dr. King and the civic and business leaders who had little executive authority. Neither the mayor nor the city council was bound by the terms of the accord. Furthermore, the Chief of Police threatened that "unless the demonstrations were called off and order restored, he would be forced to declare martial law in the city." But the accord to the extent that it went, was a victory for the black people as they proved a force to be reckoned with in weathering the racial storm.

### (B) A Pilgrimage for Harmony

The protocol of the accord called for the release on nominal bail of hundreds of black demonstrators who were proud of their activism for the much-awaited justice. But the settlement received an immediate set-back when some infuriated racists set fire to the home of an integrationist leader and some Afro-American motels triggering violent response from the black people who poured into the streets engaging in pitched battles with the police. Rev. Dr. King conducted a pilgrimage to soothe the frayed nerves of the demonstrators with an impassionate plea to abjure violence as non-violence was vital to the success of their avowed mission of harmony in Birmingham.[63]

The crisis in Birmingham was so ominous that in 1963 the attention of the entire country was focused on Birmingham and Rev. Dr. King, who spent laborious days to achieve an equitable solution to the problem. When the researcher travelled to Birmingham in preparation for the thesis, he found a strife-torn city. In 1963, 963 demonstrations had taken place in the racially tormented Birmingham and its vicinity resulting in the arrests of 25,000 civil rights demonstrators one of whom was Rev. Dr. King himself.[64] The Southern city of Birmingham created the impression that great changes were in the offing.

President John F. Kennedy, in a nationwide television address, emphasized that the events in "Birmingham and elsewhere have increased the cries for equality,"[65] and pointed out that "no city or state or legislative body can prudently choose to ignore them,"[66] calling the events "the fires of frustration,"[67] crying for "legal remedies".[68] He added:[69]

> The fires of frustration and discord are burning in every city, North and South, where legal remedies are not at hand and redress is sought in the streets m demonstration, parades and protests which create tension and threaten violence and threaten lives. We face, therefore, a moral crisis as a country and as a people. It cannot be met by repressive police force.

He took the issue with all the seriousness that it deserved and referred to the need for Congress for an antidote.[70]

> It [protest] cannot be left to increased demonstrations in the streets. It cannot be quitted by token moves or talk. It is time to act in the Congress, in your state and local legislative bodies, and above all, in all our daily lives.

He decided to send a message to the Congress urging for the promulgation of a statute, which[71] came to be known as the Civil Right Act of 1963. The historic initiative on the part of John F. Kennedy who, more than any other person, was prompted by the developments in Birmingham spearheaded so cleverly by Rev. Dr. King. "The Freedom Fighter" rose in prestige and influence to a degree that Washington almost literally conceded the wisdom in his non-violent exhortations to resolve an issue that had been tearing up the country. Kennedy was convinced.[72]

**Gandhiji and Rev. Dr. King and King Centre (Main Entrance), Atlanta**

> There have been increasing public demonstrations of resentment directed against this kind of discrimination demonstrations which too often breed tension and violence in society.

Kennedy made it clear that the Central Government had to act firmly to end racial strife in a nation where states enjoyed vast powers. He stated:[73]

> Only the Federal Government, it is clear, can make these demonstrations unnecessary by providing peaceful remedies for the grievances which set them off with serious social and political consequences.

What was the result of the initiative taken by the Central Government? Did it put an end to racial discrimination? How did the rest of the society react to the changes? We shall try to examine these important questions.

First, considerable pressure was put on school boards in Birmingham and on those in other parts of Alabama with the positive result that schools were reopened and subsequently integrated, a phenomenon that had been thither to non-existent. Afro-Americans were jubilant. The white society was not jubilant. The white-skinned students took out massive counter-demonstrations in which a bomb blast occurred. The Federal action touched off further racial violence resulting in the murder of two Afro-American youth. Rev. Dr. King's Southern Christian Leadership Conference gave serious consideration to a national civil disobedience campaign. Dissatisfied by the white resistance America's civil rights leader demanded that President Kennedy send in the army "to take over the city and run it."[74]

In order to end the crisis in the city, the president appointed a two-member committee in a serious effort to close the ever-widening gulf between the two rival groups. Rev. Dr. King had warned of reviving his campaigns unless the city authorities had acceded to the legitimate demands of recruiting black policemen. Ninety prominent whites requested the mayor to appoint an Afro-American policeman and in March 1966 was the first black person seen in a police cruise car in Birmingham. In his study tour of the South the researcher, three decades later, found several Afro-American policemen on duty in Birmingham and elsewhere thanks to the persistent efforts of Rev. Dr. King. "I am a proud police officer today with opportunities for promotion," an Afro-American in his thirties told me. "My father couldn't even think of becoming a policeman or of holding any important job in Birmingham." Many expressed the view that the non-violent path of Rev. Dr. King had been instrumental in their new profile in society resulting in a spring of hope. But the researcher could not help feeling a pang of pain at the sight of the charred images of racial antagonism. The ghastly remains of Afro-American churches, schools and homes victims of white onslaught can still be seen in several parts of Alabama, a slur on human dignity.

### (C) An Icon of Peace

Birmingham had served its objectives for Rev. Dr. King and his Gandhian non-violent movement which had received a new seal of public recognition in the United States and one that, among other considerations, had helped him win the Nobel Prize for peace. The effectiveness of his campaign grounded in Gandhian ideology of *ahimsa* had even helped him tide over the temporary smudge of defeat in Albany. Moreover, the success in Birmingham had instantly turned him into an icon of peace and reconciliation particularly in view of the fact that other black leaders had been fomenting discord in the still fertile ground of racial enmity and hatred.

Rev. Dr. King's achievement to remove racial hatred was colossal as he had been, more than any one else, the presiding genius for the implementation of the epoch-making Civil Rights Act notwithstanding the fact that John F. Kennedy was its chief architect. The Afro-American community, and for that matter, any cross-section of aggrieved human race, owed not a little to this stalwart of human dignity for having unlocked through disheartening gloom and despondence doors of hope and expectation for an equitable world order based on Gandhian non-violence.

A clarion call for a new social order to end racial struggle was heard when an August 28, 1963 over 200,000 people, black, white and brown, amiably joined hands in the now famous march on Washington. The chief goal of the demonstration was the enactment of the public accommodations measure proposed by President Kennedy barring discrimination in hiring practices. The discriminatory practices, widespread in the United States, had long kept Afro-Americans economically and educationally in the back rows of the society.

Unexpectedly, Rev. Dr. King's great dreams of social justice and harmony turned sour when a hopeless zealot fired a volley of bullets on President Kennedy's life, vainly hoping to turn back the wheels of history. Despite the momentary set-back, Rev. Dr. King revitalized the non-violent struggle with peaceful demonstrations from coast to coast—from Los Angeles to Chicago, from Seattle to New York. In the view of everyone he lit up America's racial firmament with the bright lights of non-violence and reconciliation.

We have now studied the circumstance leading up to the dawn of the historic Civil Rights Act of 1964, a significant step in establishing equality in American society. Now we will try to assess its positive implications as far as Afro-Americans were concerned.

The Act was a feather in Rev. Dr. King's cap illuminating his non-violent efforts for injustice for Afro-Americans demonstrating the effectiveness of the Gandhian ideology in a far away land. The Civil Rights

Act, for the first time in the history of the nation, forbade discriminatory practices or refusal of service in public places on account of one's racial background or of chromatic consideration in finding rooms in hotels, restaurants, social clubs, gasoline (pumping) stations and amusement parks. It opened up new windows of opportunities to Afro-Americans to seek employment and to be treated with respect and dignity. There must be no discrimination on the basis of castle, creed, sex or colour. It was a non-violent conquest.

The Civil Rights Act of 1964 was a landmark in race relations in the United States, giving credence to Rev. Dr. King's fundamental thesis that non-violent resistance was a puissant instrument for socio-political transformation. The victory of the movement was as much a glowing tribute to Gandhiji as to Dr. King, who was now absolutely convinced.[75]

> It is a method that challenges all people struggling for justice and freedom. **God grant that we wage the struggle with dignity and discipline.** May all who suffer oppression in this world reject the self-defeating method of retaliatory violence and choose the method that seeks to redeem. Through using this method wisely and courageously we would emerge from the bleak and desolate midnight of man's inhumanity to man into **the bright daybreak of freedom and justice.**

The search for truth was paramount in the life and activities of Rev. Dr. King as it was in the life of his teacher, Gandhiji. Both apostles of non-violence knew well that justice and freedom could not be won through hostility and pugnacity. The researcher could find signs of integration in the erstwhile segregated public life in Birmingham. This was a place where once violence was not only expected but accepted as well, but now there was social harmony and above all, a spirit of social reconciliation.

## SUMMARY

1. The denial of access to Afro-Americans to educational institutions and hotels; discrimination in hiring practices were rampant in Birmingham. Their complaints against such practices had failed to evoke any response from the authorities.
2. "Bull" Connor, the Mayor of Birmingham, was opposed to any move to grant equality to Afro-Americans in his extremely racist city which, according to Rev. Dr. King, was one of the worst in America.

3. Before he launched his non-violent campaign in Birmingham, Rev. Dr. King had faced a wall of opposition from his own people, but he decided to continue his struggle. Later, he received support from a number of prominent individuals in Birmingham.
4. Rev. Dr. King's recruits for his non-violent movement in Birmingham comprised a medley, some even as young as eight. Students were exhorted to fight for freedom "today" and to attend schools "tomorrow".
5. Rev. Dr. King's participation in Birmingham's struggle for justice had been greeted with mixed feelings by the black community. All were unanimous about the goal. The differences of view were about the methodology and the timing of the demonstrations.
6. The Afro-American civil rights leader inaugurated the Birmingham campaign on April 3, 1963; it lasted until the city officials had established fair hiring practices, formed a biracial committee and desegregated public facilities.
7. A month after the racial strife broke out in the city; President John F. Kennedy sent a special message to the Congress on civil rights and job opportunities for Afro-Americans.
8. The unrest in Birmingham and Rev. Dr. King's non-violent struggle in that Southern city had been pivotal in President Kennedy's final decision to promulgate anti-segregation laws. The American civil rights leader was in Birmingham, but his both eyes were fixed on the White House for the enactment of further laws to improve the racial situation.
9. In Birmingham he was arrested for leading the non-violent demonstrations, his thirteenth arrest in life for the cause of racial justice.
10. He sent a reply from jail to the churchmen who had been critical of his methods. His answer, Letter from a Birmingham Jail, is one of the most famous documents pertaining to the civil rights movement.
11. Despite the emphasis Rev. Dr. King had placed on non-violent methods, violence erupted outside the prison in Birmingham.
12. The white set fire to Afro-American churches, schools and houses while a number of black demonstrators, who had no commitment to non-violent principles, retaliated.

13. Rev. Dr. King, the Afro-American community and the officials in Washington signed an agreement to bring an end to the crisis that had engulfed Birmingham. President John F. Kennedy's timely intervention helped the process of desegregation of lunch counters and hotels.
14. A basic stipulation of the agreement was to free hundreds of demonstrators on nominal bail.
15. The situation in Birmingham served its purpose. It turned Rev. Dr. King into a hero of great stature that no other Afro-American leader had attained in the United States. Gandhian non-violence had helped him to realize his objectives in Birmingham and in other cities.

## Notes and References

1. *"What Manner of Man,"* pp. 132-33. The importance of Rev. Dr. King's non-violent struggle in Birmingham was related to the birth of the historic Civil Rights Act removing discrimination faced by Afro-Americans in employment and housing. This and other related details are also described in Alan Grides, *'Equality in Ameracia,'* (New York: Oxford Press, 1963).
2. *The New York Times,* in News of the Week in Review, p. E-3, September 22, 1953.
3. *The Times,* September 27, 1963.
4. *U.S. News and World report,* September 30, 1963, p. 39. Another version of the struggle is provided in *"I have A ream?"* L.P. Davis, op. cit., pp. 128-32.
5. *The New York Times,* May 20, 1963, p. 21.
6. *"Why We Can't Wait?"* Martin Luther King, Jr., (New York: Harper and Row, 1963), p. 103.
7. *The New York Times,* May 26, 1961, p. 32.
8. *"Why We Can't Wait?" supra.,* p. 102. Rev. Dr. King's argument was valid the sense that it was time to take appropriate action in Birmingham and in other cities for the twin causes of freedom and equality for Afro-Americans. In Birmingham he had been told to wait for the negotiation to take its course. Please see chapters 2 and 3 of the same book.
9. *New York Times,* May 20, 1963, p. 21.
10. *"What Manner of Man?"* op. cit., p. 151.
11. *The New York Times,* May 11, 1963, p. 8.

12. *The Nation,* March 9,1964, p. 23.
13. *Ibid.*, p. 14. Many people in the United States, mostly Rev. Dr. King's critics, believed that while Birmingham was winding through its torturous path of racist attitudes with the inexorability of a Passion Play and that the American civil rights leader could have prevented many of the hardships. The criticism had no valid ground. The opponents of the non-violent struggle have often out forward such arguments in subtle attempts to put off the campaign for racial justice.
14. *Editor and Publisher,* 1, p. 12, May 18, and also in *The New York Times,* 17, 1, p. 22, March 16, 1963.
15. *The New York Times,* April 17, 1963, p. 22. Still another sceptical view had much to do with Rev. Dr. King's lack of will to give Boutwell an opportunity to deal with the city's mounting racial problem. The critics ignored the fact that Boutwell would not change his attitude without outside pressure.
16. *Editor and Publisher,* op. cit. p. 12.
17. *The New York Times,* May 9, 1963, p. 17. A power struggle had been raging within the city administration complicating the already cumbersome situation. Birmingham, for a brief span of time, had two mayors, one vying against the other, to regain power. Rev. Dr. King understood the difficult nature of the situation, but decided to start the campaign facing opposition from one of the mayors.
18. *Ibid.*, The events in Birmingham and those in Montgomery demonstrated the power of non-violence.
19. *Ibid.*
20. *Ibid.*, p. 50.
21. *Ibid.*, p. 151. Rev. Dr. King wrote *"Why We Can't Wait?"* with the focus on the Birmingham campaign. He waited for "Bull" Connor's defeat at the polls.
22. *The New York Times,* April 6, 1963, p. 20. One of the Afro-American leaders willing to make the opposing views public was C. Herbert Oliver, Secretary of the Inter-Citizens Committee of Birmingham. Its members, eight Afro-American and two white-skinned ministers, had worked for the removal of the racial barriers in the city.
23. *"Why We can't Wait?"* op. cit., p. 45.
24. *Ibid.*, pp. 45-46.
25. *Ibid.*, p. 47. Rev. Dr. King had decided to hold massive non-violent demonstrations irrespective of the winner in the mayoral election

and with that aim in view he was in correspondence with Afro-American organizations attempting for racial justice and equality in the United States.

26. *Ibid.*, p. 51.
27. *The New York Times*, November 7, 1963. p. 30. After the Birmingham campaign had begun, it was necessary for the civil rights advocate to spend 7-8 days racing from meeting to meeting chiefly to receive support from Afro-American community leaders who had remained cool to the idea. Further details in "What Manner of Man?" op. cit.
28. *Public Papers of the Presidents of the United States: John F. Kennedy, 1963*," (Washington, D.C. U.S. Government Printing Office, 1964), pp. 483-84.
29. "*What Manner of Man?*" op. cit., p. 151.
30. *Ibid.*, p. 132.
31. *The New York Times*, April 6, 1963, p. 20.
32. *Ibid.*, April 7, 1963. Rev. Shuttleworth had led the first demonstration in Birmingham and it was on the same day that the so-called Battle of Birmingham had begun drawing the attention from all over the United States. Other details in L.P. Davis, *"I Have A Dream."* op. cit., in Chapter 4.
33. *The New York Times*, April 11, 1963, p. 21.
34. *Ibid.*, April 13, 1963.
35. *Ibid.*
36. The black residents of Birmingham expected the Federal government to release Rev. Dr. King from jail. Burk Marshall, assistant Attorney General, had sombre news when he told newsmen: "the Federal Government has no authority to take legal action to intervene in Birmingham." *The New York Times*, April 14, 1963, p. 46.
37. *Ibid.*, April 14, 1963., p. 46.
38. *Ibid.*
39. "Why We Can't Wait?' op. cit., p. 87.
40. *Ibid.*
41. *Ibid.*
42. *Ibid.*, despite opposition against some of Rev. Dr. King's methods of action, he had received a flood of letters supporting his campaign. Lillian Smith, a Southern writer, had sent him two letters. "You should be surprised, I believe, to know," she wrote, "the strength of

the admiration of thousands of white southerners feel for what you are doing." In *"King: A Critical Biography,"* David L. Lewis, p. 97.

43. *"Why We Can'tWait?"* op. cit., p. 87.
44. *Ibid.*, p. 87.
45. *Ibid.*, p. 91.
46. *Ibid.*, p. 93. Rev. Dr. King, based on his own experience in the United States, had great understanding of the problems of the oppressed people in his own land of birth and in the vast regions of the world. From that perspective it is understandable why the removal of injustice of the oppressed, be they in his country or in other parts of the world, had been one of his main goals in life. Please see his own work, *"Stride Toward Freedom."*
47. *The New York Times,* April 27, 1963, p. 9.
48. *Ibid.*
49. *The New York Times,* May 1, 1963, p. 26. Also in Kenneth Clark, ed., *"The Negro Protest,"* (Boston: Beacon Press, 1963) and John Hope Franklin and Isidore Starr, eds. *"The Negro in The Twentieth Century America."* (New York: Vantage Press, 1966).
50. *The New York Post,* September 7, 1964, p. 14.
51. *The New York Times,* May 4, 1963, p. 1.
52. *Ibid.*, p. 8.
53. *The New York Times,* May 5, 1963. pp. 1 and 82.
54. *Ibid.*, p. 82. According to one reporter, the demonstrators were mostly young people and that Rev. Dr. King would not allow any let-up of his peaceful campaign for the momentum to keep going. For the reflections on the power of Afro-Americans, please see Charles E. Fager, *"White Reflections on Black Power."* (Grand Rapids, Michigan, 1967).
55. *The New York Times,* May 5, p. 82.
56. *Ibid.*, Richard B. Gregg analyses Rev. Dr. King's non-violent struggle in his detailed work, *"The Power of Non-violence,"* (New York: Schocken, 1965).
57. *The New York Times,* May 5, 1963, p. 82.
58. *The New York Herald Tribune,* May 9, 1963, p. 24.
59. *The New York Times,* May 11, 1963.
60. *Ibid.*, Negotiations marked the fourth major effort in the preceding five weeks to resolve Birmingham's racial crisis. The chief police officer reported that the local law enforcement agents had been "strained to the utmost of their capacity" in their attempts to control the widespread demonstrations which were reminiscent

of numerous public marches in India against the British who also could not contain the people in several parts of India.

61. *Ibid.*
62. *The New York Times,* May 14, 1963, p. 27. Rev. Dr. King's peaceful campaign had received considerable financial assistance from the United Steel Workers of America, the United Automobile Workers and the Industrial Union Department. They had raised a total of $ 160,000 for the success of his struggle. A woman in Switzerland sent Swiss Francs to finance the campaign.
63. *Negro Digest,* May 1964, p. 46.
64. *"Vital Speeches,"* July 1, 1964, p. 547.
65. *Ibid.*
66. Attorney General Robert F. Kennedy also held talks with Afro-American leaders on May 24, 1963. They had also urged President Kennedy to deliver an address or a series of addresses on the issue of Afro-American rights starting his "moral commitment" to equal rights. *The New York Times,* May 26, 1963, p. 59.
67. *"Vital Speeches,"* p. 147
68. *"Public Papers of the Presidents of the United States,"* op. cit., p. 484.
69. *Ibid.*, p. 486.
70. ibid., p. 488.
71. *The New York Times,* September 17, 1963, p. 25.
72. *Ibid.*, At the same time, moderate Afro-Americans in Birmingham moved to regain control in their community; some of them formed a "self-enforcement committee" to restrain efforts by individuals to speed up the pace of integration by unauthorized activities. Step by step, substantial progress was being made for integration and racial harmony in Birmingham. Rev. Dr. King was still determined to end the orgy of violence that would have been the inevitable result if his non-violent attempts had failed. Please see *"Stride Toward Freedom,"* op. cit., (New York: Harper and Row, 1986).
73. *Christian Century,* No. 74., op. cit., pp. 165-67.
74. *Ibid.*
75. *Ibid.* Rev. Dr. King amplified his views on non-violence. "Here non-violence comes in as the ultimate form of persuasion. It is the method, which seeks to implement the just law by appealing to the conscience of the great decent majority who through blindness, fear, pride or irrationality have allowed their consciences to sleep. The non-violent resisters can summarize their message in the following simple terms. We will take direct action against injustice

without waiting for other agencies to act. We will not obey unjust laws or submit to unjust practices. **We will do this peacefully, openly, cheerfully, because our aim is to persuade. We adopt the means of non-violence because our end is a community at peace with itself....** We will always be willing to talk and seek fair compromise, but we are ready to suffer when necessary and even risk our lives to become **witnesses to the truth as we see it,**" as Gandhiji stressed truth in his life. "*Stride Toward Freedom,*" (New York: 1986), p. 216.

# CHAPTER-IX

# SELMA: "GIVE US THE BALLOT"

## ARTICLE -1

### (A) The Problem of Franchise

Rev. Dr. King's abiding interest in the strength of the Afro-American ballots in Selma, Alabama, may be traced back to his singular success in the Montgomery and Birmingham. The right to franchise, fundamental to democracy, was denied to Afro-American society, making American democracy a travesty. Consequently, Rev. Dr. King's demand for the constitutional right to vote became the quintessential embodiment of his struggle in Selma culminating in the historic march from there to Montgomery. This chapter proposes to discuss Selma's fight for franchise, a fight for freedom. During the Prayer Pilgrimage of May 17, 1957, held in Washington, D.C., he had proclaimed:[1]

> **Give us the ballot and we will no longer plead—we will write the proper laws on the books. Give us the ballot and we will fill the legislatures with men of goodwill. Give us the ballot and we will get people judges who love mercy.**

In his public declarations Rev. Dr. King had underlined the importance of ballot papers and the formation of an orderly society by appealing to people in the upper reaches of the society: "Give us the ballot and we will transform the salient misdeeds of the bloodthirsty mobs into the calculated good deeds of orderly citizens."[2]

In his relentless search for justice and equality Rev. Dr. King "discovered" Selma, raised the flags of Gandhian ideology on its soil and guided by the struggle of a people who longed to breathe the air of freedom due mainly to the groundwork laid by the leaders of the SNCC.

The leaders, of the freedom fighters, had entrenched themselves in Selma lighting up the flames of a new awareness in the minds of their brethren.

The situation was far from being satisfactory concerning the attainment of his individual rights. Several black people were apathetic towards their acceptance in participating in the nation-building activities and even the nominal voting power they had was not fully utilized. The sleeping giant remained oblivious of its inherent strength. Bruce R. Galphin observes:[3]

> **...without the Negro vote in key states, John F. Kennedy would not now be wearing his paper-thin mantle of victory. Negros in Alabama, Mississippi and Texas gave him their support.**

He pointed out "Negroes themselves are in no small part to blame for their failure to realize their potential,"[4] adding:[5]

> **The net increase (between 1952 and 1961) is little more than 200,000. This is true even though more and more of the South's Negroes live in cities, where they encounter little or no official opposition to registering. One of the chief causes everywhere was general apathy.**

The fact that the voting drive everywhere had fallen short of the realistic objectives was a grievous source of concern to Rev. Dr. King[6] even though Selma and other Southern cities had a large pool of skilled and semi-skilled Afro-Americans, in addition to the "cooperation" of the county registrar.[7] Robert Kennedy, the Attorney General of the United States, had strongly subscribed to the view of Rev. Dr. King, that the ballot would be vital to the progress of Afro-Americans in the entire South. *The New York Times* reported:[8]

> **Many Students of the problem, including the Civil Rights Commission, have said that Negro apathy has accounted in part for the low registration figures and that the problem of the lack of interest had to be addressed for a better future.**

(Voter apathy is common in the United States, and not just among Afro-Americans. Many individuals refuse to register to vote since they have lost confidence in what they consider a corrupt political system or from a notion that their ballots would not make much difference on the decisions taken by the elected officials.)

Against this background Rev. Dr. King set himself to work zero in on Selma. He organized a march with the specific objective of rousing his people from their sloth. That only 40 per cent of the eligible black people had been registered to vote was a definite sign of the sleepiness and the sagging confidence in the system. It was imperative to create political consciousness among his people if they wanted to survive in Selma or in other parts of the nation. If individuals are not politically conscious, they will lose their political rights.

In Selma, as elsewhere, overt intimidation and coercive methods were frequently used to prevent Afro-Americans form exercising the franchise Selma, Rev. Dr. King thought, was the right place to launch the new agitation as it had a grim record of white resistance to Afro-American franchise.[9]

Thirty-two Afro-American school teachers who had tried in vain to register had been summarily dismissed from service.[10] John Lewis, then leader of SNCC, was arrested like a thief or a convicted felon for leading a non-violent march at the court-house.[11] Was that democracy? Where is equality? Where was fraternity? The segregationists considered equality to Afro-Americans as irrelevant as beauty in a dog catcher.

Three hundred Afro-Americans were arrested between September 15 and October 2, 1963. Harassment or not the SNCC brought hundreds of black people into the Dallas County court-house to register.[12] Sheriff Jim Clarke, who was not free from racial prejudices, forbade SNCC activists from providing food to those eagerly waiting in line for hours to register.

### (B) A Humanitarian Gesture

The SNCC field workers approached the demonstrators with food disregarding the prohibition. Howard Zinn, lecturer at an Afro-American college in Atlanta, describes the violent encounter that ensued "the next thing I saw was Chico Neblett, an SNCC volunteer, on the ground with troopers all around him."[13] He continues the moving description:[14]

> **They poked at him with clubs and sticks. I heard him cry out and saw his body jump convulsively again and again; they were jabbing at him with cattle prods. At the same time, others were also subject to different forms of physical abuse.**

As the photographers were taking pictures of the violent episode, the Major yelled, "get in front of those cameramen."[15] According to *The New York Times*, Afro-Americans lay down on the sidewalk when twelve heavily armed troopers surrounded the peaceful men, prodding them with night-sticks[16] after having them picked up from the streets.

Rev. Dr. King and Sheriff James Clarke had clashed in 1963 in Birmingham before the repressive measures in Selma.

The cataclysmic saga of repressive attitude in Selma was no longer typical of the South; it was a deep-seated and widespread phenomenon in the entire United States. The Afro-American voting registration in the South had doubled in 1964 after presidential election held in 1960.[17] Two million in 1964 as against the 1.1 million in 1960 with 90 per cent of them casting ballots for the late President Lyndon Johnson.[18] It was widely recognized that Afro-American ballots swung into the Johnson camp in several key Southern states to the detriment of Senator Barry Goldwater. The Civil Rights Act of 1964 had prohibited the registrars from applying different standards to Afro-Americans and other applicants and, from disqualifying individuals on the basis of inconsequential errors. A sixth-grade education was the basic criterion of registration.

Rev. Dr. King was skeptical at best. He was too fastidious to be satisfied with subtle logistics and decided to go ahead with widespread demonstrations in Alabama and Mississippi "based on the right to vote",[19] stating that the landslide victory of President Lyndon B. Johnson should convince him that he had a "definite mandate from the American public" in favour of the black peoples' demand for political rights.

He elaborated his views:[20]

> **We hope that through this process, we can bring the necessary moral pressure to bear on the Federal government to get the Federal registrars appointed in these areas, as well as to get Federal marshals in these places to escort Negroes to the registration places, if necessary.**

An unprejudiced observer, who had followed Rev. Dr. King's non-violent campaigns in Birmingham[21] could hardly have failed to recognize the inescapable fact that he was wedded to Gandhian ideals throughout his public career.[22]

(i) Non-violent demonstrators go into the streets in order to exercise their constitutional rights and privileges.
(ii) American citizens of conscience in the interest of decency demand Federal intervention and the necessary legislation.
(iii) Racists resist by unleashing violence against the non-violent demonstrators.
(iv) The Administration, under public pressure, intervenes promptly and effectively with appropriate legislation and its speedy implementation.

America's renowned 'Satyagrahi' required a violent response to demonstrate the power of non-violence and gently feel the soul of the antagonist who could be converted by love and non-violence. Violence on the part of the opponent gave both Gandhiji and Rev. Dr. King an opportunity to prove the strength of non-violence and to prevent violence.

Wilson Baker, Public Safety Director of Selma and a moderate on racial issues, had issued a warning as early as January 1964, on the eve of the peaceful demonstration. Those whites who might foment a crisis would be barred from the area[23] and to prove his point he arrested two youth who had allegedly set off tear-gas bombs in the city's Afro-American residential areas. During Rev. Dr. King's first month in the racially afflicted Selma, he purposefully registered as an Afro-American guest, staying in a hotel built by the slaves over a century ago.[24] A member of the now-defunct segregationist National States Party kicked and punched Rev. Dr. King who, in true Gandhian spirit, did not retaliate. The assailant was fined $100, and sentenced to 60 days at hard labour for battery and disturbing the peace.[25]

On January 3, 1965, the battle lines between the officials and the civil rights leaders under the guidance of Rev. Dr. King had been drawn. He had informed a gathering of 700 cheering demonstrators that he would assist their "march on the ballot boxes"[26] from one end of Alabama to the other. The civil rights leader had openly declared that if the authorities "refuse to register strong appeals would be made to the upper echelons of the administration":[28]

> **If they refuse to register us, we will appeal to Governor Wallace, we will appeal to the Legislature. We will continue our attempts until our just goals are met for the good of our people.**

Rev. Dr. King brought the point home by eloquently declaring that he was been on taking the problem of voting rights for his people to the nation's highest judicial body by organizing non-violent demonstrators and by pointing out:[29]

> If the Legislature doesn't listen, wed dramatize the situation, and seek to arouse the Federal government by marching by the thousands to the places of registration. We know in the end we will succeed because our cause is just.

## (C) Complex Circumstances

Rev. Dr. King asked his followers to make the supreme sacrifice and "to go to jail by the thousands."[30] As a result of his non-violent methods and the wide interest he had created in the country, it was increasingly difficult to have the demonstrators handcuffed, much less victimized by violence as was the common practice in the yester-year. The Southern sheriffs, thanks in part to the American civil rights leader's persistent refusal to be provoked, were less preposterous. They showed little interest in filling the prisons with innocuous protestors who were ready to go to jail for freedom in the future. Filling the jails with non-violent demonstrators was much easier than sending them off free. *The New York Times* made the following comments on Selma's altering racial landscape:[31]

> **Dr. King found in Selma not the monolithic community that it had been in 1963. A new leadership had emerged, committed to a reluctant compliance with the Civil Rights Law of 1964 and a policy of making the minimum change necessary to preserve the peace and reputation of the community.**

Meanwhile, the new leadership in Selma had informed Sheriff Clarke to prevent mass arrest, specifically that of Rev. Dr. King in order to avoid the escalation of the explosive racial situation. Let us now analyze the progress of the non-violent struggle and its consequences.

The struggle began to take final shape. The peaceful struggle, after months of preparation, began at a slow pace just as in Birmingham in early January. 62 Afro-Americans were arrested for their brave refusal to return to a narrow path of the court-house which had been assigned to them[32] and on February 1, law enforcement agents did the great favour of arresting Rev. Dr. King along with 770 fellow Afro-Americans. Most of them were students for organizing a non-violent march in Selma without receiving an authentic permit.

The most salient aspect of the protest march was that it helped to draw the attention of the entire nation to the just and equitable demand of the black people for political rights. Rev. Dr. King was released on a bond. In the words of a reporter:[33]

> **"King now found it more dramatic to come out than to stay in." Rev. Dr. King like Gandhiji, becomes a prisoner of conscience, a prisoner for *ahimsa*.**

The non-violent march, drawing inspiration from Gandhiji's numerous non-violent marches in India, dealt a heavy blow to the policy of segregation in Selma. In Montgomery, Governor George Wallace,[34] a full-time racist, waisted no time sending troopers with trained dogs to halt nocturnal marches by the Afro-American demonstrators. A fully determined Rev. Dr. King responded to Governor George Wallace's order by calling for a non-violent demonstration to tear down the barriers to Afro-American voting rights,[35] making it clear that Afro-Americans had no intention of accepting the patently discriminatory laws.[36]

*The New York Times* observes:[37]

> **The Negroes rationale in holding night marches is to provoke the racist dement in white communities to show the wont. As a result, Negroes have often been attacked. There is no need for a repetition of such incidents.**

The national newspaper goes on to say that Afro-Americans and others "acknowledge that the risk of violence is heightened considerably after nightfall."[38] The first march took place on March 7, 1965. Although the demonstrators wanted it to be anything but violent, Alabama state troopers ripped through a large column of unarmed demonstrators using tear gas, whips and night-sticks to enforce Governor Wallace's order to crack down on the demonstrators. At least 17 black people were hospitalized while 40 demonstrators did require emergency treatment for tear gas effects and injuries sustained in the attack. The incident did not go unnoticed as the repression was widely condemned as a vile national spectacle. When violence is used against non-violent people, non-violence wins the heart of the people.

The government repression of the first march by the Afro-Americans to gain voting rights in a democratic country was abominable. The police action was the main theme of scathing editorial comments in the national media with the Newsweek portraying the ominous development as "an American tragedy"[39] while the *Alabama Journal* published an editorial on "the tragic dilemma:"[40]

> **We have stained the state and put the lie to its claims of peace and harmony given enough rope, as if they haven't already been supplied it, our strategists will hang the state in vain glorious self-immolation. By dumb, cruel and vastly excessive force we have made new civil rights legislation almost a dead certainty.**

Rev. Dr. King lamented that he had no idea that the "tragic expression of man's inhumanity to man"[41] would be the fruit of the non-violent march. During his non-violent campaigns, the civil rights advocate had violated the local court injunctions with gleeful abandon—

the regulations he deemed wrong. But he had never consciously defied a federal court injunction.[42] He was for non-violence and order.

On March 10, 1965, Rev. Dr. King led a group of 1,500 Afro-Americans and whites on a second non-violent protest march from Selma to Montgomery, only to be turned back once again by the state troopers when they reached the city outskirts. The soldiers stopped them at Pettus Bridge, which the researcher visited during his Southern field trip. Rev. Dr. King made the following statement on the non-violent demonstration by pointing out that he had no intention to break the previous agreement:[43]

> **We agreed we would not break through the [army] lines. In all frankness, we knew we would not get to Montgomery.... We knew we would not get past the troopers. We had no intention of violating any previous agreement.**

## ARTICLE -2

### (A) The Tacit Agreement

Testifying in the Federal Court, the Afro-American leader confirmed that he had no intent to lead the peaceful rally of civil rights demonstrators from Selma to Montgomery in obvious defiance of the temporary court order.[44] He informed the judge that "there was a tacit agreement at the bridge that we would go no further"[45] and that the SNCC had organized its own demonstrations independently. John Lewis states: [46]

> **If the movement and SNCC are going to be effective in attempting to liberate the black masses, the civil rights movement must be black controlled, dominated and led to have maximum impact on society.**

He studied the problem from another perspective:[47]

> **this country is a racist country. The majority of the population is white, and most whites still hold to master-slave mentality, the cause of the present problem.**

The participation by non-Afro-Americans in the crusade was evident in the second march led by Rev. Dr. King, a march in which a large number of whites, who were largely clergymen and nuns. They marched with the express purpose of supporting the noble ideals of the struggle. But the brutal attack on 38-year old Rev. James J. Reeb from Boston left a deep scar on Rev. Dr. King and other Afro-Americans.

Four white racists knocked Rev. Reeb unconscious, hitting him with an iron club. The clergyman sustained multiple skull fractures and despite the immediate medical intervention, he succumbed to the injury at the University Hospital in Birmingham. Rev. Dr. King, deeply touched by the fatal occurrence, describes the incident:[48]

> **Had policemen not brutally beaten unarmed non-violent individuals desiring the right to vote, on Sunday, it is doubtful whether this act of murder by other Alabamians would have taken place on Tuesday.**

Rev. James J. Reeb was not the only victim of the racist rage. James Lee Jackson went to help his father who, was being beaten up by a trooper, when the infuriated policemen took out his pistol and shot him in his stomach fatally wounding him. Even though Rev. Dr. King's interest in Jackson was said to be perfunctory, he did visit him in the hospital saying: "I told him we were very much concerned about him and he was very much in our prayers. I prayed with him."[49] Jackson died three days later and the cause of his death was officially listed as infection and respiratory complication and no word about the trooper's brutality![50]

Eight days into the confrontation that began on March 1, President Lyndon Johnson, who had won the election with massive Afro-American support, demanded swift action (legislation) "designed to eliminate illegal barriers to the right to vote."[51] His official announcement was an affirmative response to Rev. Dr. King's campaign based on Gandhism for justice and to end the turbulent situation in Alabama. The situation was part of the large American portrait. President Johnson informed the Congress that the development "in Selma is part of a far larger movement which reaches every section and state of America,"[52] emphasizing the commonality of the problem:[53]

> **It is the effort of American Negroes to secure themselves the full blessings of American life. Their cause must be our cause, too. Because it's not just Negroes, but really it's all of us, who must overcome the crippling legacy of bigotry and injustice. And we shall overcome.**

As *The New York Times* pointed out, the declaration "was probably the deepest commitment to the Negro cause of any American President."[53] As an aftermath, the Justice Department finally decided to implement the federal regulations and prevent the officials in Alabama from interfering with the right of the non-violent demonstrators. The American civil rights champion, it goes without saying, lauded President Johnson and reinforced by his support decided to push on until the proposed legislation became the law of the land, removing all the impediments against voting rights in Selma.

### (B) The Historic March and Sweeping Changes

Five attorneys for the Selma Afro-American voter-registration movement presented a "Proposed Plan for March from Selma, Ala., to Montgomery, Ala."[53] The non-violent march, under the plan, was to take five days, with stopovers at designated private fields, for the use of which permission of the owners of the fields had already been obtained.

It was a historic march reminiscent of Gandhiji's numerous non-violent marches and boycotts in South Africa and later in India. Let us now analyze the progress and the general effect of the historic march from Selma to Montgomery with the main objective of attaining full voting rights for Afro-Americans.

The peaceful march by Afro-Americans, a turning point in the close alliance between Rev. Dr. King's SCLC in Selma and SNCC, was a clear indication of Afro-American solidarity and within a few days preceding the development, thousands of fervid followers of Rev. Dr. King had poured into Selma. Dr. Price M. Cobbs, a practicing psychiatrist in San Francisco, describes in *Negro Digest* Rev. Dr. King's irrefutable influence on his people:[54]

> **Martin Luther King, Jr., was the ideal symbol to coalesce all these elements. He was black enough, young enough, radical enough and religious enough to appeal in some measure to all people. The appeal was just and democratic.**

Dr. Cobbs added that the Afro-American leader's "forays into mystics and vagueness...only served to enhance his appeal to all groups."[55] The demonstrators included intellectuals, liberals, religious leaders, students, ordinary folks and professionals—a grassroots movement of historic proportions.

Rev. Dr. King reminded the demonstrators who had assembled at the Brown Chapel African Methodist Church about the attendant risks involved in the famous march stressing the just nature of the cause they upheld.[55]

> **I can't promise you that it won't get you beaten. I can't promise you that it won't get your house bombed. I can't also promise you that it won't get you scared up a bit. We must stand up for what is right for us.**

The right was the guiding light. The march was held on the afternoon of Sunday, March 7, the long awaited non-violent march from Selma to Montgomery, the state capital covering a distance of 50 miles.

## (C) The Court Injunction

Rev. Dr. King derived inspiration from Gandhiji's epoch making Dandie March to the seashore covering a distance of 241 miles in 24 days leading to the Salt Satyagraha, which, according to Rev. Dr. King, had had a profound impact on the evolution of his own non-violent philosophy. His four attorneys had requested the district judge to issue an injunction to keep the state police from possible interference with the non-violent demonstrators. Nicholas Katzenbach, the Attorney General of the United States, hoped that the Afro-American leadership would call off the march as the black people seemed determined to re-enact the old drama inviting immediate retribution.

The strong support and the unprecedented success of the black man's civil rights movement were largely due to the respect paid to the laws of the land and if Rev. Dr. King pressed on with the original plan now, he would be defying a federal court order and to avert an open confrontation he decided to terminate the march in Montgomery without giving room for possible violence.

A close study of the non-violent march is important here to grasp the urgency of winning voting rights in Selma with its effect on the democratic consciousness in the Afro-Americans living in other parts of the United States as well.

1. The memorable march started on schedule with four volunteers in the front along with Rev. Dr. King and Rev. Ralph Abernathy and followed by others. When they had crossed the bridge, the American civil rights advocate stopped the march. Major John Cloud ordered:[56] "I ask you to stop the march. You will not continue.... You are ordered to stop and stand where you are." After having received Cloud's permission to pray, Rev. Dr. King motioned to Rev. Ralph Abernathy to lead the demonstrators in prayer. **It was an eloquent demonstration of Rev. Dr. King's intense faith in God, self-control and a high level of prudence to prevent a violent encounter with the law enforcement agents and to avoid bloodshed.**
2. It was a wrenching moment in the annals of Afro-American's non-violent struggle when hundreds of demonstrators knelt down to pray. Rev. Ralph Abernathy uttered the spontaneous words in a touching manner with no trace of bitterness indicating the humane face of the

Afro-American civil rights movement that had and an unmistakable Gandhian touch:[57]

> **We come to present our bodies as living sacrifice. We don't have much to offer, but we do have our bodies, and we lay them on the altar today.** Our means are just. Our final goal is equally fair and just.

3. Rev. Dr. King, with his boundless faith in the Gandhian ideology of reconciliation, had succeeded in preventing the outbreak of violence and bloodshed on previous occasions, but violence broke out in other parts of Montgomery when misguided whites without provocation ran amuck with murderous ferocity.

President Lyndon Jonson, fully cognizant of the ramifications of the problem, held talks with Governor George Wallace of Alabama, determined to send the state troopers to quell the non-violent demonstration. President Jonson appeared on national television:[58]

> **I told the Governor that the brutality in Selma last Sunday just must not be repeated. I urged that the Governor publicly declare his support for universal suffrage in the state of Alabama and the United States America.**

Rev. Dr. King's Gandhian mode of action produced a benevolent change in the general attitude of the Americans towards the race issue. It echoed in the President's words of wisdom and sanity:[59]

> **It is wrong to use violence against the peaceful citizens in the Selma.** It is wrong to deny any person equality because of the color of the skin. **The promise of America is a simple promise: Every person shares in the full blessings of this land and they shall share on the basis of their merits as a person. They shall also not be judged by their color or by where they were born or the neighborhood in which they live.**

## ARTICLE -3

### (A) Moving Forward

During the march from Selma to Montgomery, every conceivable step was taken to ensure the safety of the volunteers from tents for overnight stops to portable latrines, to ambulances. In Montgomery 600 students had assembled at the Jackson Street Baptist Church singing loudly in unison with the accent on freedom to build up a better future. (Today's Afro-American generation owes much to Rev. Dr. King's peaceful endeavours for its advancements in political and economic fields).

They sang in one voice. They sang loud and clear.

***What do you want, what do you want?***
***Freedom, Freedom, Freedom***
***When do your want it, when do you want it?***
***Now, Now, Now***
***How much do you want, how much do you want?***
***All of it, all of it.***

As the non-violent singers advanced down Decatur Street, policemen stopped them and beat them up viciously. When a policeman cornered a student against a porch, a guardian angel priest tried to protect him: "Please let the boy go," he pleaded. The policeman yelled: "You bastard priest." His impudence inflamed the passion of many of the agitators who, however, refused to be provoked in Alabama.

Despite the heavy odds Alabama found itself in the throes of the spirit of freedom as plane after plane and bus after bus brought freedom fighters into Selma in a steady stream! They included blind people and even octogenarians from as far as Montreal and New York, thousand miles away hungry for justice and freedom.

Even though there was mounting opposition to the non-violent march for freedom, the demonstrators peacefully moved on with the security net provided by the federal soldiers. It was indeed a highly remarkable non-violent exercise organized by any group in the United State in the history of the civil rights campaign. And Gandhiji was its luminous light. Rev. Dr. King and his numerous followers, black and white alike, demonstrated the power of love and *ahimsa* in their epic struggle to demolish, socio-political structure built upon injustice and reinforced by selfishness and agreed, greed for prestige and power. Greed comes in divergent forms.

Here is an account:[60]

**Backed by the armed might of the United States, 3,200 persons marched out of Selma today on the first leg of the historic venture in non-violent protest.... Hundreds of Army and federalized National Guard troops stood guard in Selma and lined the highway out of town to protect the marches.**

On March 21, 4,000 volunteers implacably marched under the leadership of Rev. Dr. King. (A) On the day, they walked 11 miles. At night they were permitted to enter an open field to bed down while soldiers would check for bombs, mines and other incendiary devices which might have been planted by the racist feudal barons. (B) On the second day, they walked 11 more miles. (C) On the third day, they covered 17 miles.

(The antagonists of the protest march falsely accused the demonstrators of engaging in illicit sexual intercourse with a view to cast a slur on the disciplined conduct of the rally. And soon came the reaction of John Louis of the SNCC: "All these segregationists can think of is sexual relationship and that is why there are so many different shades of Negro citizens."[61]

The 50-mile Negro march had ended at the entrance to the state capitol, which like a medieval fortress, had been heavily guarded; Rev. Dr. King addressed the mammoth gathering that stood in eager readiness to listen to his wise counsel:[62]

> **They told us we would not get here. And there were those who said that we would get here only over their dead bodies, but all the world today knows that we are here and also that we are standing before the forces of power in the state of Alabama, saying, 'We ain't goin' to let anybody turn us around. We have walked on meandering highways and rested out bodies on rocky byways.**

The civil rights leader tried to answer the queries of Afro-Americans who dreamed of the bright glow of freedom under the American sun.

His consoling words:[63]

> **I know what you are asking today. How long will it take? Bow long? Not long. Not long because the arm of the moral universe is long, but it bends toward justice.**

The main goal of the non-violent march was to submit a petition to Governor George Wallace for justice and against serious irregularities in voter registration. The Governor had previously informed the people that he would meet with any citizen of Alabama. Even though 20 prominent figures in Alabama had signed the petition, an aide turned them down saying, "the capitol is closed today."[64] The good Governor reneged on his promise, and appeared on television denouncing the non-violent march and its democratic overtones. Those who refuse to talk to people refuse to act for people.

The non-violent campaign of black people did not come to an end with the non-violent march to Montgomery. Every step of the vast stretch of the highway linking Selma with Montgomery today stands as a mute witness to the power of Gandhian non-violence as studied, analyzed and applied by Rev. Dr. King. The Afro-American leader had pledged to keep up the pressure on the "unlawmakers" until the civil rights bill had become the recognized law of the land. He was willing more than ever to redeem the pledge for peace and justice on Gandhian lines in the bygone era.

The present researcher stood at the highway in Selma leading to Montgomery and could not help noticing changes brought about by the march organized by the Afro-American leaders for voting rights.

Joseph Simms, an Afro-American retired school teacher and a member of the team describes his experience in the historic march from Selma to Alabama: "I was attending teacher's college," he told me. We took part in the long march for voting rights. Rev. Dr. King's non-violent efforts in Selma gave us the right to vote. The ballot paper gave us extra-power. We attained new freedom. The long march overcoming various obstacles did a lot of good to us." In similar interviews several Afro-Americans shared the view of Joseph Simms and were proud to join the march to win their rightful place in American society.

**(B) The National Boycott**

Taking a cue from the Gandhian model of peaceful boycott of British products, Rev. Dr. King adopted yet another technique of non-violent resistance. He supported the national boycott of Alabama, including the countrywide boycott of Alabaman products. The boycott had two principle aims; one was to compel Alabama to register at least half of its Afro-American population of voting age and the other, equally far reaching, was to press for a vigorous policy against the arrogant police attitude. He elaborated:[64]

> **I'm in a few days planning to call on trade unions to nfuse to transport or use Alabama products. I hope to call on all Americans to refuse to buy Alabama products. I hope to call on the Secretary of Treasury of the United States to withdraw all Federal funds that it has on deposit in Alabama banks. Such steps are essential for attaining our gods.**

He stressed, furthermore, the need to "withdraw support from a society that has refused to protect life and the right to vote."[65] Later, Rev. Dr. King stated that the proposal for the economic boycott of Alabama was eclectic besides being symbolic and not a blanket refused to purchase goods manufactured in the entire state. The decision to give up the boycott was mainly due to its possible adverse effect on the life of the Afro-Americans, most of whom depended on the local industry for gainful employment. (In the last century the ancestors of Afro-Americans worked on the rich farmlands located round the present urban areas in Alabama. They worked as slaves and later as sharecroppers but always in the deep debt to the landlords who provided them with crude farm equipments and pack animals. Today, many own houses and industries contributing to the nation's economic development, a fact that had received little attention in the United States.)

Unquestionably, the march symbolized victory for Rev. Dr. King's non-violent methods and of black Americans as a united people. President Johnson recommended a voting rights legislation to the Capitol assuring the champion of America's civil rights movement of his firm determination: "We shall overcome."[65] The march scored substantial financial gain for the campaign as a torrent of cash, cheques and money orders poured in, replenishing the pecuniary backing of the movement. Rev. Ralph D. Abernathy, who became the president of NAACP after Rev. Dr. King's assassination, exulted: "We're not in debt now.... We are going to have our first million dollar year."[66]

President Johnson completed the process by signing the Voting Rights Act into law in Alabama, Mississippi and Louisiana empowering Federal officials to deal with the issue of Afro-American registration in those states. That temporary arrangement would continue until the local registrars would be prepared to cooperate in its full implementation. 2,877 applicants were registered as voters in just two days while the total number swelled to 100,000 in thirty six counties.[67] The national statistics showed a remarkable 950,000 black American voter strength.[68] The figures represented about 40 per cent of the total number of Afro-Americans eligible to exercise the franchise, a commendable achievement of the Gandhian non-violent resistance by any standard. Rev. Dr. King could well be proud of the accomplishment, which only a few decades ago the brightest optimist could not have foreseen in his wildest dreams.[69]

Now, it is pertinent here to trace the factors that had gone into the formation of the spiritual excellence in the personality of Rev. Dr. King with his infinite capacity to suffer for common good, finally enabling him to score an astounding non-violent victory.

### (C) A Foregone Conclusion

In the autumn of 1948, Martin Luther King entered Crozier Theological Seminary for higher studies, which were to form a strong foundation for the development of his philosophy of non-violence and sacrifice. The seeds sown here were nourished by his zealous study of Gandhian thoughts. A harmonious blend of the two—the theoretical and practical, the real and the ideal—accounts for the greatness in the life and accomplishments of Rev. Dr. King, who lit up the world in the last century providing a beacon light in the turmoil of divisive forces. No wonder, America saw in Rev. Dr. King the rise of a leader to dispel the gloom in many dark dungeons of the so-called affluent nation afflicted by racial animosity which was an affront to human dignity and divine will.

In his early days, Rev. Dr. King was a voracious reader who had studied the works of several eminent thinkers such as Neibuhr, J.S. Mill, Jeremy Bentham, John Locke and Karl Marx. But Gandhiji's ideology had an exceptional appeal to him:[70]

> **At first, Neibuhr's critique of pacifism let me in a state of confusion. As I continued to read, however, I came to see more and more the shortcomings of his position. For instance many of his statements revealed that he interpreted pacifwm as a sort of passive resistance to evil expressing naive trust in the power of love. But this was a serious distortion.** My study of Gandhi convinced me that me pacifism is not non-resistance to evil, but non-violent resistance to evil.

Gandhiji's non-violent struggle and one of its foundations, the Satyagraha campaign, in South Africa and ultimately in India had strengthened Rev. Dr. King's views to crystallize his convictions.

According to him:[71]

> Gandhi resisted evil with great vigour and power as the violent resister, but he resisted with love instead of hatred. True pacifism is not unrealistic submission to evil, as Neibuhr contends.

The true Gandhian philosophy of returning love for hatred, perhaps more than any other factor, had greatly attracted Rev. Dr. Martin Luther King to Gandhian ideals, receiving much enlightenment after having familiarized himself with Gandhian views and a series of lectures given by A.J. Muste and Dr. Mordechai Johnson, who was the President of Howard University in Washington, D.C. "*The Indian way,*" according to L.G. Davies, "*seemed to offer an answer to Dr. Johnson's question of socialjustice.*"[72] Dr. Johnson had just returned from India after being imbued by Gandhiji's humane ideals. Referring to the influence of those ideals[73] on Rev. Dr. King and his conversion to the unique Gandhian way, embracing *non-violent principium,* the author point:[74]

> **King became so inspired by Dr. Johnson's talk that he began to read all of the books on Gandhi that he could find. The more he read, the more he wanted to know and the deeper he did become involved with the Mahatma's philosophy. At last he had found a philosophy that was worthwhile and offeed an answer to his sense of obligations.**

As the days began to unfold, Gandhiji's inspiration began to exert greater influence on Rev. Dr. King, who scrupulously studied his writings. In his own words:[75]

> **I had come to see early that the Christian doctrine of love operating through the Gandhian method of non-violence was one of the most potent weapons available to the Negro in his struggle.**

## ARTICLE -4

### (A) The Negative Portrayal

Several other individuals in the country, had realized the importance of the Gandhian ideals in the Afro-Americans' struggle in Selma and Montgomery. A white woman, who had understood the significance of non-violence in the Montgomery struggle strongly supported the Negro cause. She wrote a letter to the editor of the *Montgomery Advertiser* comparing the bus boycott organized by Rev. Dr. King with Gandhiji's monumental national movement in India for justice and democratic rights. The racial antagonism against Afro-Americans in Selma was so intense that many condemned her for her sympathy for the black people.[76] "Miss Juliette Morgan, sensitive and frail," Rev. Dr. King later wrote, "did not long survive the rejection and condemnation of the white community ..."[77] adding:[78]

> **...long after she died in the summer of 1957, the name of Mahatma Gandhi was unknown in Montgomery.** People who had never heard of the little brown saint of India were now saying his name with an air of familiarity. **Non-violent resistance bad emerged** as the technique of the movement, **while love stood** as the regulating ideal. **In other words,** Christ provided the religious spirit and motivation while Gandhi furnished the method.

The Afro-American society has often been portrayed in the mainstream media as crime ridden. It is a wrong allegation. Criminal minds can never digest the Gandhian ideology and participate in a non-violent struggle that calls for tremendous self-control and sacrifice. No ethnic group in the United States has launched a non-violent campaign[79] on regional or national level as Afro-American community did in Montgomery, Jackson, Mississippi and Albany. The United States has a long and bitter legacy of violence and bloodshed since its inception and through its march into the present era. The Red Indians (North

American Indians) had been the first victims of the despicable violence. Then came the turn of the African people who were bought, brought and bundled up in the crammed quarters of ships on their perilous voyage to the American shores to satiate the greed of unscrupulous fortune seekers.

In the midst of it all, Rev. Dr. King relied rather heavily on the systematic analysis of the Christian concept of "Love" interpreted by Anders Nygren, a noted Swedish theologian. The Afro-American leader was later initiated into the Gandhian approach in Alabama and committed to it so heavily that it might be difficult to draw a distinction between the well-known Indian leader and his American disciple Rev. Dr. King's words:[81]

> **Hate begets hate; violence begets violence; toughness begets a greater toughness.** We must meet the forces of hate with the power of love; we must meet physical force with love. Our goal must never be to defeat or humiliate the white man, **but to win his friendship and understanding.**

### (B) The Longing for Freedom

Rev. Dr. King, being fully aware that the principal goal of the right to vote was to gain justice and equality in and the aspiration to be free, sprang from the same longing for freedom that motivated the oppressed peoples the world over. He stressed that "the dynamic beat of the deep discontent in Africa and Asia is at bottom a quest for freedom and human dignity on the part of people who have been victims of colonialism."[82]

Rev. Dr. King made it clear:[83]

> **The struggle for freedom on the part of the oppressed people in general and of the American people in particular has developed slowly and is not going to end suddenly. The privileged groups rarely give up their privileges without strong resistance.**

As an ardent devotee of Gandhian philosophy, he would at any cost refrain from resorting to violence even in the most passionate campaign for Negro emancipation. He would never deviate from the path of *ahimsa* and seek an alternative method of violence and his faith in the unshakable victory of truth was absolute. He knew:[84]

> **The alternative to violence is non-violent resistance.** This method was made famous in our generation by Mohandas Gandhi who used it to free India from the domination of the British.

According to Rev. Dr. King non-violent resistance has five main aspects and parallel to the true Gandhian ideals they are as follows:[85]

1. **Non-violent resistance is not a method for cowards. Still it strongly resists societal evils. A person with a strong commitment to non-violent resistance vehemently opposes as evil individuals who subscribe to violent doctrines.**
2. **Non-violent resistance is not such as to bring humiliation to the opponent, not does one seek to crate a sense of defeat in the mind of the opponent. It aims at the reform and ends in goodwill and harmony.**
3. **The third point is so vital that it should be quoted verbatim. "A third characteristic of this method is that attack is directed against the force of evil rather than against persons who are caught in the forces. It is the evil we are seeking to defeat. Those of us who struggle against racial injustice must come to see that the basic tension is not between races. As I like to say, to the people of Alabama: "The tension is not between white people and Negro people. But the tension is at bottom and between justice and injustice and between the forces of light and the forces of darkness.**
4. **Any non-violent fighter should shun not only physical violence, but its evil incarnations like hatred and ill-will.**
5. **To return hate for hate can only aggravate violence, for evil cannot be overcome by evil. Love with its magic spell disarms evil.**

Viewed from this perspective, the racial problem in Alabama has a preposterous note as the ancestors of Afro-Americans were brought into the continent much against their will to work in the prosperity of the land. Their descendants are now treated as intruders and outcasts! They are not to blame for the estranged relationship, since their struggle is for justice and equality which are guaranteed in the nation's Constitution. The racial crisis in Selma and elsewhere in the United States, according to the civil rights advocate, had been the product of two cardinal factors:[86]

> **... the determined resistance of the reactionary elements in the South to the Supreme Court's momentous decisions outlawing segregation in public schools and radical changes in the Negro's re-evaluation of himself.**

(Public schools in the United States may be compared to Government run schools in India. Tax payers finance such schools under the state guidelines).[87]

The adoption of the peaceful Gandhian methods had provided Rev. Dr. King's campaign in Selma with a new image which won the sympathy of the right thinking people all over the world. The Negroes were encouraged by the development and were determined to carry the agitation to its logical conclusion:[88]

> **While the southern legislative halls ring with open defiance through 'interposition' and 'nullification,' while a modern version of the Ku Klux Klan has arisen in the form of 'respectable' white citizens' council, a revolutionary change has taken place in the Negro's conception of his own nature and destiny in the society.**

## (C) A Massive Experiment

America's first massive experiment in Gandhian non-violence led by Rev. Dr. King and his army of followers in Selma and its success lifted the spirit of the Afro-American community, especially when the movement had produced tangible results in the form of new legislation ensuring greater equality in the economic and political spheres. Rev. Dr. King pointed out that 'once he [Afro-American] thought of himself as an inferior and patiently accepted injustice and exploitation. Those days are gone now."[89]

The first batches of Africans had been brought to America in 1619, a year before the famous Pilgrim Fathers landed at Plymouth, fleeing from the flames of political and religious persecution in many parts of Europe. Tracing the early history of the Afro-American community, Rev. Dr. King points out that "throughout the era of slavery the Negro was treated in inhuman fashion. He was considered a thing to be used, not a person to be respected."[90] Afro-Americans, more than any other group in the United States, felt the need to be free, free from the clutches of inequality which was impeding their advancement. After more than three centuries, destiny chose Rev. Dr. King to lead a non-violent crusade for the emancipation of Negroes in Alabama or elsewhere in the nation.

Rev. Dr. King was the first American to propagate the Gandhian philosophy in the New World, and for that matter the first individual in the world outside India, and he did so on a level unknown in the history of the United States.[91] Herein lies the supreme qualities of a leader who strongly believed in non-violent principles which he applied on the largest scale in the United States reaffirming the efficacy of the Gandhian philosophy in our times to overthrow a system and its inner circles which had subjugated Afro-Americans for centuries.[92]

In 1966, in the shadow of the newly won voting rights, the Afro-American voting strength in Alabama soared to 228,000 constituting one-fourth of the total registration. Alabama's 11 official candidates for the office of the state governor rewrote their campaign speeches by virtually deleting the term 'segregation' as it had practically ceased to exist or at least as a key election issue since the Afro-Americans accounted for 50 per cent of the Dallas County electorate indicating a kaleidoscope of changes.

An Alabama political analyst voiced a similar reaction in his review that while covering political rallies for a whole month, he failed to hear the disparaging word "Nigger",[93] the racial slur that was frequently heard before. This was not to deny that there still isolated voices which deplored the betterment of the black commuity.[94]

During the elections to the legislature that followed, Rev. Dr. King travelled far and wide mobilizing the black people to exercise franchise prompting critics to accuse him of being racially biased. According to a reporter:[95]

> **It was a plea for support of Negro candidates and for Attorney General Richmond Flowers in his race for Governor against Mrs. George C. Wallace.**

In order to counter the charges levelled against him, he pleaded for "a unique Negro vote,"[96] justifying his appeal in the wider interest of an aggrieved community.[97]

He argues:[98]

> **But for all these years, whites have bloc-voted to keep us down, and now we got to bloc-vote to get ourselves out of this dilemma.**

In the shadow of the successful non-violent campaign in Selma, Dr. King wrote in *Saturday Review*:[95]

- **(i) Americans of conscience in the interests of decency demand legislative measures as well as Federal intervention.**
- **(ii) Non-violent demonstrators go into the streets and avenues to exercise their constitutional rights and privileges.**
- **(iii) Under popular pressure, the Administration implements measures for remedial legislation and immediate intervention.**
- **(iv) Racists resist by unleashing violence against non-violent demonstrators.**

In Selma Rev. Dr. King complained against the rigidity of the position adopted by those who had denied justice to Afro-Americans who were unable to exercise their democratic rights and found the need to disobey the law in a peaceful manner. He explained the problem to the editor of Richmond's *News Leader*:[100]

> **An unjust law is no law and an individual who discovers on the basis of conscience that a law is unjust, and is wiring in a peaceful manner to disobey that unjust law and willingly as well as voluntarily suffers the consequences, is expressing the highest respect for law.**

Referring to the same point he told *The New York Times*:[101]

> **I say obey the law when the law is right, when the law is just and when the law is in line with the moral law of the universe, when the conscience tells someone that a law is unjust, then I think a righteous person has no alternative but to conscientiously disobey that law.**

In denying the reality of democratic rights to the Afro-Americans, America's strongest defender of human rights felt the need to defy the unjust laws in a non-violent manner outmanoeuvering his opponents in various engagements in Selma and Birmingham, the two epicentres of his struggle for justice. In this way he gave a new ethical dimension to his non-violent campaigns.

## SUMMARY

1. Rev. Dr. King's interest in the Afro-American voting strength dates back to the days of the highly successful Montgomery bus boycott. During the Prayer Pilgrimage of May 17, 1957, to the nation's capitol, he had said: "Give us the ballot."
2. In 1961, experts on civil rights in the Kennedy administration came to the conclusion that Afro-Americans were on the brink of a political breakthrough in the South.
3. The repression of the black voting rights in Selma was no longer characteristic of the South, much less in the entire United States. Rev. Dr. King's attempts were directed against the perpetuation of injustice inherent in the system.
4. The distance between Selma and Montgomery is about 50 miles; the black leadership had taken the precautions necessary for the safety of the demonstrators. The walk began after a brief prayer while the entire nation and much of the world watched the momentous non-violent venture.
5. In Montgomery Governor George Wallace ordered the troops to stop night marches. Rev. Dr. King responded to the Governor's order by calling for a march on Montgomery to protest against the barriers to Afro-American voting.

6. The demonstrators had protection of the federal troops, ordered by President Johnson to prevent the outbreak of violence unleashed by the opponents.
7. Thousands of people had come to Selma by plane and by bus either to participate in the peaceful demonstration or to witness the event, unique in American history because of its strict adherence to Gandhian non-violent ideology.
8. Despite stem precautionary measures taken by the administration, the segregationists attacked the demonstrators. Several people were killed. Rev. Dr. King told his followers to remain calm, reaffirming his faith in the Gandhian ideology.
9. Appearing on national television, President Johnson urged the authorities in Alabama not to commit violence against peaceful demonstrators. He also took steps to ensure the voting rights of Afro-Americans.
10. The American President's intervention was both timely and effective; it had boosted the morale of Afro-Americans, who had been waiting for changes in the legal system.
11. Not fully satisfied with the presidential order to Congress to guarantee voting rights for Afro-Americans, Rev. Dr. King wanted a new law to that effect. He wanted to boycott Alabama, but later dropped the idea since it would adversely affect the interests of the blacks living in that state.
12. The voting rights law, the result of Rev. Dr. King's campaign based on the Gandhian ideals, improved the status of Afro-Americans, not to mention the American civil rights leader's prestige and national figure who had renounced the use of violence as a means of attaining his goal. He set an example for others to accept non-violence as a method of action to realize socio-political goals.

**Notes and References**

1. "*What Manner of Man,*" op. cit, p. 87. Rev. Dr. King was fully conscious that in the absence of voting rights, Afro-Americans would have no equal status in society. Also in Martin Luther King, Jr., "*The Measure of Man,*" (Philadelphia: United Church Press, 1959) and Nat Hentoff, "*The New Equality,*" (New York: Viking Press, 1964).

2. *Ibid.*, p. 176.
3. *The Nation*, September 23, 1961, p. 178.
4. *Ibid.*
5. *Atlanta Constitution*, September 24, 1961, p. 23.
6. *The Nation*, op. cit. In 1961, the civil rights experts in the Kennedy administration had predicted that Afro-American registration and voting would dramatically increase and that political leaders in the South would have to soften their rhetoric on the presumed white supremacy which is based on erroneous rationale resulting in racist views.
7. *The New York Times*, February 9, 1965, p. 17.
8. *Ibid.*, June 26, 1961. The same article would have been timely 1965 in that at the height of the non-violent campaign in Selma, Rev. Dr. King had organized a mass demonstration in Montgomery to encourage Afro-Americans to register to vote in that city also. He had come to the firm conclusion that voting rights were crucial for equality for Afro-Americans.
9. Selma, the governmental seat of Dallas County, had resorted to intimidation and coercive methods to prevent Afro-Americans from voting. Rev. Dr. King knew exactly what to expect in Selma and picked the city precisely for its vehement opposition to Afro-American voting rights. The SNCC voter campaign had begun in February 1963, following the arrival of Rev. Bernard Lafayette and his wife. Further details on the problem can be found in Robert Wan-en Penn, who Speaks for the Negro." (New York: Random House, 1964).
10. "*SNCC: The New Abolitionists*," Howard Zinn, (Boston: Beacon Press, 1964), pp. 126-27.
11. *Ibid.*, p. 143.
12. *Ibid.*, p. 145.
13. *Ibid.*, p. 163. *The New York Times* provided a considerably different version of the violent development. The reporter John Herbers wrote that Afro-Americans lay down on the sidewalk while the police tried to push them. October 8, 1963. Mistreatment of other Afro-American demonstrators has been reported in other papers.
14. "*SNCC: The New Abolitionists*," op. cit., p. 163.
15. *Ibid.*
16. *The New York Times*, October 8, 1963, p. 21.
17. *Ibid.*, September 30, 1964, p. 22.

18. *Ibid.*, November 5, 1964. As far as Rev. Dr. King's position was concerned, the legislation might just as well never have been written. Soon after the election, he told reporters that he planned to organize peaceful demonstrations in Alabama and Mississippi. An observer who had studied the developments in Birmingham even in the most casual manner could see that the civil rights leader was about to zero in on Selma with yet another campaign for justice and equality.
19. Ibid., November 6, 1964, p. 17.
20. *Ibid.*, p. 1.
21. *Ibid.*. p. 33.
22. *Saturday Review,* April 3, 1965.
23. *The New York Times,* January 3, 1965, p. 20. The police arrested two white-skinned youths for allegedly setting off a tear gas in an area where Afro-Americans had predominantly resided in an effort to provoke them and cause considerable damage to property. In January, prior to the start of a rally, it was reported that the opponents of the campaign would be kept out of Selma's Afro-American residential area to prevent the escalation of violence.
24. Ibid., p. 25.
25. *Ibid.*, January 20, 1965, p. 18. A great part of the civil rights demonstration had taken place near the Dallas County Court-house.
26. *Ibid.*, January 19, 1965. pp. 1 and 20.
27. *Ibid.*, January 4, 1965, p. 58. Rev. Dr. King, after arriving in Selma, told a gathering of Afro-Americans: "I have made my choice. I have to march. I do not know what lies ahead of us. There may be beating, jailing and the use of tear gas." His views were based on the past experience of Afro-Americans. More details of similar experience are also given in *"I Have A Dream,"* L.G. Davis, op. cit., Especially Chapters 7 and 8.
28. *The New York Times,* January 4, 1965, p. 58.
29. *Ibid.*
30. *Ibid.*
31. *Ibid.*, News of the Week in Review, p. 5E. The police tried to avoid arresting Rev. Dr. King so much so that his arrest was two weeks behind schedule. Prior to that, Mr. Frederick D. Reese, Rev. Dr. King's principal aide in Selma, had requested the members of the registration board to set aside Friday for registration of teachers. The chairman of the school board informed them that they would

be allowed to leave any school at any time to register but that they could not come at that time as the board was not open. Afro-American leaders replied that they wanted to see themselves if the board was open. At that time, authorities sent force to dispel them using extreme force.

32. As in Birmingham, the campaign in Selma had a slow beginning, but with encouraging results. There was no gainsaying the fact that the demonstrators, mostly students hungry for a better future based on equality and justice, found satisfaction in taunting Clark who was their arch rival on the road to equality. A student leader said to his fellow protesters that the police did not want to arrest them adding that "we want to make them arrest us. Well lock arms in front of the court-house." (*The New York Times,* February 4, 1965, p. 22). Ironically, Clark was on the verge of being hospitalized for severe exhaustion as a result of handling the demonstrators for a considerably long period of time. Nothing that had occurred during that turbulent month could have justified the action which Clark took on February 10, 1965 when he and a group of policemen used sticks and electric cattle prods to lead 165 demonstrators, mostly children and teenagers; they were forced to march more than two miles. The young demonstrators, suffering from fatigue, fled into a large private compound. This inhuman and thoughtless act by the police infuriated Afro-American parents, besides instilling new spirit into the civil rights campaign strengthening the will of the demonstrators. More than 3,400 demonstrators were arrested yielding to pressure to halt mass arrest creating additional problems for the police. *The New York Times,* February 12, 1965, p. 58.

33. More demonstrators were arrested. The police handcuffed 520 Afro-Americans and the majority of them were kept overnight in penal camps. *The New York Times,* February 6, 1965, p. 10.

34. *Ibid.*, February 21, 1965, p. 14. In 1971, Governor George Wallace was shot while he was campaigning as a candidate for the office of the President of the United States. He was paralysed from the waist down. He was a strong segregationist. Before his death in 1998, he took a conciliatory attitude towards Afro-Americans and asked them for forgiveness which should be given to him with open hearts.

35. *Ibid.*, February 23, 1965.

36. *Ibid.*, Judge Thomas ordered the board of directors to relax its literacy test and to speed up the Afro-American registration. *The*

*New York Times* reported that the "initial reaction of civil rights leaders to the judge's order was one or jubilation and hope."

37. *Ibid.*, February 24, 1965 p. 28.
38. In March, Rev. Dr. King had received strong intimations from important business leaders of a desire to see an early end to racial discrimination and violence in Alabama. *Ibid.*, p. 28.
39. *Newsweek,* March 22, 1965, p. 18. *Washington Post* depicted a moronic "Special Trooper" chuckling with satisfaction as he cleaned his club, which had an Afro-American lady's blood stains after she sustained injury.
40. *Alabama Journal,* March 19, 1965, p. 27.
41. *The New York Times,* March 8, 1965, p. 20. Also in *Reader's Digest,* August 1967, p. 128.
42. *Congressional Record,* March 18, 1965, p. 5444.
43. *The New York Times,* March 8, 1965, p. 22. Governor George Wallace had intended to avoid violent confrontation by the police with the demonstrators despite his strongly antagonistic attitude toward Afro-Americans.
44. *Ibid.*, March 12, 1965, p. 1. Rev. Dr. King's testimony saved him from contempt of court citation. Judge Johnson asked him: "Is it correct to say that when you started across the bridge, you knew at that time that you did not intend to march to Montgomery?" Rev. Dr. King replied: "Yes, it is. There was a tacit agreement at the bridge that we would go no further."
45. *Ibid.*, p. 19.
46. John Lewis., op. cit., p. 197.
47. *Ibid.*, The demonstrators had kept a 24-hour prayer vigil for Rev. Reeb; 200 people had prayed in the torrential downpour.
48. *The New York Times,* March 12, 1965, p. 1.
49. *Ibid.*, February 12, 1965. There was yet another death during the civil rights campaign. A trooper had shot Jimmy Lee Jackson in Marion, Alabama. On that day three generations of his family were into hospital, the hapless victims to the assaults by the police. Jackson's 82-year old grandfather was severely wounded at the back of his head.
50. *Ibid.*
51. *The New York Times,* March 16, 1965.
52. *Ibid.*, The irony was that while the Justice Department was protecting the civil rights demonstrators in Alabama, it was ejecting the Afro-American demonstrators and others from its own building

in Washington D.C. for demanding justice. The security guards forcibly ejected those who were squatting on the fifth floor of the office of Attorney General, Nicholas Katzenbach.

53. *Ibid.*, March 21, 1965, p. 1.
54. *Negro Digest,* July 1967, pp. 65-67.
55. *Ibid.*
56. L.G. Davis, "I Have A Dream," op. cit., p. 191. Governor Wallace had been silent until then without making any plea for peace and stability in Selma. After he had heard of the planned non-violent march, he forbade it. But the march had gained considerable momentum for him to stop since thousands of Afro-American heeding the call of Rev. Dr. King were willing to move forward.
57. *Ibid.*, p. 197.
58. *Ibid.*, p. 198. President Jonson also made it clear that he had "advised Governor of my intention to press with all the vigour in my command to assure that every citizen of this country if given the right to participate in his Government at every level through the complete voting process." His assurance revitalized the Afro-American campaign for voting rights.
59. *Ibid.*, p. 198.
60. *The New York Times,* March 22, 1965, p. 26.
61. *"I Have A Dream,"* op cit., p. 201. He reached of the speech and cried out with a rhythmic chant: "Glory hallelujah! Glory hallelujah! Glory hallelujah!" Roger Lee, 82-year old grandfather of Jimmy Lee Jackson, might have been the most apologetic pilgrim fall. He could only walk a few miles and was forced to quit with tears in his eyes while others went through the ordeal with sheer determination to attain their goal of attaining equality.
62. *The New York Times,* March 20, 1965, p. 1.
63. *Ibid.*
64. *Ibid.*
65. *Ibid.*
66. *Ibid.*, March 31, 1965, p. 17 Rev. Dr. King's I main goal of the boycott was "to arouse the consciousness of the good people of the state, so they can rise up against the irresponsibility of Governor George Wallace." Governor George Wallace, who had considerable support of the segregationist elements in the province, was strongly opposed to give even an ounce of equality to Afro-Americans.
67. *Ibid.*, August 13, 1965, p. 19.
68. *Ibid.*, March 1, 1965.

69. *Ibid.*, April 17, 1966, p. 63. Also in New South, Spring, 1966, pp. 74-75. In 1964, hardly anyone walking along Times Square in New York City could locate Selma on the map. By the end of....it had become a widely knowing the result of an avalanche of date about the Afro-Americans-American struggle, its officials and the emphasis on non-violence. In that year, Selma, an important city in Alabama, had been turned into the staging ground and the wheels of publicity began turning with an almost computer-like speed when Afro-American demanded justice with mom vigour than ever facing opposition. *The Times Journal* in Selma (April 20, 1965) reported that Mayor Joseph Smitherman had given orders to Baker to have the police join the state and county troopers to break up the scheduled march for voting rights. The serious developments in Selma drew national attention. Baker stated that he would resign rather than respond to mayor's order to use force to discourage the demonstrators. Some members of the Selma City Council backed Baker's stance, trying to reach a compromise to ensure that the police would not use violence against the demonstrators bent on marching for justice. Before that, mounted police had spurred their horses against a retreating group of protestors in full view of television cameras. Ron Gibson, who was a reporter of *Birmingham News,* (May 2, 1965) pointed out that he had seen Sheriff Clark lead others trying to force the Afro-Americans back into their church. Undaunted by such violent reactions, they continued their struggle under Rev. Dr. King's leadership. Such repressions became the topics of editorial comments in different parts of the country demanding an end to unnecessary violence, which had tarnished the image of the nation as a whole as a truly democratic country. Officials in the nation's capital were closely watching the deteriorating situation in Selma to seek a peaceful resolution to the problem which had been dislocating the social equilibrium.

70. "*Stride Toward Freedom,*" Rev. Dr. Martin Luther King Jr., (San Francisco: Harper and Row Publishers, 1986), pp. 97-98. Rev. Dr. King strongly felt that pacifism was a "courageous confrontation" of the forces of evil by the strength of love. And in that respect "it is better to be the recipient of violence than the inflicter of it, since the latter only multiplies the existence of violence and bitterness in the universe ...."

71. As a serious student of theology, Martin Luther King had great admiration for Professor George W. Davis who taught Systematic

Theology. Martin said that Dr. Davis was "marvelous teacher" and "sincerely religious". L.D. Reddick, "Crusader Without Violence." (New York: Harper and Brothers, 1959).

72. *"I Have A Dream,"* Lenwood G. Davis, (Westport: Connecticut, Negro Universities Press, 1973), p. 25.
73. *Ibid.*, p. 25. "Love" in this context means understanding and goodwill. Greek New Testament contains three words for love, viz., "eros," "philia" and "agape." Eros, in the Platonic philosophy, meant yearning of the soul for the realm of the divine. Philia meant intimate affection among friends. Agape meant nothing sentimental or fundamentally affectionate; it meant understanding, redeeming goodwill toward others. These ideas were contained in Rev. Dr. King's article titled, "Non-violence and Racial Justice", appeared in "*Christian Century*," 74, February 6, 1957, pp. 165-67.
74. Except from pages 65-72 of Rev. Dr. King's "Stride Toward Freedom." The article appeared in *Jubilee,* (September 1958).
75. *Montgomery Advertiser,* January 16, 1957. Rev. Dr. King's non-violent activities were reported in major newspapers in North America and hundreds of local papers also.
76. *Jubilee,* op. cit.
77. *Ibid.*
78. *Ibid.*
79. *Ibid.*, In *"Stride Toward Freedom"* and in other speechess and writings, Rev. Dr. King has explained his personal hardships and the bitter experiences of his people in their struggle for justice.
80. *Ibid.*
81. *Ibid.*, In another context, Ceasar Chavez, an advocate of non-violent methods, organized The Mexican migrant farmers in California for better wages and working conditions. They had been severely exploited. Chavez urged the American consumers to boycott grapes and other produce grown in California to dramatize the plight of the migrant labourers. He received death threats for his non-violent methods meant to improve the lot of the Mexican farmers.
82. Rev. Dr. King heavily relied on the systematic and spiritual evaluation of the Christian concept of "love" as advocated by Anders Nygren. A noted Swedish theologian, Nygren argued in his significant study titled, "Agape and Eros" (1953) the love as described in the New Testament, translated from the Greek as "agape" is the most powerful creative force in the universe.

83. *Jubilee,* op. cit.
84. *Christian Century* op. cit., pp. 165-67.
85. The five salient points were first published in an article by Rev. Dr. King titled, "Alternative to Violence," appeared in *Christian Century. Ibid.*, They were also the basis of his struggle in Selma.
86. *Ibid.*
87. In the United States public schools are financed by Government as opposed to private schools. Black children were not permitted in many schools before they were integrated. Educational institutions for the Afro-American children were poorly equipped. Today, they have the freedom, perhaps without complete equal treatment, to attend schools and colleges in the North and South.
88. *Christian Century,* op. cit.
89. *Ibid.*
90. *Ibid.*
91. *Salt Satyagmha,* the pinnacle of the achievement of non-violent struggle, had had a great influence on Rev. Dr. King. On March 12, 1930, Gandhiji, against the views of some members of the Congress Party, left Sabarmati on foot along with 75 volunteers, for Dandi beach where they reached on April 5. They broke the law by picking up salt on the sea shore. Gandhiji openly proclaimed: "My advice is that workers should everywhere manufacture salt" even if "they run the risk of being prosecuted." The Salt Satyagraha was the harbinger to the eruption of unprecedented protests in the whole country. *"British Rule in India,"* R. Gopal, chapter XIII, op. cit., and *"Gandhi And Modem India,"* P. Moon, pp. 144-58., op. cit.
92. Rev. Dr. King talked about the divine aspects of his suffering. "Perhaps the suffering, frustration and agonizing moments which I have had to undergo occasionally as a result of my involvement in a difficult struggle have drawn me closer to God. Whatever the cause, God has been profoundly real to me in recent months? In Chapter 6, *"Stride Toward Freedom"*. He has expressed similar views in publications like *Jubilee* and *Century.*
93. In "A Testament of Hope: The Essential Writings of Martin Luther King. Jr.," Ed. by James Melvin Washington, (San Francisco: Harper and Row, 1986).
94. Rev. Dr. King's important contribution to the civil rights movement should be viewed against those, including the slain black leader, Malcolm X, who had preached violence. Further details in 'The Autobiography of Malcolm X, '(New York: Grove Press, Inc., 1965)

and "The Death and Life of Malcolm X," Peter Goldman, (New York: Harper and Row Publishers, 1973). Especially Chapters 4 and 7.

95. *Alabama Journal.*, June 14, 1965.
96. *Ibid.*, Also see *Christian Century,* February 6, 1957, op. cit.
97. *Ibid.*
98. *"What Manner of Man,"* Lerone Bennett, (Chicago: Johnson Publishing Co., 1963, pp. 33-34.
99. *Saturday Review,* March 7, 1965, p. 21.
100. *News Leader,* April 3, 1965, p. 17.
101. *The New York Times,* Sunday Magazine Section, August 25, 1963, p. 9.
102. *Saturday Review,* April 3, 1965, p. 16. We also have to taken into account the religious aspect of the difficult struggle in Selma to restore Afro-Americans' democratic rights. Small groups of nuns, with no colour differences had travelled from far away Midwest to Selma, the city under siege, either to join or relieve those who were already in the front line of protest. A spokesman for the Diocese of Detroit said: "They have done it and they will continue to do it with our blessing." (*Detroit Tines,* May 25, 1965). Hundreds of priests and nuns, in all, had made the special trip to Selma from Baltimore, Boston, Chicago, New York, Oklahoma, San Antonio, Tulsa, Pittsburg, Washington and Wilmington. John Cogley, a former editor of *Commonweal,* a religious publication, spoke of a "crisis of obedience" among the young nuns and priests, as they had not received clearance from the regional chancery offices. Rev. Dr. King's constant emphasis on the religious principles of his ideology had attracted wide attention, which no other Afro-American leader was able to receive. Governor George Wallace's strong opposition to the voting rights proved a blessing in disguise in as much as his opposition to a just cause and the brutality of the police had resulted in sympathy and support for the struggle in Selma. Gandhian non-violence would never fail.

# CHAPTER-X

# EPILOGUE

## Gandhi's Influence and Rev. Dr. King's Legacy

### ARTICLE -1

**A Case Study**

Gandhiji's life and philosophy exerted a profound influence on the brilliant career of Martin Luther King Jr., creating a new legacy in a country born of military strength and guided all along by the principle of physical force and the rule of might. No biographical study of Rev. Dr. King can be complete without a probe into the Gandhian ideology for which he stood. The great Indian leader had his political pioneering in South Africa, as something thrust upon him by an inscrutable destiny. Man is driven by the tide of time, but some have in them the inherent strength to stem the tide and change its course to a direction of their choice. Gandhiji belongs to this illustrious group and therein lies his greatness.

Before Gandhiji arrived in South Africa, the Indian residents provided a case study in imperial futility and moral bankruptcy, instrumental for a political and social structure based on the denial of equality. The Government was primarily interested in the Indian labour and acted on the fundamental premise that any improvement in their condition would be counter productive. They were treated no better than chattels and denied even civil rights and human status. The Indian community in South Africa was a flock without a shepherd until Gandhiji had set foot in the South African soil and filled in the long lacuna. Gandhiji's visit to the Dark Continent was official to defend his clients in a local court. He decided to stay and fight for their cause. He developed a new strategy with no precedents in the world and wrote out the most remarkable chapter in man's struggle for freedom. A great endeavour with no precedents definitely called for exceptional skills and resourceful mess, which he abundantly possessed. He called his technique Satyagraha, a strict adherence to truth in putting up peaceful resistance with a strong will to win the goal by being kind to the opponent. The world in utter dismay and the enemy in utter confusion watched the creation of an invincible weapon in warfare. In a decade or two the hard-core racists submitted to the spiritual and moral strength of Non-violent resistance, leading to a new era of peace, compassion and co-existence.

The whites were infuriated to see an organised Indian movement to resist injustice and they unleashed violence and terror. The parliament in Pretoria adopted Act 37 of 1919, viz. The Transvaal Asiatic Land and Trading Amendment Act. The main goal of the Act was to curtail the rights of the Indian settlers, either as companies or as persons to own property. The ownership of property played a major role in an individual's social status. The Transvaal Asiatic and Trading Amendment Act was meant to deprive the members of the Indian community of any opportunity for improvement. In the same manner, the Mines and Works (Amendment) Act of 1926, commonly called the Colour Bar Act of 1926, reserved certain aspects of the mining industry for settlers from Europe while slamming the doors on the Indians. Several laws with similar intent had been passed with crippling effects on the interests of the Indians. During the 1930s a number of rigid measures mainly to limit the Indian occupation of land was introduced. In South Africa, the Indians under Gandhiji's able leadership inaugurated the history's first Non-violent campaign with its message that non-violence was a potent instrument for social changes. The treatment the Indians received in South Africa reinforced by Gandhiji's bitter experiences impelled him to resist the evil of racial discrimination with his new instrument of Satyagraha. Thus as a method for change in society Satyagraha was born in South Africa and Gandhiji became its progenitor.

## ARTICLE -2

### Legitimate Rights

We have to understand the special circumstances in South Africa in order to realize the significance of Gandhian ideology and its practical application as a unique tool. Pitted against a barbarous colonial machinery headed by an unscrupulous General Smuts, Gandhiji was constrained to try every feasible weapon in his armour, when the truth dawned upon him that the victory in the war depended not on British physical force but upon what he himself called "soul force." He knew that the path before him was by no means smooth, for the new technique called for tremendous patience and capacity for immense sacrifice. Gandhiji was intensely grieved to see the condition of his Indian fellowmen in an alien land, subjugation to a vast array of discriminations and indignities. He decided to take up the challenge and lead them like Moses into a new equitable order of things. He despised greed.

The First World War was the product of the insatiable greed of the European powers, which fell out in apportioning the fruits of conquests and exploitation. Nevertheless, Britain claimed that it was a noble war, fought in the interests of "equality, justice, fairness and equity." The hypocrisy of this claim and the consequent juxtaposition were exposed when Gen. Smuts openly declared: "White and black people are different, not only in colour but also in soul; their political institutions should be different."

The Boer War and the existing political situation had added a new dimension to the South African imbroglio. The Dutch settlers turned against the English, alleging injustice and discrimination. This rift in the white camp worked to the advantage of the Indian community by providing them with a little more bargaining tool. Although this historical development might have softened the adamant attitude of the imperious Smuts, Gandhiji had to face severe odds in his campaign to remedy the evils of the policy of apartheid. He tried Satyagraha for the first time (which later went down in history as a powerful device for reform and emancipation) and its uniqueness and novelty stunned even his fiercest opponents who finally veered around to an amicable settlement of the long-tormented problem. Ahimsa had the final say in the matter and Gandhiji scored the first victory in his long career as a defender of justice and fraternity in society.

What the society would gain depends to a great degree on how creative and committed its members are. The amount of energy a single person is capable of releasing is simply amazing. Gandhiji proved with his own work that a will backed with faith can work miracles and take the world on its stride. Thanks to Gandhiji's sacrifice the world today is a better place to live in!

Gandhiji's religious upbringing and faith in God guided his life, notably in the realm of his political work as he firmly believed that politics without a religious prop up is "a dangerous pastime, resulting in nothing but harm to individuals and nations indulging in it" and his concept of religion was thoroughly philanthropic: "For me, humanitarian service or service of all that lives, is religion." This basic humanistic aspect was unquestionably a determining factor in Gandhiji's political life. He could identify himself with the common man in the lowest echelon of the Indian society, but was able to rise above its blind adherence to time-barred customs and conventions and its fatalistic inertia. He could renounce worldly gains with the careless ease of a typical Indian sage, but would defend unto death the basic human rights and dignity with the zeal of a crusader. No wonder, he became a saint among the politicians and a politician among the saints. He might more justly be called a practical philosopher believing in Non-violent actions.

Non-violence, the basis of all great religions, was the nucleus of the Gandhian philosophy, which he unflinchingly practised all through his life in South Africa and India. We have to consider two aspects here.

First, in South Africa Gandhiji gave a new impetus to the cause of the justice of South African Indians and in the process devised a new strategy—Satyagraha, which was nothing but care and concern saddled with truth and blended together without leaving any residue of ill-will. In sharp contrast to the traditional heroes who made their presence felt through audacious feats of violence and adventure, Gandhiji worked with patience and persistence, diligence and caution. He was a responsible leader, who would take no chance in fighting for the just cause of his fellow Indians, facing oppression and ill-treatment in a foreign land.

Secondly, the most distinguishing aspect of history's greatest anti-colonial movement in a foreign land was its strict adherence to non-violence in its opposition to the brute force by world's mightiest colonial power in India. Gandhiji, who should be given the greatest credit for toppling the greatest imperial nation in recorded history, adhered to non-violence knowing it to be far superior to any method violence could dictate. But the new technique demanded infinite patience and remarkable power of endurance. It was a weapon invulnerable to the coward and the sceptic, but it could work miracles in the hands of the brave and the confident.

**Researcher at the Museum, King Centre, Atlanta**

## ARTICLE -3

### Contradictions

History testifies to the fact that Gandhiji was right in choosing the Non-violent path for resisting racism and colonalism in South Africa, for it withstood every external effort to choke it and ultimately succeeded in bringing about the desired changes in that British colony. The new struggle produced enough pressure that compelled the officials to listen to reason and repeal the numerous laws introduced to suppress and subjugate the South African Indians who toiled for the country's prosperity. Gandhiji's success was the victory of *ahimsa* as a means of fighting out evil and left a glorious legacy for the prosperity to cash on.

Gandhiji had only one ideologically sustainable alternative to violence. "We need," he argued, "not force of arms, but force of will .... If we develop the force of will, we shall find that we do not need the force of arms." It is time that we heeded his call to develop a culture of peace as a prerequisite for human progress. Violence could solve nothing: for, violence begets only violence and results in total destruction. The two World Wars brought misery and suffering to the world as a whole. We shall decide now if we should survive or perish. How Gandhiji transformed a hope into a reality! At a time when Rev. Dr. King was cracking his brain to evolve a *modus operandi* to resist racism in America, Gandhiji flashed in his mind a "Saving Grace". He knew at once that he had got the answer. Rev. Dr. King's Non-violent campaign was one of the most remarkable developments in the recent history of the United States for constitutional rights for millions of its own citizens. The persecution of the Japanese during the last war in the intern camps in the United States or the saga of ill-treatment suffered by the Chinese are pale in comparison with the institutionalised racism against the black people who lived in constitutional wilderness. Rev. Dr. King took Gandhiji as his ideal and scrupulously followed his method of resisting injustice. And he succeeded in his efforts to a large extent. The price he had to pay for Negro emancipation was the same that Gandhiji himself paid for the upliftment of the down-trodden, but in any case, it was trivial in comparison with the wealth they have brought to the entire world—faith in abiding human nature and hope in the future of mankind. Rev. Dr. King's efforts were crowned with success. Schools, Colleges and public places are no more forbidden fruits to the Afro-Americans. By subscribing to the Gandhian dogma of non-violence, Rev. Dr. King influenced federal legislators, by means of peaceful demonstrations and boycotts, to introduce laws for Afro-Americans and to remove the unjust ones which blocked the path to their progress.

The accolades in America and the Nobel Prize for Peace, bestowed on the American civil rights leader were a glowing tribute to his great services. Educational and philanthropic institutions vied with one another in bestowing on him their covetous awards and highest honours, besides being booked for lectures even two years in advance. There came his way notable prizes like the Spingagn Medal of the N.A.A.C.P. There was one thing that everyone agreed on: Rev. Dr. King fully deserved all these and even more. But the greatest of all the distinctions that encrowned him was that he had got entombed in the hearts of the millions of right thinking people all over the world. Violent men do not receive social acceptance.

## ARTICLE-4

### The Concept of Civil Disobedience

The non-violent struggle helped the Afro-Americans gain access to public facilities and in its wake generated in them a large degree of dignity on the part of the Negro had undermined the South's negative peace, since the white man refused to recognize the change.

The concept of civil disobedience was not entirely new to America as one of its greatest protagonists. Henry David Thorean was an American, whose philosophy admittedly was yet another source of inspiration to Rev. Dr. King. The first vehement demonstration of civil disobedience could be traced back to the famous Boston Tea Party when 60 colonists expressed their strong protest against the import duty by hurling 342 chests of tea into the Boston Bay on December 16, 1773. It was a masked raid conducted by American settlers on three British Cargo vessels, disguising themselves as the native Red Indians. The tax on imported tea was so high that many had recourse to smuggled Dutch tea and in a desperate attempt to counter the move the British allowed the East India Company in 1773 a substantial tax rebate on tea shipped to America. It misfired when it infuriated the colonists who saw in it a sinister scheme to create tea monopoly to the detriment of the local merchants. Promptly came the reaction known as the Boston Tea party.

The idea of the civil rights campaign as a reaction to racism came out of its flickering existence into the public domain in our times with the massive civil rights movements organized by Rev. Dr. King who perfected and elevated it virtually to the higher level of constitutional validity. The explicit approval it received from the Congress, the Supreme Court and the President himself amply testified to its credibility. The Non-violent movement gained legitimacy in a relatively short span of time.

Despite the obvious parallels between the Gandhian version of Non-violent movement and that of Rev. Dr. King, one can certainly discern a few differential strands arising chiefly from the heterogeneous societal forces, lurking in the background. In a trenchant article, Ved Mehta points out certain differences between the genuine Gandhian view of Non-violent ideology and its American graft "Dr. King unlike Gandhi is fighting for minority rights," adding that the struggling people in British India constituted the entire labour force. Rev. Dr. King upheld favourable legislation for Afro-Americans effectively harnessing disobedience to unjust laws.

Rev. Dr. King's efforts against unjust laws assumed even more importance in so far as he had to uphold non-violence against considerable challenges held out by several other advocates of the collective Negro cause. They strongly believed that violent confrontations alone could tame the white arrogance and force them to listen to reason.

## ARTICLE -5

### A Different Perspective

One of the leaders, Malcolm X, a black Muslim, was in the forefront of those who supported violent overthrow by incessantly reminding Afro-Americans that they had "tilled his (white person's) fields! Cooked his food! Washed his clothes! You have cared for his wife and children when he was away. In many cases, you have even suckled him at your breast.... You have sweated blood to help him build a country so rich that he can today afford to give away millions even to his enemies ... And still, this Christian American white man has not got in him the human decency and enough sense of justice, to recognize us, and even accept us, the black people who have done so much for him, as fellow human beings." Before he was assassinated, Malcolm X had followers in many parts of the United States. Rev. Dr. King's speeches and conduct were free of the rancorous rhetoric, which had stained the exhortations of those who pleaded for an armed conflict to achieve the goal. When he was only 28 years of age, Rev. Dr. King had organized the first successful Non-violent campaign in America—the now famous bus boycott in Montgomery. The lengthy, Non-violent and highly successful boycott had lifted the curtain of his Gandhian heritage in the United States. When the peaceful boycott escalated and the news spread all over the country, Rev. Dr. King meant so much to his followers that his very presence worked as a tonic for the zed black people of Alabama. He told a huge audience: "We have been exploited economically, excluded socially and dominated politically. The Negro can endure. He can smile. He can also keep hoping and striving." His influence and popularity grew by leaps and bounds as he continued to lead peaceful demonstrations in several parts of the United States for one purpose or another, for voting rights, job opportunities for Afro-Americans, for equality or to end discrimination in housing. Gandhian philosophy formed the basis of his struggle for justice and his approach was interlinked with Gandhiji's Non-violent methods. It might be yet another irony in history that when Thomas Jefferson wrote the Declaration of Independence, he owned 110 slaves in the nation's capital. The very concept of slavery was ingrained in the life-blood of American society and Rev. Dr. King had to strive for justice and equality against this highly hostile background. As heard in his historic speech in Washington Rev. Dr. King dreamt of a democratic society in which liberty, equality and fraternity reigned supreme. The American civil rights leader wanted to achieve this by appealing to human conscience and not by bloodshed, that was bound to leave behind a cult of hatred, revenge and retaliation.

## ARTICLE-6

### Testimony

The American civil rights leader had shaped a policy based on the Gandhian philosophy of *ahimsa* in order to attain justice for his people who had been denied democratic rights in a country that prided over its government of the people, by the people and for the people. Deriving inspiration from Gandhiji, Rev. Dr. King strove to give his people a great lesson in fighting for a just cause using a new irresistible device to the exclusion of violence in all its forms. He re-enacted the Gandhian drama in America with equally conclusive results, thereby demonstrating once again that it was a universal panacea for every social ill, irrespective of caste, creed or colour. Besides, it provides the right answer, for it not only offers a permanent solution to the contention but also brings about a lasting reform in the opponent. Thanks to its salutary effects, every party to the conflict is at peace with himself with goodwill to all men and malice towards none.

All right-thinking men had always questioned the morality of a social and political system which judged individuals on the basis of the pigmentation of the skin. In the tight of Gandhiji's successful Non-violent campaigns Rev. Dr. King's demonstration of the effectiveness of Satyagraha paved the way in later years for the oppressed in different parts of the world to adopt Satyagraha in their struggle for freedom and equality. In this manner the new mode of fighting received universal acceptance as the best way to undo man-made tyranny and aggressive politics and in the process he opened a new road to social harmony.

The researcher does not venture to overestimate the achievement of Rev. Dr. King by indulging in exaggerated statements and hasty generalisations. Rev. Dr. King might have fallen short of the expectations of the most ambitions of his fellow Afro-Americans. It was equally true that he had been instrumental in ameliorating the sufferings of his black fellowmen and lighting up their spirits with hopes for the future.

In the sixties, when black people were struggling for equality, public demonstrations were banal, as some turned violent, particularly during the summer season, euphemistically called the hot, hot summer. Today, hardly anyone talks about the hot steamy summer or violent demonstrations by black people. They are, thanks to Dr. King's sacrifice, optimistic enough to envisage a tolerant and homogeneous American society in which their children will have greater roles to play in a truly democratic atmosphere. But for the timely appearance of this great man on the American political scene, Negro leadership would have slipped into the hands of a band of short-sighted, reckless individuals who advocated quick remedies thereby plunging the entire nation into the cauldron of anarchy and terror.

Rev. Dr. King's principles predicated on the Gandhian philosophy taught the black people patience, restraint and self-control which served as a beacon-light on the face of dire provocations and averted a national pandemonium.

Mohandas Karmchand Gandhi and Rev. Dr. Martin Luther King are indeed two glorious names that deserve a special place in the annals of history as champions of the poor, who in word and deed stood by them. They died for them. The history of the most eventful twentieth century can never be complete without an analytical study of these two personalities: there lies their greatness! Both men were assassinated.

The assassination of Gandhiji took place at 5.17 p.m. on January 30, 1948 on the prayer Ground at Birla House and his violent death resulted in a great tremor in the world. "It is dangerous to be too good," lamented Geroge Bernard Shaw in his message of condolence. Another rude shock came exactly twenty years later: "King fell over a second-floor railing to the concrete. Blood gushed forth from the right jaw and necktie. His necktie had been ripped off by the blast," moaned Rev. Jesse Jackson, a close associate of the slain American civil rights leader. Rev. Dr. Martin Luther King Jr., was pronounced dead at 8.30 p.m. on April 4, 1968. Gandhism was conspicuous in the life and career of Rev. Dr. King. Both veteran leaders in two different parts of the world strove for and sacrificed their lives to *pacem et justitiam pro omnibus*. Both have left us a rich legacy: *tamasoma jyotir gamaya.*

At the sad news of the assassination and the demise of Gandhiji, Jawaharlal Nehru, the then Prime Minister of India announced to the whole world:

> "Friends and comrades, the light has gone out of our lives and there is darkness everywhere. I do not know what to tell you and how to say it. The light has gone out I said, and yet I was wrong. The light that shone in this country was no ordinary light. The light that has illuminated this country was no ordinary light. The light that has illuminated this country for these so many years will shine for many years and a thousand years later that

> light will be seen in this country and the world will see it and it will give solace to innumerable hearts .... It represented the living truth... the eternal truth reminding us of the right path, drawing us from error, this ancient country to freedom."

Einstein said of Gandhiji: "Generations to come it may be, will scarce believe that such a one as this ever in flesh and flood walked on this earth."

## ARTICLE -7

In short, those who study the science of Non-violence and the technique of Satyagraha dispassionately and equanimously will get convinced that they are the greatest contributions of Gandhiji to the whole world. Since Satyagraha is the holding fast to TRUTH, adherence to TRUTH and means to 'Truth realisation' and since Truth is God for Gandhi, Satyagraha is the most powerful and invincible weapon for the establishment of the Kingdom of God on earth, where Truth alone triumphs and eternal values are preserved.

Non-violence, on which the great edifice of Satyagraha is built, is the universal love on which the whole universe survives. If we turn our eyes to the time of which history has any record down to our time, we shall find that, man has been steadily progressing towards Non-violence. If it were otherwise, human species would have been extinct by now. It is love that sustains our planet. We should further progress in this great virtue of universal love, which can create a new Heaven and a new Earth. Satyagraha aims at this.

Further, the application of Satyagraha in our daily life to solve the conflicts becomes the greatest weapon, as it is based on the soul-force against the brute-force which is not employable by all. If 'might is right', then the weak, women and children cannot apply that brute-force for achieving their goals. The Soul-force, (the *atma sakti*) derives its force from God the all-powerful. It is available for all and hence applicable by all. Non-violence can be practised by anybody, both by the physically weak and strong as well. What holds good even to the weakest (physically) is possible for all in the universe. According to Gandhi, it is a blasphemy to say that Non-violence and Satyagraha can be practised only by the individuals and not by nations. To him the Non-violence and Satyagraha which can be practised at the individual level can be extended to larger, national and international scales. Therefore, as B.G. Gokhale said, "the credit of putting the Non-violence and Satyagraha on the map of

Researcher at Raj Ghat, New Delhi

King Centre, Atlanta. The centre's second floor is devoted Gandhiji with his large portrait, his words of wisdom, charkha and home-spun cotton.

collective action must go to Mahatma Gandhi. Non-violence is a power which can be wielded equally by all—children, young men, women as well as the grown up people—provided they have a living faith in God of Love and have therefore equal love for all...."

Gandhiji first experimented this in South Africa and later he tested its veracity in the Indian Freedom Struggle. Having realised its invincibility, it was taken up by late Rev. Dr. Martin Luther King (Jr.) for the liberation of the Afro-Americans in the U.S. and got it proved further. Thus, it appears that **Satyagraha can triumph over any opposition and it can be applied to any situation.** But being the strongest weapon, one should think twice before its application.

## *APPENDICES*

## *APPENDIX-1*

# CHRONOLOGY OF GANDHIJI'S FAST

Fast, an extreme form of self-sacrifice, can result in serious illness or even death. It was one of the selfless methods Gandhiji had used, out of his love for India and as a nonviolent resister, without causing injury to anyone except to himself.

| | | |
|---|---|---|
| November 13, 1931 | — | Gandhiji proclaimed before the Minorities' Committee in London that he would be against separate electorate for the Depressed Classes and that he would show his protest by fasting. |
| March 11, 1942 | — | Gandhiji dispatched a letter to Sir Samuel Hoare clearly expressing his intention to fast until death in accordance with his announcement to that effect in London. |
| April 13 | — | Reply from Sir Hoare. |
| September 9 | — | Gandhiji's letter informed the Prime Minister of his final decision. |
| September 19 | — | Leader's Conference held in Bombay. Bombay delegates interviewed him in prison. |
| September 20 | — | Fast began and Gandhiji gave his first press interview. |
| September 23 | — | Gandhiji's health deteriorates. |
| September 26 | — | Doctors said that Gandhiji's health was in a critical state. Government declared the acceptance of Yervada Accord. Fast terminated. |
| September 27 | — | Gandhiji laid down his condition for cooperation. |
| September 30 | — | Restrictions placed on Gandhiji. |
| November 4 | — | Gandhiji announced plans for yet another fast over the issue of entry into Guruvayur temple. |

## *APPENDIX-2*

# A CHRONOLOGICAL LIST OF SOUTH AFRICA'S ANTI-INDIAN LEGISLATIVE MEASURES

---

1. Statute Law of the Orange Free State, 1891.
2. The Dealer's Licences Act, No. 18. 1897—Natal.
3. The Immigration Restriction Act, 1897—Natal.
4. Law 3 of 1897, regulating the Marriages of Coloured Persons within the South African Republic (Transvaal).
5. The Immigration Restriction Act of 1903—Natal.
6. The Immigration Act, 1906—Cape Colony.
7. The Immigration Act, No. 15 of 1907—Transvaal.
8. The Education Act, No. 25 of 1907—Transvaal.
9. The Townships Amendment Act, Law 34 of 1908—Transvaal.
10. The Asiatic Registration Amendment Act, No. 36 of 1908—Transvaal.
11. The Public Service and Pensions Act, No. 19 of 1908—Transvaal.
12. The Education Act, No. 6 of 1910—Natal.
13. The Immigrants Regulation Act, 1913.
14. The Indian Relief Act, 1914.
15. The Townships Franchise Ordinance, 1924—Natal.
16. The Rural Dealers' Ordinance, 1924—Natal.
17. The Durban Land Alienation Ordinance, 1924—Natal.
18. The General Dealers Control Ordinance, 1925—Transvaal.
19. The Colour Bar Act, 1925.
20. The Minimum Wages Act, 1925.
21. The Local Government (Provincial Powers) Act, 1926.
22. The Immigration and Indian Relief (Further Provision) Act, 1927.
23. The Asiatics in the Northern Districts of Natal Act, 1927.
24. The Immigration Amendment Act, 1931.

25. The Transvaal Asiatic Land Tenure Act, 1932.
26. The Transvaal Asiatic Land Tenure Amendment Act, 1934.
27. The Transvaal Asiatic Land Tenure Amendment Act, 1935.
28. The Rural Dealers' Licensing Ordinance, 1935—Natal.
29. The Transvaal Asiatic Land Tenure Amendment Act, 1936.
30. The Marketing and Unbeneficial Land Occupation Act, 1937.
31. The Immigration Amendment Act, 1937.
32. The Transvaal Asiatic Land Tenure (Further Amendment) Act, 1937.
33. The Asiatics Transvaal Land and Trading Act, 1939.
34. The Motor Vehicles and Road Traffic Regulations Amendment Ordinance, 1940—Natal.
35. The Durban Extended Powers Ordinance, 1940—Natal.
36. The Asiatics Transvaal Land and Trading Act, 1941.

*APPENDIX-3*

# THE ASIATIC LABOUR IN INDUSTRIES

| | Year | Number |
|---|---|---|
| Indian workers on farms | 1937 | 13,196 |
| Privately-owned factories | 1937-38 | 12,674 |
| Sugar mills and refineries | 1937-38 | 3,351 |
| Coal mines | 1939 | 625 |
| Gold mines | 1939 | 138 |
| Electricity | 1937-38 | 125 |
| Diamond fields | 1939 | 8 |
| **Total** | | **30,117** |

## *APPENDIX-4*

# BORN IN HOME COUNTRIES AND DOMICILED IN SOUTH AFRICA (1936)

| | | |
|---|---|---|
| Indians | : | 26,254 |
| Europeans | : | 1,494 |
| **Total** | : | **27,748** |

*APPENDIX-5*

# RELIGIONS OF THE ASIATIC PEOPLE IN SOUTH AFRICA (1936)

| | | |
|---|---|---|
| Hindus | : | 159,823 |
| Muslims | : | 42,590 |
| Christians | : | 10,720 |
| Confusius | : | 1,888 |
| Buddhists | : | 1,771 |
| Others | : | 1,097 |
| Unknown (not stated) | : | 899 |
| No religion | : | 716 |
| **Total** | : | **19,691** |

## *APPENDIX-6*

# DEMOGRAPHIC COMPOSITION OF THE UNION

| | | |
|---|---|---|
| Natives | : | 6,596,689 |
| Europeans | : | 2,003,857 |
| Coloured | : | 769,661 |
| Asiatics | : | 219,691 |
| **Total** | : | **9,589,989** |

*APPENDIX-7*

# ASIATIC MARRIAGES (1936)

| | **Males** | **Females** |
|---|---|---|
| Married | 42,405 | 36,203 |
| Never married | 72,444 | 38,826 |
| **Total** | **114,849** | **75,029** |

(The rest were widowed, divorced or unspecified)

*APPENDIX-8*

# PROPORTION OF THE ASIATIC SEXES (1936)

| Province | Males | Females |
|---|---|---|
| Natal | 97,073 | 86,558 |
| Transvaal | 15,379 | 10,114 |
| Cape | 6,677 | 3,831 |
| Orange Free State | 22 | 7 |
| **Total** | **129,151** | **100,510** |

## *APPENDIX-9*

# THE APOSTLE OF NONVIOLENCE

In Birmingham jail, Rev. Dr. Martin Luther King, Jr. wrote page after page scrawling replies to eight fellow clergymen who had strongly criticized his role in nonviolent civil rights demonstrations as "unwise and untimely."

His letter, reflecting strong Gandhian influence, has become a classic statement of his conviction that "injustice anywhere is injustice everywhere"—a belief which he strengthened his public life as an apostle of nonviolence.

Rev. Dr. King's invaluable contribution to the Afro-American struggle for justice by nonviolent methods won him the 1964 Nobel Peace Prize.

The letter he wrote while sitting in the Birmingham jail was the strongest advocacy in favour of nonviolence.

He cautioned "Human progress never rolls in on wheels of inevitability; it comes through the tireless efforts of men willing to be co-workers of God, and without this hard work time itself becomes an ally of the forces of social stagnation."

# Bibliography

## Bibliographical Note

In this brief bibliography are listed only those works which have been found to be of immense help to the research. For a comprehensive understanding of the position of Afro-Americans in the United States, the following books are recommended: *"The Negro in the United States,"* by Franklin Frazier, *"Stride Toward Freedom,"* by Rev. Dr. Martin Luther King Jr., and *"An American Dilemma,"* by Gunnar Myrdal.

A number of works by and on Gandhiji and Rev. Dr. King (as mentioned in the introduction) have proved invaluable in the preparation of this thesis.

## Primary Sources

### *Books*


Ahmann, Mathew, ed., *The Negro.* (Notre Dame: Fides, 1962)..

Bakshi, R: *Gandhi and Salt Satyagraha.* (Bombay: Viswa Vidya Publications, 1954).

Belfrage, Sally: *Freedom Summer.* (New York: The Viking Press, 1965).

Chakrabarti, Mohit: *The Gandhian Humanism.* (Boston: Concept Publishing Co., 1992).

Clark, Kenneth., ed., *The Negro Protest.* (Boston: Beacon, 1963).

David, Jay: ed., *Growing Up Black.* (New York: Morrow and Company, 1968).

Fischer, Louis: *Gandhi: His life and Messsage for the World.* (New York: Bantam Publishing Company, 1961).

----------, Louis: *Gandhi and Stalin.* (New York: Harper and Row Publishers, 1950).

---------, Louis: *The Life of Mahatma Gandhi.* Second Impression. (London: 1951).

Franklin, John Hope and Isidore Starr, eds., *The Negro in Twentieth-Century.* (New York: Vintage Press, 1966).

Gandhi, M.K. *Autobiography: My Experiments with Truth.* (Bombay: Hindi Kitabs Ltd., 1951).

----------, M.K.: *My Philosophy of Life.* (Bombay: Pearl Publications Pvt. Ltd., l961).

----------, M.K.: *Satyagraha in South Africa.* (Ahmedabad: Navjivan Publishing House, 1950).

----------, M.K. *Man and Machine.* (Bombay: Bharatiya Vidya Bhavan, 1966).

----------, M.K.: *Young India.* (Bombay: 1940).

----------, M.K.: *Collected Works.* (Delhi: The Ministry of Information and Broadcasting, Government of India, 1958).

Gregg, Richard B: *The Power of Non-violence.* (New York: Schocken, 1965).

Grier, William H. and M. Cobs: *BIack Rage.* (New York: Basic Books, 1968).

Hofstedter, Richard and Michael Wallace: *American Violence: A Documentary History.* (New York: Alfred A. Knopf, 1973).

Huttenback, Robert A.: *Gandhi in South Africa—British Imperialism and the Indian Question, 1860-1914.* (Ithaca and London: Cornell University Press, 1984).

Jwwin, Julius: *The Native in South Africa.* (Johannesburg: Witwatersrand University Press, 1942).

Joshi, P.S: *The Tyranny of Colour A Study of the Indian Problem in South Africa.* (Durban: Commercial Printing Co., 1942).

King, Martin Luther, Jr.: *Stride Toward Freedom: The Montgomery Story.* (New York: Harper and Row, 1959).

---------, Martin Luther, Jr.: *The Measure of Man.* (Philadelphia: The United Church Press, 1959).

---------, Martin Luther, Jr.: *Strength to Love.* (New York: Harper and Row, 1963).

---------, Martin Luther, Jr.: *Why We Can't Wait?* (New York: Harper and Row, 1964).

--------, Martin Luther, Jr.: *Where Do We Go From Here?: Chaos or Community?* (New York: Harper and Row, 1967).

---------, Martin Luther, Jr.: *The Trumpet of Conscious.* (Harper and Row, 1968).

Kuiper, Leo: *Passive Resistance in South Africa* (New Haven, Connecticut: The Yale University Press, 1957).

Mukherji, S.B.: *Indian Minority in South Africa.* (Delhi: New Ages Printing House, 1959).

Myrdal, Gunnar: *An American Dilemma. The Negro Problem and Modern Democracy.* (9th edition). (New York: Harper and Row, 1944).

Nair, Shankaran: *Gandhiji and Anarchy.* (Bombay: 1954).

Nanda, B.R.: *Mahatma Gandhi.* (London: George Allen and Unwin, 1958).

Nehru, Jawaharlal: *Glimpses of World History.* (London: Lindsay Drummond, 1949).

--------, Jawaharlal: *The Discovery of India.* (London: Meridian Books, 1947).

Preston, Edward: *Martin Luther King, Jr.: Fighter For Freedom.* (New York: Doubleday and Company, 1969).

Rao, Kauleshwar: *Indians and British Colonisation of East Africa—1883-1939.* (Patna: The Associated Book Agency, 1979).

Saunders, Doris, Ed., *The Day They Marched.* (Chicago: Johnson, 1963).

Singh, Ranjee: *Gandhi and the Modem World.* (Bombay: Classical Book Company, 1988).

Sterner, Richard: *The Negro's Share.* (New York: Harper and Brothers, 1943).

Tendulkar, D.G.: *Mahatma* in 8 vols. (Bombay: Times of India Press, 1951).

Thompson, Daniel C.: *The Negro Leadership.* (Enlgewood Cliffs: Prentice Hall, 1963).

Thompson, L.M.: *Indian Immigration Into Natal (1860-1872).* (Cape Town: 1952).

Unnikrishnan, T.K.N.: *Gandhi and social Change.* (Bombary: Raisat Publication, 1985).

Vadakumthala, Rev. Dr. Alexander: *Human Rights of Indians in South Africa.* (Kochi: Viani Rintings, 1992).

Woodward, C. Vann: *Origins of the New South, 1877-1913.* (Baton Rouge: Louisiana State University Press, 1951).

Wright, W.W.: *The Cultural Life of the American Colonies.* (New York: Harper and Row Publishers, 1957).

Zengerin, Robert and Albert Blauser: *Civil Rights and the American Negro.* (New York: Trident Press, 1961).

Zinn, Howard: *The New Abolitionists.* (Boston: Beacon Press, 1964).

***Secondary Sources***

Agar, Himilton: *South Africa.* (London: 1934).

Ashe, G.: *Gandhi.* (New York: Stein and Day, 1968).

Calpin, H.R.: *Indians in South Africa.* (Pietermaritzburg: Shuter and Shooter, 1949).

Carrington, C.E.: *The British Overseas.* (London: Cambridge University Press, 1950).

Cudjoe, Prof. Selwyn.: *Tacarigua: A Village in Trinidad.* (Welesley, Massachusetts: 1995).

Davie, Maurice, R.: *Negro in American Society.* (New York: McGraw Hill Book Company, Inc., 1949).

De Keiwiet, W.: *A History of South Africa.* (Oxford: Oxford University Press, 1941).

Desai, D.M.: *The Indian Community in Southern Rhodesia.* (Salisbury: Herold, 1949).

Frazier, Franklin: *The Negro in the United States.* (New York: The McMillan Company, 1957).

Gandhi, M.K.: *Nonviolent Resistance.* (New York: Schocken, 1965).

Green, M.S.: *The Making of the Union of South Africa.—A Brief History, 1487-1937.* (London: Longman Green and Company, 1946).

Grimes, Alan P.: *Equality in America.* (New York: Oxford University Press, 1964).

Hancock, W.K. and J. Van Der Poel: *Selections from the Smuts Papers.* 4 vols. Cambridge; At the University Press, 1960).

Hentoff, Nat: *The New Equality.* (New York: The Viking Press, 1964).

Hoshi, P.S.: *Apartheid in South Africa.* (Kimberley: 1950).

King, Mrs. Coretta Scott: *My Life with Martin Luther King.* (New York: Holt Rinehart and Winston, 1969).

Kondapi, C.: *Indians Overseas, 1838-1949.* (Bombay: Oxford University Press, 1951).

Kuper, L.: *Indian People in Natal.* (Pietermaritzburg: Natal University Press, 1960).

Kuiper, L., H. Watts and R. Davies: *Durban: A Study in Racial Ecology.* (London: Jonathan Cape, 1958).

Lewis, L. Davis; *King: A Critical Biography.* (New York: Praeger Publishers, 1970).

Lokos, Lioness: *House Divided.*—The Life and Death of Martin Luther King (New Rochell, New York: 1968).

Lomax, Louis E: *The Negro Revolt.* (New York: Harper and Row Publishers, 1962).

McGill, Ralph: *The South and the Southern.* (Boston: Little Brown and Company, 1963).

Miller, William Robert: *Nonviolence: A Christian Interpretation.* (New York: Schocken, 1968).

---------, Willarn Robert: *Martin Luther King, Jr., His Life, Martyrdom and Meaning for the World.* (New York: Weybright and Talley, 1968).

Narain, Iqbal: *The Politics of Racism.* (Ahmedabad: Navajivan, 1965).

Palmer, Mabel: *The History of the Indians in Natal.* (Cape Town: Oxford University Press 1957).

Patil, Dr. S.H.: *Gandhi and Swaraj.* (Delhi: Deep and Deep Publications, 1983).

---------, H.S.L.: *The Indians South Africa: A Tragedy of Empire.* Part 11. (Madras: G.A. Nateshan, 1909).

Price, H.D.: *The Negro and Southern Politics.* (Westport, Connecticut: Greenwood Press, 1957).

Pyarelal: *Mahatma Gandhi: The Early Phase.* (Ahmedabad: Navajivan, 1965).

Pyrah, G.B.: *Imperial Policy and South Africa, 1902-1910.* (Oxford: Oxford University Press).

Sacks, Benjamin: *South Africa: An Imperial Dilemma.* (Albuquerque: University of New Mexico Press, 1967).

Singh, Chanan: *The Indian Case Against the Immigration Bill.* (Nairobi, 1947).

Sridar, Sen: *The Position of Indians in South Africa.* (Calcutta, 1950).

Smith, William, R.: *Nationalism and Reform in India.* (New Haven: Yale University Press, 1938).

Washington, James Melvin: *A Testament of Hope: The Essential Writings of Martin Luther King, Jr.,* (San Francisco: Harper and Row Publishers, 1986).

Webb, Maurice and Kirkwood, K.: *The Durban Riots and After.* (Johannesburg, 1949).

Williams, John A.: *The King God Did'nt Want to Save: Reflections of the Life and Death of Martin Luther King, Jr.,* (New York: Coward McCann, Inc., 1970).

Woods, C.A.: *The Indian Community of Natal: Their Economic Problem.* (Cape Town: Oxford University Press, 1954).

Young, Whitney M., Jr., *To Be Equal.* (New York: McGraw Hill and Company, 1964).

***Magazines***

*Christian Century.* (Selected issues, 1959-1968).
*Commonwealth.* (Selected Issues, 1957-1968).
*Crisis* (Selected Issues, 1962-1965).
*Ebony.** Johnson Publishing Co. Inc., Chicago, Illinois (Selected issues, 1956-1967).
*Harper's Magazine.* (Selected Issues, 1963-1972).
*Nation.* (Selected Issues, 1965-1973).
*Negro Digest.* Johnson Publishing Co. Inc., (Selected Issues, 1967-1969).
*New Republic.* (Selectell Issues, 1955-1962).
*New Yorker.* New York, (Selected Issues, 1963-1966).

***Newspapers***

*Atlanta Constitution.* Atlanta, Georgia. (Selected Issues, 1958-1960).
*Birmingharn News.* Birmingham, Alabama. (Selected Issues, 1958-1961).
*Chicago Defender.* Chicago, Illinois. (Selected Issues, 1958-1969).
*Detroit Times* (Selected Issues, 1955-1956).
*Trinidad Guardian,* (March 15-16, 1997), Trinidad, West Indies.
*Kesari.* (Bombay).
*Liberation.*
*Montgomery Journal.* Montgomery, Alabama. (Selected Issues, 1956-1966).
*National Observer.* Silver Springs, Maryland. (Selected Issues, 1957-1966).
*New York Herald Tribune.* New York. (Selected Issues, 1961-1967).
*New York Times.* New York. (Selected Issues, 1955-1969).
*Trinidad Express,* (September 12-15, 19981, Trinidad, West Indies.
*Washington Post.* Washington, D.C. (Selected Issues, 1958-1960).

***Magazine Articles***

Adler, Renata. *Letter from Selma.* New Yorker, April 10, 1965, pp. 121-57.
Alexander, Robert: "Negro Business in Atlanta". *Southern Economic Journal,* 17: 451-64.
Bosmajian, Hugh A.: "Rhetoric of Martin Luther King's 'Letter from Birmingham Jail": *The Midwest Quarterly,* 8: 66-67.
Boyd, Malcolm: "Violence in Los Angeles." Christian Century, 82: 1093.

Galphin, Bruce M.: "Political Future of Dr. King." *Nation,* September 23, 1961, pp. 177-80.

Good, Paul: "Bossism, Racism and Dr. King." *Nation,* September 19, 1966.

Alberstam, David: "The Second Coming of Martin Luther King." Harper's, August, 1967, pp. 39-51.

Hentoff, Nat: "A Peaceful Army ." *Commonweal,* June 10, 1960.

King, Martin Luther, Jr.: "My Trip to the Land of Gandhi." *Ebony,* July 1959.

----------, Martin Luther, Jr.: "Advice for Living." *Ebony,* December, 1958.

----------, Martin Luther, Jr.: "Behind the Selma March." *Saturday Review,* April 3, 1965.

----------, Martin Luther, Jr.: "Bold Design for a New South." *Nation,* March 30, 1965.

----------, Martin Luther, Jr.: "Let Justice Roll Down." *Nation,* March 15, 1965.

----------, Martin Luther, Jr.: "Luther King, Jr. and Mahatma Gandhi." *Negro Historical Bulletin,* (January 15, 1951. No. 124).

Rustin, Bayard: "The Meaning of Birmingham." Liberation, June 1963.

# Index